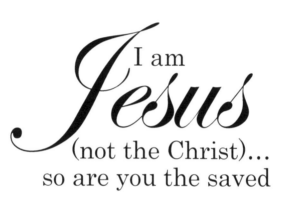

I am
Jesus
(not the Christ)...
so are you the saved

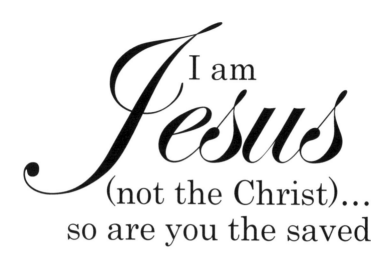

I am Jesus

(not the Christ)...
so are you the saved

OUR HERITAGE AS 'NATURAL RESOURCES' IN CHRIST
- A LETTER TO THE CHURCH

Chimezie Okonkwo

I AM JESUS (NOT THE CHRIST)…SO ARE YOU THE SAVED OUR HERITAGE AS 'NATURAL RESOURCES' IN CHRIST - A LETTER TO THE CHURCH

All Scriptural texts has been taken from the King James
Version of the Holy Bible except otherwise stated.

iUniverse books may be ordered through booksellers or by contacting:

iUniverse
1663 Liberty Drive
Bloomington, IN 47403
www.iuniverse.com
1-800-Authors (1-800-288-4677)

ISBN: 978-1-4917-6846-4 (sc)
ISBN: 978-1-4917-6845-7 (e)

Library of Congress Control Number: 2015907898

Print information available on the last page.

iUniverse rev. date: 05/26/2015

This book has been written to the glory of
God and to the shame of the devil.

As you read this testament, let your thought, mind and meditation be solely on Jesus Christ, not on the author of this letter but on the Author and Finisher of our faith. Read it with literary intentionality. This means that you'd try to understand what the author has in mind, not what you think. God bless you.

Contents

Dedication

This book is first dedicated to my Father - the living God; to my Lord, saviour and inspiration - Jesus Christ and most importantly to my teacher, advocate, mentor, discernment and guide – the Holy Spirit.

To my loving wife, three children – Kingdom, Freedom and Wisdom and to my unborn children (if any); this book is for you and will not be complete without you. Thank you and God bless you indeed.

I will also dedicate this book especially to the loving memory of my parents, lecturers, angels, bosom friends and living legends: my late mum – Mrs Faustina Nwebube Okonkwo (nee Ubaja) who ascended to eternity in the very early hours of Monday 28 January 2002 after she fell into a diabetic coma and never came back to life; and my late Dad – HRM Eze Professor Chuka Okonkwo who passed on to eternity on Sunday 06 April 2014 shortly after that dreadful tumour and unfortunately cancerous surgery. In his language my late Dad always said that – "one thing must kill a man", he encouraged me to keep writing because *'practice makes perfect'* and to never be discouraged in life because "as long as there's life, there's hope." My parents were the first to identify the star in me above all and I'd never take that recognition of trust and truth for granted.

Finally I'd also dedicate this work to all the preachers who have spoken into and affected my life positively. To name some: the Right Reverend Bishop Ngozi Durueke who God used at the city of my birth Owerri in 1995 to heal me when I had a mental challenge, he had also instructed me to study [Hebrews 11] from where my Bible study journey actually took off; Apostle Ebenezer Ajitena who was my pastor here in London for over seven years and he baptised me at Jesus's baptismal site on the Jordan River in Israel on 17 May 2012 during my first Holy Land Pilgrimage tour of Israel from 14 May 2012 – 23 May 2012; Pastor Chioma Emmanuel who was the first pastor in life to *categorically* tell me in clear words that I have the call of God on my life on 14 January 2009; Pastor Alex Omokudu who is a very unique and dynamic pastor, a great spiritual drive to many and a man I easily considered in my last book as one of the best pastors in the world yet; Pastor Bill Winston who is a man of radical faith that I admire unreservedly and hope to meet someday soon; Pastor John Hagee and other preachers who have been unrelenting in their support of/for the people of Israel; Pastor David Ibiyeomie who is a man I respect so much plus meeting you face to face at *your* Church in Port Harcourt on 29 June 2014 was really transforming; greetings to Bishop Francis Wale-Oke who I met at a Christian conference here in London on my birthday 20 February 2015; I also salute Dr Pastor Paul Enenche of DIGC worldwide who I also met at another Christian conference in London on 17 April 2015; Pastor Benny Hinn; Bishop David Oyedepo; Pastor Enoch Adeboye; Pastor E Isaiah; Pastor Abbeam Danso who are all giants of the gospel of Jesus Christ and to the Late Dr Myles Munroe who I met for the first time in July 2007 at a Church in London United Kingdom and was a great source of encouragement towards my writing endeavour, plus I have safe-guarded and kept for a memorial the personal letter of encouragement you wrote to me dated 14 March 2014 praising the great effort I made in my first book. I must also say that I sent my first book to many pastors but Dr Myles Munroe was the only pastor that actually wrote me personally, and acknowledging the contents of my first book felt like a signature from God saying – 'well done my son'. Yet the glory was intended for God and still belongs to God. Thank you.

I applaud you all and others who I have not mentioned their names. May God bless you all.

Preface

The words of my writings are the words of my mind turned into the art of God through God. I acknowledge them but I don't despise them. I use them but I don't abuse them. I conceived them but I don't construct them. I write them but I don't comprehend them. The Psalmist said in [Psalm 45:1b] – "My tongue [is] the pen of a ready writer", whilst I say 'my pen (itchy fingers) is the tongue of a ready speaker/preacher/student-teacher'.

It is truly a daring and very controversial topic indeed, I have been terribly frightened about writing it and have repeatedly refused to start writing it but the Spirit has been steering me back to it and may I say that I have in no way any intention to blaspheme the name of the living God rather that the authority *in the name of the Lord* is unveiled from a user perspective being that we pray (*in*) the name of Jesus and take authority (*in*) *the name of Jesus* [John 14:13-14], not 'through' the name of Jesus. We do not however pray to Jesus rather we pray 'in his name'. This is a revelation many may not have caught yet. When my sons were much younger, any time they saw our pastor on TV, they always said - "Dada see Jesus". Today when my young daughter sees one of our pastors and another pastor we normally watch as well on TV, my daughter shouts "Jesus". The reason is because they are 'Jesus' by the authority in that name, not the Christ. Even young children understand this truth. However I discovered that it is not all pastors who my young children saw on TV that they called 'Jesus', although I don't know the reason for this. Also I started praying to God through the power of the Holy Ghost after I caught and understood this revelation, but I pray in the name of Jesus thereby appearing as Jesus before the throne of God. A lot of times when we pray 'in the name of Jesus', people often think about Jesus as a totally different entity or being but that is the picture of the

Christ. I'd explain that assuming authority as Jesus is different from the image we put in our heads and minds of who the Lord Jesus or Christ is. It's entirely not the same from my understanding and has he not asked that we take authority *in his name*? This means that we're stepping into Jesus's shoes every time we pray because he has authorised us to, however this does not make us *the Messiah or the Lord and Saviour, surely not the Christ*. This was an understanding that I had clearly comprehended from the owner of that name (the Lord Jesus Christ) sometime in 2009 whilst meditating on the word of God that ***I am Jesus*** and I had put it up on my Facebook account at the time. Fortunately or unfortunately with close to a thousand friends on Facebook at the time who were very willing to comment on virtually every Biblical quotation or comment I'd always write on my page, however though, I did not receive any replies to this particular post and I felt terribly embarrassed about this to the point that I started deleting a great number of those so-called friends who I'd expected to comment on my *out-of-this-world* 'new great revelation'. Events passed and as *upset* as I got, unfortunately I decided to deactivate my original Facebook account eventually sometime in January 2010. Having done this, I still nurtured this thought in my heart through all those years until the Lord began to stir me back to it again in September 2014. Even while writing this book, I have been attacked immensely in many ways and got to points where I almost deleted this book multiple times because in my mind I thought – '*surely I have offended God*' by writing this book, but God kept silent even after praying on numerous occasions asking him to tell me to delete this book if it would amount to a sin against him or if it wouldn't bring him glory. The incessant attacks eventually made me aware to the light that this is a book of destiny. In [Mark 16:17-18] Jesus said – "And these signs shall follow them that believe; ***In my name*** shall they cast out devils; they shall speak with new tongues; {Verse 18} They shall take up serpents; and if they drink any deadly thing, it shall not hurt them; they shall lay hands on the sick, and they shall recover." This Scripture summarises the truth that miracles happen (in) *not* (through) the name of Jesus and the Lord Jesus made this possible to the believer *in his name*. Subsequently God has been using situations around me to drill this mentality into me somehow to a point where I needed to depend on his total grace in faith for specific victories, particularly over my health and children's lives.

The place of Supernatural:

My first son (Kingdom David) as much as my other children (Freedom Justice and Wisdom Majesty) easily conquers the devil whenever he throws an attack. Kingdom David has always conquered challenges the quickest and this has made it obvious to me that there may also be a divine eternal covenant in the kingdom of David which may as well be a disguised representation in the Old Testament for the power in the name of Jesus, although the New Testament covenant of grace and triumph came in the name of 'Jesus'. Kingdom David is also my only child among the three who never knew the dreadful experience of a coma and I celebrate God for him and even for his siblings that had the experience and came out alive, particularly my daughter who was afflicted multiple times and was victorious in all. We dreaded the many nights that we had to leave our daughter (Wisdom Majesty) in the hospital to go home while she remained in a coma state but today those challenges and experiences have become the triumph I write as my testimonies. This is also why in my last book I argued that David was the Jesus of the Old Testament. I still very strongly believe this thought. However, my other two children (Freedom Justice and Wisdom Majesty) got quite sick in late 2014 and were choke-coughing seriously, it was the kind of coughing sessions that had always previously taken them to the intensive care unit in a coma state until I'd ring our pastor and after he'd pray, God intervenes and they would eventually get better. However on this attack session that I call '*the last attack*' (it surely was), I and my wife got so nervous and panicked as usual and my wife said – "let's take them to the accident & emergency unit" at the St. Thomas' hospital here in the United Kingdom which is also where they were born. Taking them to the hospital we know may quite possible end up in another unwanted coma state again because between 31 January 2014 and 07 July 2014 my daughter had at least four hospital admissions and three of these ended up at the intensive care unit while she remained in a coma state for days until full recovery. Horrific experiences they really were indeed!! So with this recent attack and believing the God that we serve I said to my wife boldly – "my children will never go to that hospital again for an admission and they will not die. I dare the God I serve and worship to act now. Why do we worship God if he will not answer us when we pray in the name of Jesus?" My wife just sat there crying because of the possibility ('no possibility' I'd call it) of maybe the unknown. I was very upset in my spirit, and I said in supplication to the Lord - "Holy Ghost of the living God, I have told you before that I will never bury any of my children according to your word in [Exodus 23:26] which says that – '***There shall nothing cast their young*** or be barren, in thy land: the number of thy days I will fulfil'. Lord I say it again instead of taking any of my children, Lord if I have finished the assignment you sent me to do here on earth take me in my children's place but if I have not keep my children and keep me. Lord I know and still believe that I have not finished my course yet otherwise why did Jesus die on the Cross of Calvary for me and my children to have life? Father remember your promises through your servants, the declarations and specific words you've spoken to me through them as they were led by your Spirit. Holy Ghost over to you." I was really upset and believing the Scripture mentioned above and [John 11:4] with [Psalm 118:17] is the reason why I've always known that I will never bury any of my children as I spoke it over them in that state and in the name of Jesus. After my prayer nothing happened and my children were still feeling and looking very poorly. So I knelt down to God again with my hands lifted up to heaven and burst into tongues of fire. I ended that prayer session by these words – "God of my pastors over to you, Holy Ghost of the living God over to you in Jesus name it is done Amen." I looked again and nothing seemed to have changed. So I took the anointed oil and I said - "Holy Spirit if you have anointed this oil, defend your word because my children will never be admitted in the hospital ever again and will not die. Lord I will never bury any of the three children that you have given me – Kingdom, Freedom and Wisdom!" I was really under pressure, so I poured anointed oil all over my children while they (Freedom and Wisdom) lay breathing very fast while sleeping and then I said to my wife – "let us go to bed, God has heard us." I did not wait to see what my wife was going to do or how she felt because I knew it was not an emotional battle, rather a spiritual one and the only choice we now had was to be unperturbed and strong in faith believing God. I had handed it over to the Holy Spirit, so I slept off. Meanwhile couple of hours after I'd slept off, I remembered my children in my sleep and jumped up again from where I lay. I had intended to see how they were doing and heard the Lord's voice very audibly say to me – "can you help your children…can you heal them? I said 'No'. Then I heard him say again – "enjoy your sleep, I am taking care of your children for you." Wow. Reluctantly but trustingly I forced myself to sleep off again. By the time I woke up in the morning, I had *'believed God with fear…not knowing'* [Hebrews 11:7-8] what the Lord will do and did not just rush into my children's room. I was very nervous but my spirit, soul, body and mind; everything was eager to see what the Lord had done. I had fear through exercising my faith in God. But when my children (Freedom Justice and Wisdom Majesty – who were attacked) woke up, the Holy Ghost had made then whole again 'supernaturally'. I was just shedding tears of joy and shaking my head in awe of what the power of the Holy Spirit could do. I always prefer addressing the Spirit of God as the 'Holy Ghost' rather than as the 'Holy Spirit'. I know that they are the same Spirit but with a particular unbiased preference or attachment I believe, feel stronger and more comfortable calling on the 'Holy Ghost', however as normal I use both names interchangeably.

These previous challenges taught me how to make my life easier and thereby stay away from certain challenges in the future particularly the ones that involve my children; because anytime any of my three children developed a health scare or challenge, I learnt how to remind God that they are his children (not mine) and I'm only a care-taker employed in that parenting role by God because every parent is employed by God. I'm responsible for them but they're not necessarily my responsibility. That responsibility belongs to the God as their real parent because he employed me in that care-taking position, therefore everything my children will ever need is the business of the Spirit of God to provide for it and this is why I'm confident that my three children will never be admitted in hospital ever again for any health challenge and will never lack any thing that God could provide; and I say all this as a testimony in the name of Jesus also because [Acts 10:38] says – "How God anointed Jesus of Nazareth with the Holy Ghost and with power: who went about doing good, and healing all that were oppressed of the devil; for God was with him." During my trying moments and particularly on that night's ordeal when my children (Freedom and Wisdom) were having that *last attack*, I remember picking my phone to call or text our pastor and I heard the voice of God ask me – "For how long will you depend on your pastor to pray for the children I gave to you to oversee? Does it mean you are not capable of this task given to you?" Immediately I just dropped my phone before I went back into prayers by myself because my wife had resolved that the hospital was the only alternative at that stage. It dawned on me that parenthood is the greatest and most priceless trust in leadership. Parenthood means that God trusted you capable enough to take care of, lead and manage young lives and you don't want God to see that you are not fit enough for a role he counted you worthy and fit for. It's unbelievable, what trust! Hence I was able to see (not only physically but also in spiritual terms) my children as totally God's responsibility given to me to oversee as a care-taker. We could once in a while ask our pastors (as our spiritual leaders in the Churches) to pray for us but when it becomes a routine it undermines our personal God-given authority and the relationship we have with the incomprehensible God. So from the foregoing my short word of advice is this - *if you ever get sick, run to the throne before you run to the hospital because God still heals when you ask him to heal **in the name of Jesus***. Did the Lord not speak to Moses and Aaron saying in [Numbers 14:28] – "Say unto them, As truly as I live, saith the LORD, as ye have spoken in mine ears, so will I do to you…"?!

The place of Faith:

Faith is simply 'stupidity'. I've also depicted faith to stand for - *'Facing All I Thank Him'*, that means through our challenges we must thank God. This enables or ensures that we're always in that 'thanksgiving' mode, but you cannot talk about faith by side-lining fear. So it's very important to understand the meaning of both faith and fear. Fear has two and (one) meaning(s) and the later summarises the former two in my opinion. I personally believe that Fear means good and works for our good, therefore has either of two initial meanings - *'Forsake Everything And Rise'* (or) *'Find Everything And Rule'*. By 'forsaking everything and rise', believers tend to forgo their fears or worries and rise up in faith over the feelings of such fears or worries. That means we neglect or ignore the symptoms of the sicknesses in our bodies for instance and acted like they actually didn't exist. We ignore the lies and images of death painted in our bodies by the enemy. I've personally lived through this in the past and often ended up not realising when the pain or discomfort left my body. Then by 'finding everything and rule', believers make discoveries and innovations that eventually launch them into the limelight. This approach ensures that we dare to think beyond our limits and act beyond our abilities. It becomes a choice that has only one sure outcome – 'victory', rather than the alternative of failure, but to summarise both arguments, it behoves me to base my conclusion with the (one contrary) interpretation of fear that I've always chorused in my thoughts thus - *'Fake Evidences Appearing Real'*. Drawing from this very critical and audacious analytics, I had concluded that *'I had believed God with fear...not knowing'* [Hebrews 11:7-8] (as already seen from *above*) because that was my faith working. I was simply facing all in thanksgiving to Jesus whilst also dealing with those fake evidences that appeared real, yea though I was scared-stiff! In fear (you may ask)? Yes indeed. I discovered that fear is an advantage that causes faith to prosper more *'through fear'* and without fear, faith has absolutely no meaning. I'd explain this please. It is fear that purifies faith for it to be credible as faith and all other contrary debates on faith I'd insist remains balderdash. Towards the end of May 2014 I was preparing to travel to Nigeria for my late Dad's funeral. I was born into a hugely polygamous home and the battle was rife and clear from the onset. However from my late Dad's children that we know about or are aware of, I was the fourth child but the third son by the order of our birth. My late Dad regardless had made it very clear in words and actions that he intended and appointed me to stay in the place of and in the position as his first 'capable' son for some reasons which was (to me) an unfortunate position to be put in because I would have ended up making more enemies than friends within the family line. My elder brother who was born by my mother had no problems with this, however the wider family had concerns. This was the case because growing up I had emerged the biggest rebel the family had ever produced and some relatives disliked my aura for it. I put myself through some radical experiences growing up and these subsequently affected my lifestyle and vain choices during my younger years. As a young child growing up I had to deal with the confusion and stress accumulated from a lot of unanswered questions (particularly about the sovereignty of God) in my heart and my parents couldn't even really answer them. I wanted to know how God came into existence and why it must be God that came into existence first, why wasn't it another? My Dad once said to me that if I'd dared to ask the Anglican Bishop that ordained my *Confirmation* in the Anglican Church, that he'd not have '*confirmed*' me because he didn't even know the answers to my questions. With all these mix up of questions that I'd grown in my mind about the deity, whenever I got upset I'd curse God telling him that he didn't actually exist. But I was quite young at the time and now I understand better and I still can't stop asking God for forgiveness and I know he has already forgiven me. I and my siblings all grew up in the same home, neighbourhood and environment but my siblings had different experiences from what I personally was exposed to growing up and this had influenced my reaction or attitude towards everything in life since I had a very strong belief in violence (in every meaning of it) until God changed my life for his glory. But these unique experiences made me to understand that indeed it is very possible to live in the same house with somebody, have possibly the same daily routines or chores with them yet you both face different challenges and hence react to those challenges from the way your individual personalities *see* or rather *feel* them. Everyone's challenges are different because each person is endowed with very unique personalities and mine was a queer one. They may be similar experiences but the reception will always have individual interpretations, impact and peculiarity. For instance some 'personal' challenges God intentionally brings them 'to you' as a man or human being, not to your wife or family. So you may need to tackle these challenges by yourself (without the intervention or help of your wife or family) although with the help and power of the Holy Ghost. Yes the Bible has said that you are '*one flesh*' with your wife but your destinies will never be the same. For instance a man having a headache does not mean that his wife would have the same just because 'spiritually in Christ' they are one flesh, because physically they are totally different individuals. In life we may be so close, yet we're so different because experiences and challenges determine or define the personalities of different individuals even after we give our lives to Christ. Our challenges remain different and so does our individual reaction(s) to them.

Having lived away from Nigeria (where I was born) in the United Kingdom for just over ten years at the time, the threat to my life was more apparent. I received threat texts from the extended family who I referred to as "the Taliban" at the time and being a changed personality I had become quite scared of the unknown. I knew my late Dad's soul will not rest if I did not attend his funeral. He was my friend and always fondly called me by either of these three *names* (depending on the situation or the message he was trying to convey):

1. Ugochinyeremba - (meaning 'global eagle' or 'international eagle' or 'intercontinental eagle'. My Dad always preferred calling me by this name because he believed that I'm as precious as an eagle yet the Lord had chosen to give me away to go and be a blessing to the entire world)
2. The Prince - (this *name* he called me at random)
3. Chimezie Okonkwo – (my late Dad only called me by my birth first-name and surname when he wanted an advice or a warning to stick in my head).

Whenever I rang my Dad or whenever he saw me, his calm demeanour and echo of "Ugochinyeremba" always boosted my morale and enthusiasm in life giving me a sense of *not just belonging*, but acceptance. He had this noble picture in his mind about me that could not be taken away from him. Although when I was a child my late Dad fondly called me "my little boy". A tag I disdained so much and he'd always joke about it with his friends. He was genuinely quite fond of me and my siblings knew I was (without any doubt) his favourite child of all his children (as well as my mum's) because they never failed to very proudly tell people about me even in my absence and I've never known a parent believe in their child so much the way my parents believed in me. So for some of the extended family it was okay, for others there was this undeniable aura of hatred and envy snarling everywhere. This therefore meant that I couldn't have disappointed my late Dad by not being present at his funeral and the word of God had already advised men to – "Honour thy father and thy mother: that thy days may be long upon the land which the LORD thy God giveth thee" - [Exodus 20:12] and [Ephesians 6:2]. My mum was no more and this was my last shot at obeying God to honour my late Dad, so I could not just falter at this great responsibility that suddenly fell on me.

However during these trying times that came in May 2014 whilst preparing for my late Dad's funeral, I had always knelt down to pray seeking counsel from God and asking God for a word for June 2014 (the month that I was supposed to travel to Nigeria to be able to attend the funeral of my late Dad scheduled for Friday 4th July 2014). The Lord never spoke to me by any means; not even in a dream regarding any word that I'd asked for and I only grew more worried as the days drew nearer. On Sunday 01 June 2014 I was in the Church where I and my family usually attend Church service and worship, by the time the pastor mounted/ascended the altar the first words he said on that marvellous first day of the month was - "*This is your month of faith.*" I jumped up shouting, giving praises to the Lord. I knew instantly that it was the word I needed to conquer this journey ahead of me. I went home excited and on getting home, I jumped on my Hole Bible as led by the Lord to study [Hebrews chapter 11] which I already knew was all about faith. This was the chapter that the Right Reverend Bishop Ngozi Durueke of 'Powerline Living Water Ministries a.k.a He Reigns Chapel' in Owerri Nigeria had given me to study in 1995 after I had a mental challenge from smoking an over-dose amount of the Indian hemp (weed). That experience actively motivated my life journey through the Holy Bible. I knew it [Hebrews 11] was on *faith* and I was excited to refer to this Scripture again, a Scripture that God used to heal the mental challenge which I sometimes cheekily refer to as '*the mental mountain*' I had in the past just because in that almost *ruined* state I'd dared to believe God and study his word. I was excited, however on getting to {Verse 7} and the {Verse 8} of that passage, I was shocked with the revelation that jumped into my spirit. Permit me to start from {Verse 6} please for the purposes of better comprehension [Hebrews 11:6-8] – "But without faith it is impossible to please him: for he that cometh to God must believe that he is, and that he is a rewarder of them that diligently seek him. {Verse 7*} By faith Noah, being warned of God of things not seen as yet, ***moved with fear***, prepared an ark to the saving of his house; by the which he condemned the world, and became heir of the righteousness which is by faith. {Verse 8} By faith Abraham, when he was called to go out into a place which he should after receive for an inheritance, obeyed; and *he went out, not knowing whither he went*." As a little boy growing up, I desperately wanted to build an ark for God because Noah's history motivated me through my Christian Religious Knowledge (C.R.K) classes. What I may not have realised was that Noah only obeyed the voice of God in faith and as a result the journey became easy for him. I gathered a few logs of wood and nails (quite a few) during this period and would not just find myself building that ark for some reason even though I had a great zeal to do it.

The catchphrase in this Scriptural account [Hebrews 11:7] above was that *'Noah moved with fear'*. This could have been the fear of God, the fear of the enormous task ahead, the fear of the unknown or the fear we do not even know what it is because it was not mentioned in this Scripture. The Holy Bible was not very clear on this so we don't know for sure but what we do know and understand is that Noah *'moved with fear'* and became the heir of righteousness which is by faith. Also in [Hebrews 11:8] of the same Scripture we're told that *'Abraham went out, not knowing whither he went'*. It must be mental to leave your home not knowing where you're heading to but these Scriptures explain to me and clearly to anybody I'd believe that against what virtually most (if not all) our Bible teachers have taught us, faith is not necessarily the opposite of fear and fear is not the opposite of faith. If I relied on these particular verses, then faith is also quite arguably not the absence of fear and fear is not the absence of faith. These verses make it clear that in my definition and by the grace of the understanding and revelation through the Spirit – *'Faith is the presence of fear and a corresponding action towards the cause of that fear'*. There are five stages in movement: sit, crawl, stand, walk and run; but there is yet the supernatural stage I'd call 'fly'. These are the birth process and the growth stages of faith from my own understanding. I figured out that this is because faith has supernatural wings, faith is like an aeroplane that flies you out of intimidation but arguably through fear. Faith is a fight so it cannot be the opposite of fear because that fight is against the spirit of fear. You'd probably have to pass through fear for the action to be considered as faith. It is a resisting force applied to conquer and devour the entirety of fear with that sort of Esther's *'if I perish I perish'* kind of mentality as detailed in [Esther 4:16]. The Bible remarkably admonished us to "fight the good fight of faith…" – [1 Timothy 6:12]. This revelation coupled with prayers from my pastor (at the time) gave me the crude boldness to step into that challenge that I dreaded for months. I eventually went to Nigeria very courageously and against all odds we victoriously and triumphantly gave our late Dad an *envious* farewell because I dared and moved with fear like Noah did.

If Noah *moved with fear* and succeeded, that means fear is an advantage. How could faith then be the absence of fear if faith needed fear's presence to be considered as faith? If there's no fear then there's no faith because everything is normal and natural and there would be no need to exercise anything called faith. Faith works like light, at the presence of darkness light shines through. If there's no darkness, the presence of light would then be meaningless and considered natural or normal making light common place because without darkness light cannot be light. It is darkness that gives light value, just as fear gives faith value. A condition of normality cannot warrant the use of faith because it just doesn't make sense. Faith is about the strongest force I know of in life. Everybody applies faith everyday through life and this therefore means that everybody uses fear through life. You don't have to believe in faith but you can only live in faith. No believer has ever seen God, neither have we seen Jesus, yet we believe. The believer's faith is often seen as stupidity by the carnal mind. When your young child wakes up from sleep in the morning, they leave their rooms and run to your room to meet Daddy and mummy. They come (in faith) believing that Daddy and mummy did not die in their sleep at night. That thought may not even have crossed their mind(s) because naturally a young child may not normally think about this. They saw Daddy and mummy before they went to bed last night, so naturally/automatically they believe Daddy and mummy are alive and definitely somewhere at home. This is your young child exercising the force of faith. When you got up from your bed this morning, why didn't you think about death and whine away the day on your bed scared-stiff? It is only because you believed in life and continued your normal daily routines 'as usual'. Your belief was your faith. When you picked up this book to read, you only trusted that your eyes weren't going to fail you, then you opened the pages of this book and started reading with ease. It was your faith at work. When you went to sit for that examination, you had no clue what the outcome will be, but you sat for it anyway. Merely sitting for it not knowing if you'd pass or fail is faith. When you went to apply for a foreign visa, who assured you that it'd be granted? But you still went for it bearing in mind that if your application got refused, that money you paid for the application would have just developed wings and flown away because money has wings and can actually fly (spiritually). Whatever it was that pushed you to that embassy was faith. You've heard and read that people are killed and maimed daily in Nigeria and some other parts of the world, yet you bought your flight tickets and went on vacation there regardless. That was the force of faith at work in you and through you. You don't have to believe in faith but you cannot doubt the works of faith because you exercise faith every day. Faith is like the Lord Jesus. That you can't see faith physically does not mean that it does not exist, just like you not being able to see God or the Lord Jesus physically does not mean that they don't exist. I believe God and the Lord Jesus in the name of Jesus because if faith can work by the spirit, then God and the Lord Jesus surely work by the spirit too and being that we have the Spirit of God in us, which means we (like bags) carry the person of Jesus in us.

Therefore if faith is alive then the Lord Jesus is even more alive. So if an unbeliever ever doubted my belief in the name of Jesus or questioned the realness of Jesus as a living person in or through me, I'd assure them that the day they stopped exercising faith (being alive) will be the day I stopped believing in the Lord Jesus. If it then be that the unbeliever cannot live without faith, then it means that I (as a believer) cannot live without the Lord Jesus, albeit '*in his name*'. This is why we need to start serving God like we were God himself (the way we believed he'd have done it if he had to ever serve himself) because '*we were made in his image*' - [Genesis 1:27]. We need to serve God as though we were self-serving and as well worship God as though we were self-worshipping. We are not God but we were created like God. How do we wish ourselves to be served by others? Do the same in faith to God. If faith then is action that brings about a change, it then goes to say that for every action there is a reaction and for every change there is an exchange. Something has to go for something better to come. Evil has to go for good to come. In faith flesh has to go for the Spirit to come, just as Jesus had to go (as Christ) for the Holy Ghost to come; but the name of Jesus never went with the Christ. In faith *action is pertinent*. For instance I chose to give my children a verb (each) for their third name(s). I called my first son *'spring'* for his third name because apart from the fact that he was born during the spring, we also understand that in the part of the western hemisphere where I live *'time winters backwards towards the end of the year and then springs forward after the winter but just before the summer'*. Spring therefore is a natural symbol of faith (movement) I'd assume. I also called my second son *'shine'* as his third name to naturally trigger his destiny into bright shining motion which I call *the faith mode*. Then I called my daughter *'amaze'* as her third name to automatically place her life in an action mode because action is a symbol of life and if a verb is an action word, then action is an evidence that there's life which equally prompts movement and neither (life nor movement) could be achieved without faith. Men of faith usually don't seem normal and surely don't speak the normal language. They usually do strange things and speak strange language. They are stupid men (without any disrespect) to the natural mind because stupidity makes faith what it is. Faith is therefore that bridge or force that covers the gulf that the enemy tries to put between God (at his level) and us (at our level), and that force is empowered or activated in the bold name of Jesus.

The place of History:

This is where history should probably have come good because God could equally have used my previous lifestyle to instil fear and panic to the same group that tried to frighten me not to go to Nigeria. Who could cover history if it's been allowed by God for a testimony? It is history that gives birth to the future and God never wastes experiences no matter how terrible they may seem. After all it was God who watched over us during the dark years of our lives and it was God who brought us through them. It is what you go through in life that gives birth to who you really become tomorrow. God uses our past experiences and failures to build the foundation of our future character. Also remember [Romans 10:17] – "faith cometh by hearing, and hearing by the word of God." If I did not have a psychological challenge that made me open to receive the word the pastor had declared on that Sunday, I may never have remembered to study [Hebrews 11] and if I did not study it, how could I have made reference to these experiences in this book if I did not have them? This tells me that every tiny seemingly insignificant challenge builds the bricks and the walls of one's destiny. History is equally like doing a kindness because you can never do a kindness too soon as you never know how soon it will be too late. You can equally not get rid of your past experiences because you do not know how soon God will require you to testify or speak or write or even teach about them. It's like a need to take action against injustice in an environment where injustice prevails and one refuses to take action without realising that the absence of action in the face of injustice could be considered equal to participation in the eyes of God. In [John 15:2] Jesus said – "Every branch in me that beareth not fruit he taketh away: and every [branch] that beareth fruit, he purgeth it, that it may bring forth some fruit." This is another reason why you must write your books, compose your poems, sing your songs, preach the kingdom of God, teach the gospel of Jesus Christ and strive to release all the gifts and talents that *God has put in you* for you to *put out to the world*. Do not let your friends, enemies or friendly-enemies (*frenemies*) discourage you, not even your pastors because the Scripture lays emphasis that God's ways are higher than our ways and his thoughts higher than ours. As you do this, God will begin to prune and purge you just to make you bear better fruits for his glory; and God will surely preserve you. On the contrary if you don't, you risk being taken away as the Scripture above said. My message through this book is a summary of just some of my numerous encounters and experiences through life so-far although I understand also that the real attraction to anyone reading this book I'd assume is pondering over the title of the book – 'I am Jesus, not the Christ...so are you the saved' and thinking that this writer must be insane, so let's read some of his insanity. It must be insane indeed to write such a title. Hence I share this divine-insanity (culled from a spiritually-led free-thinker) with you. It's an invitation into my world and experiences. Therefore no experience(s) as much as no action(s) is/are considered invalid in response to a justified necessity and history is brought to life through action as inaction is subdued. Being so action (again) is very strong and that action is your faith in many terms; action as much as faith is a language and that language speaks through fear into triumph. Generally people 'may' forget what you say (words) to them, but they will never forget what you do (action) to them and this is where the saying *'action speaks louder than words'* comes in. The reason for my writing is not to say, but to do. How? To cause the readers to do by bringing their experiences (history) to life, thereby being an encouragement to someone hence causing a change in their lives. This will mean that I have used words of my testimonies to do (stir) action in them, hence my mission in writing is to evangelise the kingdom of God with emphasis on the gospel of Jesus Christ through these personal experiences, revelations and ideas from God with supernatural miracles, signs, wonders and undeniable testimonies manifesting; to encourage and to change by the intervention and power of the Holy Spirit. I need people to read my writings or hear my words and get transformed by the God that caused me to *'pass through'* these experiences (history) and therefore write and speak these words.

The place of Grace:

From the foregoing I discovered a correlation between what the Holy Bible calls faith and grace that I believe and I am obliged to explain here. Having been through different churches under different pastors for the vast majority of my life and having had the privilege to humbly study through the Holy Bible a few times I discovered that people (most preachers and teachers included) misinterpret grace just as they have often misinterpreted faith as seen above and I say this with all humility, respect and a teachable spirit (if I'm found wrong in any way). The definition of grace by many believers is quite appalling and has been a bit of a moral maze. Some call grace 'unmerited favour' which they interpret gives people the right to commit whatever sins they like and grace would cleanse it automatically because of the price Jesus paid. This wrong perception has made me to very carefully interpret grace as '**unmerited favour *without sin* and yet not by works**'. Scripture in [Titus 2:11-14] says – "For the grace of God that bringeth salvation hath appeared to all men, {Verse 12} Teaching us that, denying ungodliness and worldly lusts, we should live soberly, righteously, and godly, in this present world; {Verse 13} Looking for that blessed hope, and the glorious appearing of the great God and our saviour Jesus Christ; {Verse 14} Who gave himself for us, that he might redeem us from all iniquity, and purify unto himself a peculiar people, zealous of good works." This Scripture emphasizes that grace is not for sinners. Grace actually teaches the saved to do things right. Apostle Paul questioned whatever grace that encourages sin in [Romans 6:1-2] – "What shall we say then? Shall we continue in sin, that grace may abound? {Verse 2} God forbid. How shall we, that are dead to sin, live any longer therein?" Apostle Paul in his words in [Ephesians 2:8-9] further shows us the relationship between grace and faith – "For by grace are ye saved through faith; and that not of yourselves: [it is] the gift of God: {Verse 9} Not of works, lest any man should boast." From the foregoing I'd conclude that *whatever teaches you to be in control of what is supposed to be your dirty habit(s) is the gift of grace.* This simply explains our right-standing with God guaranteed because of the shed blood of our Lord Jesus. Living righteously does not therefore imply that we are helping the finished works of Jesus, it only means we show appreciation to God for what Jesus did on the Cross of Calvary by not abusing this *'privilege turned right'* through unrighteous living, thereby avoiding the extravagant waste of this gift called grace.

After I published my first book, the day I mentioned my worries regarding expected criticisms aimed at my book, it was my 'now' late Dad who said to me "No! No! No! It's okay. It'd help you a lot. Don't worry about the criticisms, let them come in." These words encouraged me to write again. I am in no way qualified to write about our God but the more I tried to hesitate the more the urge to write these words kept coming. As a graduate in the business and management field and a former employee in the same sector, I should have no prior Biblical knowledge, education or understanding in what I write; but when one hears the voice of God, you will know that it is the voice of God and then obey thereby putting your trust in God to make the seemingly impossible task ahead of you to be accomplished spiritually (first) before it's physical manifestation. The voice of God is not your mind talking to you because your mind speaks with doubt and would always give you an alternative but God's voice is specific, firm and commands authority. The book of [John 10:27] reminds us that - "My sheep hear my voice, and I know them, and they follow me." If I did not hear God's direction, this revelation will never have come through and even if some other person got this revelation, they may either have had a different perspective to it or worse still may not have been courageous enough to write, teach or preach it. *I am writing this book totally against my will* and this makes me to know or rather to strongly believe how pertinent God wants this knowledge made available to every child of God out there and even non-believers alike that the name of Jesus is the only name given [Acts 4:12] to connect men to God. If I want to access God, I do not go in the name my parents called me 'Chimezie' or in my surname 'Okonkwo', rather I call on the living God 'in the name of Jesus'. If the Scripture said "Therefore **if any man be in Christ**, he is a new creature: old things are passed away; behold, all things are become new" – [2 Corinthians 5:17], this explains to us that because Jesus was in Christ, that's why we call him Jesus 'that became' Christ. It's like my name and surname – 'Chimezie Okonkwo', from the natural perspective I am supposed to be Chimezie in Okonkwo which also could be interpreted to mean Chimezie in the Okonkwo family or Chimezie that became part of the Okonkwo family. But thank God for salvation because I may be Chimezie Okonkwo physically but spiritually I bear the name of my daddy in heaven – the Lord Jesus which could equally be summarised as 'Chimezie Okonkwo in the Jesus family'. My name 'spiritually and supernaturally' changes from Chimezie Okonkwo to 'Jesus' if I must bear witness of the power of God in my life and for God to hear me. It's the same for any believer in Christ. This is because every saved of God is a member of this family and we all share in the same name, body and blood given for the salvation of all men and we all equally have the legal rights to use that name with dignity and respect. It's like a shared responsibility, so we must represent that name responsibly well.

The psalmist says in [Psalm 82:6-7a] – "I have said, Ye are gods, and all of you are children of the most High. {Verse 7a} But ye shall die like men." This scripture can quickly bring 'Jesus' to my mind although it was clearly referring to us 'the saved'. Apart from calling us gods (small letter 'g'), that statement actually started with 'Ye' (capital 'Y') right in the middle of a sentence. This depicts us as the children of God, exactly like the Lord Jesus was when he walked the earth. This is equally written in [John

10:34-35] – "Jesus answered them, Is it not written in your law, I said, Ye are gods? {Verse 35} If he called them gods, unto whom the word of God came, and **the scripture cannot be broken**." From this rendering if God called us gods, this tells me that we are a peculiar and younger version of God as children (like Jesus – who later became the Lord and Christ). This is equally true from [Genesis 1:27] where the of God said – "So God created man in his own image, in the image of God created he him; male and female created he them." Therefore we truly know that God cannot lie because he had said that he made us in his image and as such would then call or refer us to as 'gods'. If God has made us his children and in his image even calling us 'gods', then truly "we have a high calling, of God, in Christ Jesus" – [Philippians 3:14]. The book of [Galatians 4:6-7] explains that – "And because ye are sons, God hath sent forth the Spirit of his Son into your hearts, crying, Abba, Father. {Verse 7} Wherefore thou art no more a servant, but a son; and if a son, then an heir of God through Christ." It says that we have become the heir of God (like Jesus was, who has become Christ) through Christ. So we must pass through the phase where we sometimes will face challenges maybe not exactly like Jesus did and believing in that renewed name and identity *in that name Jesus* who has now become Christ and Lord for us. Jesus said in [John 15:20] – "Remember the word I said unto you, The servant is not greater than his lord. If they have persecuted me, they will also persecute you; if they have kept my saying, they will keep yours also." So persecutions are surely inevitable for a believer in Christ because it is through him (Christ), in his name (Jesus) that we become heirs of God in the form that he was in on earth, which is the same form we are in today on earth. What a glorious honour indeed, it's truly a privilege to be a son and servant of Christ. Please bear in mind that I am not comparing us with or to God thereby giving the unreasonable impression that we '*rub shoulders*' with the deity, however I am identifying our likeness to God (howbeit as Jesus) in that name Jesus and [1 John 4:17] declares – "Herein is our love made perfect, that we may have boldness in the day of judgement: because *as he is, so are we in this world*." This means his current nature is our present nature in this world and we know that Jesus Christ has never changed [Hebrews 13:8], since he has always maintained his nature from yesterday, till today and even for ever. I'd also love for my readers to pay particular attention to this eye-opening Scripture from Apostle Paul [Philippians 2:5-8] – "***Let this mind be in you, which was also in Christ Jesus***: {Verse 6} <u>Who, being in the form of God, thought it not robbery to be equal with God</u>: {Verse 7} But made himself of no reputation, and took upon him the form of a servant, and was made in the likeness of men: {Verse 8} And being found in fashion as a man, he humbled himself, and became obedient unto death, even the death of the cross." The [Verse 5 and 6] of this Scripture particularly sends cold shivers through me because it really gives us a visible picture of who we are. Jesus took upon himself the form of a servant even though he was the Son of God so that he would die on the Cross of Calvary that we may live and that life we live in his name. Just think about how awesome it is that we 'immediately' have the mind-set of Christ through the power of salvation. Having the mind-set of Christ entails functioning or living with a totally renewed and sound mind-set above the forces of the world as established in [Romans 12:1-2]. It's an utter privilege indeed. Unbelievably true but this truth was reiterated in [1 Corinthians 2:16] – "For who hath known the mind of the Lord, that he may instruct him? But ***we have the mind of Christ***." I therefore believe that if we have the mind of Christ, the priority of grace enables us to serve others before ourselves and our service follows this order: God, children, wife/husband, others and then ourselves. Therefore this book will attempt to expound on this exceptional and undeserved grace which God has endowed and enabled us with in the name of his Son our Lord Jesus. As you study this book, I'd advise you not to restrict your thoughts with a closed or linear mind. Open up your mind and digest the details in this book and God will bless you as you do this in Jesus name Amen.

Acknowledgements

To God be the glory.

Introduction

Many will ponder how on earth an ordinary man will have the audacity to call himself by the name of the Lord without the understanding or realisation that the word of God called us so in [2 Chronicles 7:14] – "If my people, **which are called by my name**, shall humble themselves, and pray, and seek my face, and turn from their wicked ways; then will I hear from heaven, and will forgive their sin, and will heal their land." So clearly we bear, have the legal right (by grace) to bear and are called in the name which the Lord appeared with in human form which is Jesus! The book of [Isaiah 43:7] attests to this grace – "…Even every one **that is called by my name**: for I have created him for my glory, I have formed him; yea, I have made him." Having said this, many critics may be quick to identify that the word of God warned us to beware of false Christs in the last days in [Matthew 24:24] which testifies thus - "For there shall arise false Christs, and false prophets, and shall shew great signs and wonders; insomuch that, if it were possible, they shall deceive the very elect". However I will remind us that the Lord gave us the authority 'in the name of Jesus' and not 'in the name of Christ'. Our Lord Jesus only became the Christ after triumphing over his ordeal on our behalf at the Cross of Calvary as Jesus. Before the Cross, he was the man Jesus and would not have become the Christ without victory at the Cross of Calvary. Hence we were authorised to use his name '*while he was a man on earth*' - which is Jesus, not as the glorified Messiah, Lord and Christ. I have never said a prayer 'in the name of Christ', but everyday millions of believers (including myself) say their prayers either 'in the name of Jesus' or when we attempt to cross the boundaries we pray 'in the name of Jesus Christ' and the same is the Lord's name, regardless that we are not the Lord and Christ. The reason is this, the name 'Jesus' gives us a bridge into the name of the Christ and

Lord which is into the Holy of Holies, a place of fellowship with God. God recognises us by that name 'Jesus' because it is our real identity in and through Christ before (in the presence of) God. Consequently the Holy Ghost was sent 'in the name of Jesus' [John 14:26] and we must assuredly ascend the spiritual throne of God 'in the name of Jesus'. This means the Holy Spirit was sent to make the name of Jesus real to us by opening our spirits up for 'schooling' and that is why this Scripture above assures us that the Spirit of God shall teach us all things as well as show us things to come. Therefore not receiving the Spirit of God means that we may never understand our name or identity before God. What happens most times is that ignorantly when we pray, we pray to God as though we were coming to God through a representative or through a channel or an image called Jesus. That's not true because when we pray 'in his name' and the channel is Christ, God responds as though it were Jesus (the Christ) himself praying. Why? Surely because this is the name he identifies us with regardless whatever challenge we may come to God with.

The place of Discernment:

From the above we can understand that there is a difference between 'Jesus' and 'Christ' from both a natural and spiritual perspective. Jesus was born by a woman, walked the earth as a man, died like a man, resurrected and was then glorified 'as' Lord and Christ. If you pay particular attention through this routine, apart from the glorification phase as Lord and Christ you may concur that this is the true journey of any child of God – born, walk, die and be glorified 'with' (not 'as') Christ [Romans 8:17]. Meanwhile Christ was not born, never died but Jesus rose from the dead 'with' and/or 'as' Christ [Colossians 3:1] and this is where that mystery remains – Christ never died as Christ but as Jesus, yet was risen 'as Christ'. In [1 Corinthians 15:3] Apostle Paul made reference to Christ dying for our sins. In hindsight we could understand that he was referring to the later glorified Jesus as Christ who has always existed and lived [John 17:5] before the world began. In [Romans 10:9] Apostle Paul made reference to God having raised the Lord Jesus from the dead. He referred to Jesus here as the Lord Jesus (Christ) because he was already exalted by the time of his writing. This is made even more complex to comprehend by its rendering in [Romans 8:11] where Apostle Paul uses 'Jesus' and 'Christ' in reference to the dead and risen (resurrected) Lord thus - "But if the Spirit of him that raised up Jesus from the dead dwell in you, he that raised up Christ from the dead shall also quicken your mortal bodies by his Spirit that dwelleth in you." My question is this – was Christ really ever dead? Did Christ ever rise if he was never dead? The answers to these questions are clearly 'no' and 'yes' respectively. It is 'no' because Christ was never dead and 'yes' because Jesus rose as Lord and Christ. Remember when God said in [Genesis 1:26a] - "Let (us) make man in (our) image, after (our) likeness", who was God referring to as 'us' and 'our' in that verse? It was Christ and the Holy Ghost because they had existed from the very beginning. Jesus was not there at the beginning, however 'as Christ' he was there. The Holy Bible says in [1 Corinthians 1:24] - "But unto them which are called, both Jews and Greeks, **Christ the power of God, and the wisdom of God.** This is equally repeated in {Verse 30} of the same Scripture. Well this does not prove that Christ was there at the beginning, I know. But in [Proverbs 3:19] it was written that - "The LORD by wisdom (which translates to 'by Christ') hath founded the earth; by understanding hath he established the heavens." This testimony was equally confirmed in [Psalm 104:24] - "O LORD, how manifold are thy works! In wisdom (in Christ) hast thou made them all: the earth is full of thy riches." If then God created all things by 'wisdom' and since 'Christ is the wisdom of God' as seen from these two Scriptures above, which means Christ was truly there from the beginning of creation and was instrumental to it. On the other hand, [Genesis 1:2] also tells us that the Holy Ghost (Spirit of God) was there from the beginning – "And the earth was without form, and void; and darkness [was] upon the face of the deep. And the **Spirit of God** moved upon the face of the waters." So they (God, Christ and Holy Spirit = Trinity) were there right from the beginning. Also if God created the world by wisdom, which means everything in the world is God's intellectual property (including man) since it was God's wisdom that made all things. The registered trademark or copyright registration that God has over all flesh is the blood of his Son our saviour Jesus Christ. Life (Christ) is therefore the only guaranteed and original trademark (given to man but owned by God) that cannot be duplicated because God owns life and that life is Christ (the never-dead but risen Son of the living God).

The place of Authority:

This mysterious dilemma is what this book intends to delve into – The difference between Jesus the Saviour, Messiah, Lord and Christ and Jesus the man which is also the name given for 'authority' where the word 'author' can be derived from; hence Jesus is in [Hebrews 12:2] defined as - 'the author (because he has authority and responsibility) and finisher (because his authority is complete and defined through his responsibility) of our faith' while in [Hebrew 5:9] this is detailed further thus – "And being made perfect, he became the author of eternal salvation unto all them that obey him." Here obedience is emphasized. In the book of [Acts 3:6] where it was recorded by Luke that Apostle Peter referred to the Lord as Jesus Christ, he was talking about an event that had already occurred and transformed. It was the reformed man Jesus that was transfigured and glorified to become Christ or Jesus Christ as already stated above. But we may have equally noted that at certain events through the Holy Scriptures, emphasis was either sometimes laid on the name of the man Jesus or on the name of the Lord and Christ who are Spirit-beings. Drawing from when Jesus asked Peter who men said he was, Peter answered "thou art the Christ, the Son of the living God [Matthew 16:16] and [Mark 8:29]." I believe Simon Peter saw the glorification of Jesus as Lord and Christ ahead and refused to call him Jesus; moreover Jesus always spoke to his disciples about what the 'Son of man' was going to face. Simon Peter dared to boldly step into the future. In the following verse, Jesus admonished '*them*' (his disciples) not to tell any man [Mark 8:30]. He did not want his future identity to become known or common to men. Subsequently in the book of [Matthew 16:17] Jesus responded to Simon Peter thus "Blessed art thou, Simon Barjona: for flesh and blood hath not revealed it unto thee, but my Father which is in heaven." I'd love my readers to take a minute and ponder this Scripture in depth. Jesus was adamant, convinced and assured that the Holy Ghost had revealed his not yet manifested and glorified personality to Peter. In [John 17:6a] Jesus said – "I have manifested thy name unto the men which thou gavest me out of the world…" How could one manifest a name they do not bear? This makes it evident beyond reasonable doubt that Jesus was and remains a name for both God and man (the saved man). Then in [John 17:22] Jesus continued – "And the glory which thou gavest me I have given them; that they may be one, even as we are one." Meaning that we carry the same glory exactly as Jesus and therefore exactly as God. God gave to Jesus and Jesus gave exactly the same to us; confirming that we bear an express image of Jesus. If so, then surely I am Jesus (just not the Christ) and so are you if you are saved and only believe. Jesus received the name and glory of God and empowered us with the same. The book of [John 17:12a] confirms this – "While I was with them in the world, I kept them in thy name…" Here was Jesus testifying to God what he used the gift of God for and how he achieved this '*in the name of God*' and that name was Jesus. To back up this unbelievable argument and responsible authority Jesus said in [John 17:18] – "As thou hast sent me into the world, even so have I also sent them into the world." I hope we understand this? ***God sent Jesus in the name of God and then Jesus sent us in the name of Jesus.*** The Scripture said Jesus was sent in the name of God and we know that name was Jesus being that God is a supernatural deity who operates with and in uncountable names. For every challenge, God has a specific name to conquer it. For instance God sent Moses to the children of Israel by the name 'I AM THAT I AM' [Exodus 3:14], but sent Moses to Pharaoh in the name of 'The Lord God of the Hebrews' [Exodus 3:18]. However after Pharaoh king of Egypt would not budge, God sent Moses and Aaron back to him by the name of 'Jehovah' saying in [Exodus 6:2-3] – "And God spake unto Moses, and said unto him, I am the LORD: {Verse 3} And I appeared unto Abraham, unto Isaac, and unto Jacob, by the name of God Almighty, ***but by my name JEHOVAH was I not known to them***." In like manner when God saw the need to send a redeemer to save mankind, he had to complete this task using a name that was compatible with both God and man. A name that both God and man could be identified with; and that name is Jesus. For this same reason God sent Jesus in human form and therefore in flesh to live like man, face the same challenges that man would later encounter including persecutions and tribulations but Jesus was able to overcome every challenge because he was both God and man and had the ability and supernatural power to adapt regardless the situation. This is also because as an intermediary, he would eventually transfer the power of God to man through the indwelling of his Spirit.

The book of [2 Corinthians 5:17] states - "Therefore if any man be in Christ, he is a new creature: old things are passed away, behold, all things are become new." Old things are passed away because the old man was flesh but after salvation the old man became a new man (a spirit being) because giving your life to Jesus is a spiritual act rather than a physical one that is why we must worship God through the new man 'in spirit and in truth' [John 4:24]. The new man therefore takes the person and the name of 'Jesus' (not Christ). What makes that name 'Jesus' meaningful and powerful is the power of death and most importantly resurrection. If Jesus did not rise from the dead his name would make no meaning more than any ordinary name. This is why the unbelievers called believers *Christians (not Jesus-ians) because we have already been made Jesus and we are now trying to be like Christ* through grace which is the power of resurrection that causes or stirs righteous living in us and that resurrection power came into Jesus through the Spirit of Christ. I particularly have concerns about the title of Christianity which I'd deal with later in this book. Therefore we (as the Jesus of this day) are in Christ and he is in us just as Christ is in God and God in Christ [John 17:21] hence 'if any man be in Christ...' – [2 Corinthians 5:17]. So whatever Jesus was on earth, that's who we are today on earth. The mystery again is that Jesus was fully God and fully man; this is why he is called 'the Son of God' and 'the Son of man'. No wonder the word of God refers to the recreated man as "heirs of God and joint-heirs (as Jesus) with Christ (not Jesus)" – [Romans 8:17]. It is only the name of Jesus that gave us such royal majesty to be heirs of God and joint-heirs with Christ.

The word of God in [Colossians 1:27] laid similar emphasis thus – "To whom God would make known what is the riches of the glory of this mystery among the Gentiles; which is Christ in you, the hope of glory." The Scripture says 'Christ in you', not Jesus in you. It is Christ through his Holy Spirit who resides in us (as today's Jesus), not Jesus residing in his own body again. This means that the one we call 'Jesus' is not just merely Jesus but rather our Lord and Saviour Jesus the Christ who has been exemplified and glorified. This also explains why the Church is called the body of Christ (1 Corinthians 12:27) rather than the body of Jesus? Christ is called the head of the Church [Ephesians 5:23 and Colossians 1:18] and the head carries the functioning and control of the entire body through the power of the mind; so then the head tries to control this body to live right because if the body suffers any pain as a result of the sins of the body, it affects the functioning of the mind which is the thoughtful part of the head and this pain or discomfort affects the functioning of Christ in our lives because he is the head thereby also undermining the cause fought and won through death on the Cross of Calvary. If I have Christ inside of me by the Holy Ghost, then I pray in the name of Jesus; this means that I become Jesus before God in my dealings in life and as the body of Christ, however not Jesus the Lord. Ever wondered why Hispanics bear 'Jesus' as their personal or given names? Could it be this understanding that motivated their courage? Again inside the name of 'Jesus' is 'Christ' that has never died, so while Jesus still walked the earth he had Christ in him and it was the Christ in him who never died with him that was able to resurrect him. Christ in man is the Spirit of God and if the Spirit had refused to raise Jesus from the dead, Jesus wouldn't be relevant today. This goes to truly confirm that it is Christ in me that gives me the hope of glory. If I am the body and Christ the head [Colossians 1:18] and [1 Corinthians 11:3], which explains that all my sense organs (brains, eyes, ears, nose, and mouth) belong to Christ. So this goes to say that I can think Christ because I think through Christ's mind and don't forget that *we have the mind of Christ* [1 Corinthians 2:16], I see Christ because I see through Christ's eyes, I hear Christ because I hear through Christ's ears, I breath Christ because I breath through Christ's nostrils and I talk Christ because I talk through Christ's mouth which is why my words have authority (to declare) and power (to establish), but all as Jesus the body and remember the *holy communion* which 'is' (not 'represents' but 'is') the body and blood of Jesus. Therefore I feel pretty brazen to declare without any reservations or apologies to any man's thoughts, ideologies or criticisms that I am Jesus (not the Lord, not the Saviour, not the Messiah, not the Christ and not the King of kings) in the world today and so is any child of God. This is augmented by the realisation that 'Christ is our life and we shall appear with him in glory' [Colossians 3:4], albeit as Jesus because we will appear before God in the saving name of Jesus.

In [Revelation 2:17] the Holy Bible says that "to the overcomer (in Christ), God has given a white stone with a new name in it which no man knoweth saving he that **receiveth** it". I am fully convinced that the new name is Jesus and again this does not make us the Christ. The white signifies purity, the stone being the solid rock on which we stand and the new name being Jesus because when we got born again, we **received** Jesus. Again the white stone bearing that name in it is a clear picture of Christ having washed our sins from scarlet to white as snow [Isaiah 1:18]. I strongly believe that God refined Jesus to become the Lord and refined his name for us to be able to bear and hide under that covering – 'the name of Jesus'. I will say something that may be considered very stupid here that *you don't even have to be a believer or what we call a Christian before that name 'Jesus' begins to work for you in life as long as you use it but you must be a believer in Jesus to get saved* and I'd prove it from a little encounter I personally witnessed. In my previous role a few years ago I observed a Hindu lady shout "Jesus" when she almost got into trouble and it saved her from that trouble instantly. I got very curious and asked her why and how she managed to shout that wonderful name 'Jesus'? She confessed that she had no idea how it got into her mouth. I became even prouder of the name of Jesus that day and ever since. It dawned on me that even non-believers or non-Christians alike make use of it (the name of Jesus) consciously or subconsciously when there is trouble around the corner and it gets them out from trouble because without a shadow of doubt they know quite well that Jesus Christ is the Lord. Their greatest battle hindering or stopping or rather preventing them from conversion is pride (first) and then the spirit of religion that they've worshipped for so long because religion is as strong as the spirits of unbelief, shyness, doubt or fear. Let's quickly go through this very short account recorded in [Mark 9:38-40] – "And John answered him, saying, Master, we saw one casting out devils in thy name, and he followeth not us: and we forbad him, because he followeth not us. {Verse 39} But Jesus said, Forbid him not: for there is no man which shall do a miracle in my name, that can lightly speak evil of me. {Verse 40} For he that is not against us is on our part." If the man was casting out devils in the name of Jesus yet he was not a follower of Jesus, it sends a message across.

Often times we believers judge people who God has not yet judged only because they are not believers like us. No man can judge or determine who makes Heaven or not, this is why in our faith we must guard our minds on what we think about the so-called unbelievers. Even Jesus addressed this concern in [Matthew 8:11-12] – "And I say unto you, That many shall come from east and west, and shall sit down with Abraham, and Isaac, and Jacob, in the kingdom of heaven. {Verse 12} *But the children of the kingdom shall be cast into outer darkness*: there shall be weeping and gnashing of teeth." If you went through other Bible versions of this text, you'd discover that Jesus was surely not referring to the children of the kingdom of darkness if he said *'the children of the kingdom'*. This therefore tells us that it is not necessarily our best behaviour that guarantees our eternity because the Holy Bible called all our righteousness *'as filthy rags'* - [Isaiah 64:6]. After all in [Romans 3:29] Apostle Paul asked and answered thus – "[Is he] the God of the Jews only? [is he] not also of the Gentiles? Yes, of the Gentiles also." This categorically says that God is equally the God of unbelievers. Was he not called the God of all flesh - [Jeremiah 32:27]? Therefore that name 'Jesus' can truly save anybody regardless of what we actually think or believe about them! Surely 'Jesus' saves you – believer or unbeliever and actually Jesus said in [Matthew 9:13b, Mark 2:17b and Luke 5:32] that – "I came not to call the righteous, but sinners to repentance". So against what many Bible teachers teach us today, I know surely that God speaks and seeks to win sinners. How do I know this (you may ask)? Who tells sinners to change and who instructs unbelievers to convert? However there is even a stronger need for confessing Jesus Christ as Lord because the Holy Bible says that it is *'the only name given' by which 'men' can be saved* - [Acts 4:12]. By which 'men' can be saved, not by which 'only believers' can be saved. Does this however mean that there is no need for redemption? No. Jesus was only emphasizing how pertinent it is for believers to have an undying fear of God thereby remaining committed and vigilant so as not to miss the kingdom of God through a lackadaisical or carefree attitude towards the things of God in the belief or mentality that they are already saved just because they believe and thereby being firm in their relationships with God. Jesus was marvelled at the great faith of the centurion who had told him to *'speak the word only'* [Matthew 8:8] rather than visiting his home because he counted himself unworthy to receive Jesus at his home. Jesus simply did not want men to take salvation or the grace of God for granted and in [Romans 13:1-7] a detailed statement on the power and relevance of authority is rendered.

The place of Royalty:

I'd break this down further with the realities of life. If our Lord is called Jesus Christ, naturally from a lay point of view if his first name is Jesus then his surname (Father's name) has to be Christ. Being our own father, we as his son have the legal authority to use and be called by his name 'Jesus'. This means in our daily routines and chores at school, work, ministry and other endeavours, we can actually in real terms be referred to as 'Jesus' or the sons or children of God and this is because Jesus was and still is the Son of God. For instance [Acts 10:18] writes about Apostle Peter – "And called, and asked whether Simon, which was surnamed Peter, were lodged there." From this short passage it is clear that Apostle Peter had a name (Simon) but even the Holy Bible repeatedly addressed him by his surname 'Peter'. In the same light we automatically inherited our Daddy's name and therefore his identity naturally and it is not a stolen identity because we have the right to the name of Jesus. However the Holy Bible sometimes referred to him as Christ Jesus which (again from a lay point of view) stirs up debate but equally occurs in real life situations with many societies preferring to address an individual by their surname(s) first. Scripture in [Colossians 3:3-4] declares – "For ye are dead (with Jesus), and your life is hid with Christ (*not 'with' but 'in' that name 'Jesus'*) in God. When Christ (*not Jesus*), who is our life, shall appear, then shall ye also appear with him in glory." Our life is hid in Christ because he is our *Daddy in heaven and the head of the Church* (as seen earlier in this book) who died as Jesus and rose as Christ. Therefore I (we – the children of God) have become Jesus today in this world and as such we are believers who are also referred to by the world as Christians (Christ-like or anointed-ones) because of Christ that is resident in us through his Holy Spirit and also because we have the very nature of Christ. Jesus is practically re-incarnated in us thereby effectively creating a sure destiny for us in Christ and God. We are the property of the name of Jesus as much as the name of Jesus is our property. Therefore what we are to the name of Jesus and what it is to us is for instance similar to, although a lot higher than what the British Passport and its holder is supposed to be to her majesty the Queen – her property. The authority that issues the British Passport (her majesty's passport office) does so in the name of her majesty the Queen. The authority is under and is controlled by her majesty the Queen. This therefore means that the department (issuing authority) that issues the British Passport is owned by the Queen and subsequently the property called a British Passport legally belongs to her majesty the Queen. It's a property she issues her subjects to give them visa-free travel access to the vast majority of the world as her subjects (as royalty)…owned by her majesty the Queen. This argument that portrays us as *'royalty'* and heirs of God is for instance being applied by Great Britain today hence confirmed by the crown on the cover of a British Passport being that a crown is the symbol of royalty. Many other nations adopted this initiative from Great Britain, for instance nations like Canada, Poland and some others whose passport covers have crowns on their covers. So the passport of the United Kingdom identifies the holder as a citizen of the United Kingdom and as a subject of her majesty the Queen. In the same way what the British Passport is to a British Citizen as already explained above is even less than what the promises of God in the Holy Bible and the name of Jesus are to a child of God. The British royal family understands this very much and have always put God first in all their affairs. The name of Jesus is a spiritual treasure that identifies exactly who we are, just as the British Passport is a physical treasure used to identify its holder. I'm sure every British Passport holder has at some point read the words written on it by her majesty's secretary of state, however and unfortunately I'm equally sure there are millions of believers who have not dared to read through one verse in the Holy Bible yet they are supposed to be or are believed to be members of the Church who bear the name of Jesus, particularly during prayers.

The United Kingdom (UK) is one nation I know out of all the nations on the planet earth that took or adopted it's governing principles and doctrines from the Holy Bible which we fondly refer to as the word of God just the same like it was in the ancient times kingdom of Israel. From having a monarchy, through keeping the prime ministerial position, to the words on the national anthem and the national symbol(s) or what we may call the coat of arms that bears the crown. Regardless I observed that a nation like the United States of America (USA) for instance encourages believing (Christianity) and believers (Christians), however they may not have applied such great insights (and I'm not being disrespectful in any way) from the word of God as has been inculcated in the norms and doctrines of the United Kingdom although the USA was equally founded on some core Biblical values. The United Kingdom (a nation I love, admire and cherish so much) on the contrary could easily be viewed as a nation that encourages believing (Christianity) but not necessarily the believers (Christians). It's a very complicated gamble and I'd explain my comments please. In the United Kingdom if you talked about God, people stared at you weirdly making you look and feel out of place as though you were discussing the right topic in a wrong environment for it. However in the United States if you talked about God, the atmosphere was suddenly lit up and made you feel comfortable. You'd hardly hear an American make a complete sentence in any living day without talking about God at some point but it is not exactly so in the United Kingdom which is actually the nation that took more from the Holy Bible, even though both nations have unfortunately in recent years seen a huge decline in the numbers that profess belief in Christ. Pertinently God has used these great nations to bless the world regardless the observed shortfalls. The United Kingdom is a nation I'm very proud of belonging to, being the only nation on earth with 'greatness' attached to its name – Great Britain; more so it gave the world their central language called the 'English language' which remains the language of the world even for many centuries to come I believe. However there is yet a better language than the English language, which is the language of the Spirit or the language of heaven (*speaking in Tongues*). The United States being arguably the next great nation after the United Kingdom and the most powerful nation in its own right is unique in its own way because it gave the world their currency (the United States Dollars) and without currency the world goes hungry and sterile. However also there are better currencies which are the currencies of the Spirit or the currencies of heaven. It's in four phases: the **word of God** which involves - Godliness/Holiness/Righteousness - [Matthew 6:33 and Hebrews 12:14], the **blood of Jesus** [Romans 5:9, Revelation 1:5 and Revelation 12:11], **faith** [Hebrews 11:1] and **charity** [Proverbs 10:12 and 1 Peter 4:8]. Yes charity because giving attracts equal measure, therefore arguably giving is a currency. Although 'physically' *language is an exceptionally unique form of identity whilst currency may not necessarily be,* however 'spiritually' both language and currency are divine proofs of our identity and strength as royalty. Naturally language tells people a lot about an individual hence the role of 'language education'.

In my opinion after the nation of Israel (God's acclaimed nation and people), the United Kingdom and the United States of America are the next two Scripturally-founded nations in the world respectively. Greece, Italy (Rome) and Spain seem to have long lost their Biblical identities and foundation(s) which has made their economic systems very complicated in recent times. All through British history and culture one would find traces of a nation hinged on the core values and principles taken from the Holy Bible which I believe has been this great nation's guide. Hence grasping the role and effects of royalty or the realm of the royal-majesty is imperative because it puts us in charge as authority is exercised through us as children of God just as her majesty the Queen is in charge of and a spiritual mother to all British and commonwealth citizens and residents. I'd define royalty simply as having an unreserved fear and knowledge of God with the understanding of the kingship that it brings with it or attracts to it. The United Kingdom is probably the only nation on earth that adopted the core values and principles of the kingdom of God as has already been said earlier because the nation was drafted and written on the word of God (Holy Bible) even though in recent times deviations have started to manifest gradually in the system like the issues of gay marriages and other flaws. It has also unequivocally maintained these royal attributes and core values in its culture ever since regardless these perceived or known flaws. In principle every citizen of any royal kingdom is a potential heir to that throne and this equally means that arguably every British subject is heir to the throne only that one would have to find out their millionth position as heir, however in practice and reality it cannot just be so. Also in the kingdom of God every believer (as one) was made for the palace. It's often been rumoured that her majesty the Queen does not need a passport to travel out of the country and therefore cannot be subject to passport controls at airports. I'm particularly not sure how true this information is but I tend to believe it because if people (her majesty the Queen's subjects) are covered and protected by God's glory and majesty 'in her name', how could she then be subject to her own self or to the power, authority and majesty God has already bestowed on her as Queen or in her name? If her majesty the Queen could never be a subject of her own self, then how could she use a passport endorsed and issued to her subjects in her own name? Sensibly it cannot be possible. This is exactly how it is for every child of God, we are customised by the name of Jesus. We have a crown on our royal head(s) and that crown is the name 'Jesus', thus making us joint-heirs (of the kingdom of God) with Christ [Romans 8:17]. This means that heavenly-royalty is made one for all believers by the Spirit of God. It is bigger, greater and more powerful than any man-made political position. Nobody votes royals into authority. So if you're wondering why or how it's possible that her majesty the Queen does not need a passport to travel, then the answer is already obvious – as already stated above that her majesty the Queen cannot use a document she issues to her subjects because it is an insult to her authority as the head of state and Queen just as the word of God was not written for God but for every child of God. It can therefore be reasonably argued or implied that real and true royals don't need man-made passports to travel. The Bible says that 'the world belongs to the children of men' - [Psalm 115:16]. But I know a nation where there is a rife competition amongst men at a certain stage of their lives to start battling to become *traditional rulers*, yet all are subject to passport controls whenever they travel out of their own territories. Therefore as children of God, we are not controlled or under the systems of this world.

Royalty is different from loyalty just as much as the world has witnessed the classification of human beings. The *sweet consolation* is that we're all equal in the eyes of God but the *bitter reality* remains that we've all been segregated from ourselves and classed into different grades. For instance it is quite disappointing that when God creates, man tries to recreate. As a child of God you cannot be recognised or associated with colours because we are made in the glory and image of God and **no human being was painted at creation**. This means that you cannot be tagged black or white. That idea of being black or being white is only man-made. It was a concept initiated, coined and/or formed by the colonialists or what you may call the *colonial masters*. It was not from God and must be dropped by the humans of this age and generation. The only place(s) in the Holy Bible where 'white or black' were used as colours (not as identities) in the Scriptures was in [Matthew 5:36] where it says – "Neither shalt thou swear by thy head, because thou canst not make one hair white of black". Through the Scriptures everywhere it makes reference to the colour 'black', it was referring to – reproach, shame, languish, suffering, punishment, slavery, hurt, emptiness, pain, void, waste and everything abhorable (again not identities) as can be seen in the following Scriptural verses [Jeremiah 8:21, Jeremiah 14:2, Songs of Solomon 1:5-6, Lamentations 4:8, Nahum 2:10, Joel 2:6, Jude 13]. Jesus was neither white nor black, he wasn't even what we call a Christian but Jesus was a Jew from Nazareth in Judea who gave birth to the Church (not Christianity) in a place called 'the upper room'. I've insisted that Jesus never gave birth to Christianity here because when Jesus gave birth to the Church, there was no place in the Holy Bible where it was recorded that Jesus called us Christians, just as he never called us 'whites' or 'blacks'. In the beginning God created them *male and female* as it is written in [Genesis 1:27] and in [Genesis 5:2] and then in [Matthew 19:4] and again in [Mark 10:6], not black and/or white. Man recreated by identifying God's creation with colours thereby tagging them white and black. Kingdom royals cannot be tagged by the colours of men because they undermine the glory bestowed on men by God, psychologically. Nevertheless that is the order of the world of men, it's not of the kingdom of God. Again I say, God never attached any colour to his creation, man did. No human being is 'white' in colour and none is 'black' in colour. It would be easier, more meaningful and easily acceptable if the world addressed the so called 'whites' and 'blacks' of the earth by their continental or national heritage and identities for instance as – Israelis, Africans, Europeans, English, Americans, Canadians, Australians, Asians etcetera because we are yet to see a white or black human being to justify that man-made tag. Actually if I see a white human being I may run away because I'd probably think it's a ghost and if I see a black human being I will *surely* run because it must be the devil or some other demonic spirit. Again these colours have spiritual meanings and representations, with white being a colour attached or associated to all things angelic, clean and Godly (light) whereas black is a colour attached or associated to all things dirty and devilish or ungodly (darkness) and I say this without any racial prejudice in my heart because my wife is a European originally from Poland and I'm African holding British citizenship which automatically makes you a European citizen as well but I'm an origin of Nigeria, this should make our children be identified as multi-racial yet there's no such thing being that there's only one race created by God which is the human race. Jesus the Lord and Christ was not 'white' and was not 'black'. Jesus was a Jew and the so called 'whites' and 'blacks' of the earth believe in the same Jesus who became the Christ. So if we believe in the same God, how can we then be different? Meanwhile the word 'black' is synonymous with the word 'lack', making me consider that its real meaning was intended as 'b-lack' or more clearly as 'be-lack'. I believe this argument could be the real reason why the United States of America has wisely opted to use the terminology 'African-American' in addressing its 'black' citizens, as opposed to 'black-Americans' and subsequently people from the Caribbean are referred to as 'Afro-Caribbean' rather than as 'black-Caribbean'. Could this be traceable to the financial results (failures or poverty-dominance) prevalent and predominant in the so-called black communities within our societies today, particularly in Africa where the poverty rate is astounding and keeps rising? Well that would be an argument for another day since it does not directly address the core or central message of this book and I have not written these one-hundred thousand plus words for my books to gain world-class fame or for them to be the best among the best-sellers; and though they may but ultimately I write with a truly genuine conviction stemming from the mind-set of creativity and revelation.

This book could easily have been expanded to accommodate a few more chapters which may have included the following:

- Jesus: God the Son
- Jesus: the Son of God
- Jesus: the Son of Man

- Jesus: the Son of David
- Jesus: the Son of Joseph
- Jesus: the King of the Jews

But for the purposes of immediate clarity and conciseness, I have decided to break these down into just two chapters below and a number of sub-heads:

- Jesus: Son of God
- Jesus: God the Son

However, a revised and more comprehensive volume/version of this book on the 'Ideas from GOD series' could be edited in the future to incorporate all originally planned or intended six chapters as mentioned above by the merciful grace of God and for his glory and majesty.

Chapter 1: Jesus – Son Of God

(MAN OF GOD)

The place of Name:

JESUS arguably denotes

J – Justice (brings Freedom)
E – Evangelism (for Eternity)
S – Scripture (teaches Gospel)
U – Upright (fears God)
S – Saviour (righteous Salvation)

Jesus signifies stewardship. Jesus – Son of God was Jesus the 'man of God' and most importantly the servant because he was born with the character of stewardship and an attitude of servitude. Jesus as the Son of God identified us equally as the sons of God. In [John 14:12-14] Jesus said "Verily, verily, I say unto *you, He* that believeth on me, the works that I do shall he do also; *and greater [works] than these shall he do*; because I go unto my Father. {Verse 13} And whatsoever ye shall ask <u>in my name</u>, that will I do, that the Father may be glorified *in the Son*. {Verse 14} If ye shall ask anything <u>in my name</u>, I will do [it]." So why did Jesus say "and greater works than these shall *he* do?" Why would we be able to do greater works than the Son of God himself? This is because we as the Jesus on the earth today have overcome by the power of Christ (the resurrected Jesus) in the new and recreated Jesus (Christ) living in us. It is because we have absolutely no restrictions whatsoever stopping or hindering us from doing greater works than Jesus did because we do all <u>in his name</u>. In the middle

1

of this Scripture above, Jesus said "…He that believeth on me…" and the word 'He' starts with a capital 'H' because this I believe was to lay emphasis on our new authority as Jesus. Jesus had to go through the ordeal and searing pains of the Cross of Calvary and although we don't have to do the same, yet to prove his love for us we may be required to go through some challenges sometimes for the glory and love of God to be revealed in and through us. This also means that although we may sometimes experience these challenges, we are not hated by the Lord and it does not make Jesus's works null and void or invalid or devoid of power to deliver but what it does explain is that in all and through all *we are more than they that have already conquered* - [Romans 8:37]. This means that we are more than just one man because of the authority in the name of Jesus and the power of the Calvary's Cross on which Jesus was slain, although the Cross posed a kind of barrier to Jesus. It really did! That was why on the way to the Cross Jesus 'kneeled' down to pray to the Father in [Luke 22:42] - "Saying, Father, if thou be willing, remove this cup from me: nevertheless not my will, but thine, be done." Then an Angel came to strengthen him in the following verse, yet in agony Jesus prayed more earnestly. Jesus clearly saw the Cross as a hindrance, yet he understood that the will of the Father must be done. The sacrifice on the Cross of Calvary tried to stop him, however Jesus came out victoriously that we might take up his name and reign in the earth [Revelation 5:10]. Therefore the name of Jesus being the name of God and man (as already stated above) is more than just one man because God represents the Trinity (three persons in one God) and because we bear that name Jesus, hence we are more than mere conquerors. The name of Jesus is not for Christ because he is called Christ, it is not a name for a *'psychological spiritual man/being'* called Jesus, it is for us. Furthermore while Jesus was on earth, Jesus could still not do any mighty works in Nazareth because of their unbelief [Matthew 13:58] and [Mark 6:5-6]. This was somewhat a form of restriction or barrier to him and if it wasn't, then Jesus would have performed miracles in Nazareth; after all he was both God and man so why not?! No wonder Jesus said "Verily verily, I say unto you, He (again notice that the 'H' is in capital letters because Jesus knew we must take up his name and earthly position here on earth with his Spirit in us if only we believed on him) that believeth on me…[1 John 14:12-14]". In the book of [John 6:47] Jesus said "Verily, verily, I say unto you, He (again 'H' in capital letter) that believeth on me hath everlasting life." Jesus always reemphasized the truth by using the word 'verily' twice, thus - 'verily verily' and the word of God makes it clear that although Jesus was referring to us; starting the word 'He' with a capital letter 'H' gives us a lead to function in his name. It was not an error, neither was it an insult to him that we should bear his name and authority. So we only have to believe in Jesus to become like Jesus and even 'better' than Jesus was on the earth (by the divine power of salvation) for us to be empowered to do *'greater works'* than Jesus did. This is only possible because we have greater power now than Jesus while he was 'on earth' since he died and rose from the dead for us, yet nobody equipped Jesus similarly by dying for him because he was the power of God and also because he came to fulfil the will of God as established in the Holy Scriptures. For instance because Jesus died to give me strength in his name, it then goes to say that the name of Jesus has the power and authority to heal me of any disease as well as to keep me in health more than any false power or false authority that the devil may be exercising as a weapon used to afflict the people of God.

By the power in his name and as the present 'Jesus' in the earth, believers carry and represent light anywhere we are and everywhere we find ourselves. The Holy Bible says (actually Jesus said this himself) in [Matthew 5:13a and in Verse 14] – "Ye are the salt of the earth: {Verse 14} Ye are the light of the world. A city that is set on an hill cannot be hid." As the salt of the earth and like Jesus did, we give taste to the world. Again, Jesus never said 'Ye are the "whites and blacks" of the world', he said "light". He knew what he wanted to say and said it, Jesus was very conscious of his words. The glorification of Jesus quickened us to assume his earthly office and ministry. Jesus called himself "light" and called us "light". So we are truly the Jesus of now by the power of revelation in his name. This can be verified in [John 9:5] where Jesus said – *"As long as I am in the world, I am the light of the world."* Jesus said 'as long as I am in the world' because immediately he ascended to God as Christ and Lord, with he (as a Spirit) in us we automatically became that light…bearing his name and same authority, doing exactly what he did and even more. So we know that Jesus called us 'light', just as the word of God called Jesus 'light'. So we now represent Jesus as light since [1 Thessalonians 5:5] confirms - "Ye are all the children of light, and the children of the day: we are not of the night, nor of darkness." 'Light' here I believe connotes salvation, which means we are the children of Christ since *Christ is the horn of our salvation* - [Psalm 18:2] and like begets like. That means our salvation was made and moulded in Christ from Christ. Subsequently if Jesus did not resurrect from the dead (as Christ), salvation would have had no life and meaning in it. Without salvation Jesus's name would have had no power in it and would have been like any other ordinary name as already explained from the introduction of this book. Therefore the power in that name was grafted in us through salvation and Jesus had no choice or any other option to reject being used by God for this selfless and compassionate purpose because the word of God could not have lied and had to be fulfilled. Jesus was and Christ is/ remains (in us) a burning and a shining light just like Jesus testified about John the Baptist in [John 5:35]. We became *branded* by the same power of resurrection and our brand name changed *spiritually* from whatever we were called at birth by our parents to 'Jesus' immediately we accepted Christ as Lord and Saviour of our lives. It is the same Spirit that raised Jesus from the dead (as Christ) that dwells in us transforming us to make commands and declarations in the name of Jesus. The blood-bought brand name of Jesus is a supernatural name for spiritual ascension. I'd define a brand as a processed and established (transformed) thought because it is not a brand until there is a metamorphosed transformation. A brand is whatever you make it to be. Whatever you believe and call a brand becomes a brand to and for you, at work in you and a testimony through you. Therefore every child of God is branded in that name – 'Jesus'.

In business terms, God was the innovator while Jesus was the innovation from God and through God whereas we are the re-invented and remodelled Jesus. In many hi-tech and multi-national organisations today for instance, re-invention is the new form of innovation because the future of the world are (from a natural perspective) in the hands of the unknown and many organisations cease to invent new things because they are in business *without God*. If you're in business on your own, you're not in business. Similarly if you're in business without God, you're already out of business. Therefore organisations avoid taking risks by re-inventing well established products and making them supposedly 'better' but the future of the child of God is in the sure hands of God because Jesus was re-invented in us and empowered by the Holy Ghost in us for our profiting. Jesus became tested, trusted and well established after he gave salvation to mankind and took the name as 'Christ', hence Jesus Christ. Jesus was elevated to *Christhood* while we were elevated to *Jesus-hood*. Equally so Abram after he met with God became Abraham [Genesis 17:5] as much as Jacob after he had wrestled with God and prevailed had his name changed to Israel [Genesis 32:24-30]. Whenever a man has an encounter with God his identity either changes or improves dramatically regardless of his immediate circumstances at the time of the encounter. The Holy Bible in [Jeremiah 29:11] declares – "For I know the thoughts that I think toward you, saith the LORD, thoughts of peace, and not of evil, to give you an expected end." Therefore the future of organisations constantly face uncertainties because they are controlled by the economies of the world, but the children of the Most High have a defined and assured destiny in Christ. This is because **the 'Spirit of Christ' can only dwell in the 'body of Christ'.** The world will always have the choice and the hope to change if the Lord tarries, but until then should the world rest their faith in hope? Well, until there's absolutely no hope; hope must exist. This is why Christ (through his Spirit) is always receptive of sinners that are willing and eager to change and be changed. I remember my late Dad always advising me "Chimezie Okonkwo take your destiny into your own hands!" I could not really understand this advice but the only way I knew how to take my destiny into my own hands was by giving my life to Christ and I did through numerous challenges and circumstances that would eventually force me to him; although I am still trying to improve and constantly learning in the **school of change** which is a combination of the study of the word of God as detailed in the Holy Bible and some personal life experiences. Yet regardless our belief, God made his name on earth 'Jesus' accessible and useable to and for us all. This does not in any way encourage unbelief or sin because as we may already know this - *'grace is grace, yet without sin'* because grace overshadows or overcomes the sinful nature in man.

At some point in my life I'd pondered on God's love and why he made available that power in the name of Jesus to us out of the thousands of names that we (as his children) identify him with. So I decided to write a book titled "The names of God" and got frustrated writing that book. That single experience taught me a very strong lesson that *you cannot name God*, however *God names himself* by the miracles he does in and around us. God represents every great thing and every great thing is made of God [Psalm 104:24]. My intended motive on attempting to write that book was to keep track of the names of God as recorded in the sacred word of God and to understand the specific reasons and situations that caused or stirred God to often change his names from time to time and from situation to situation but I easily lost count. I also discovered that every name of God was attached to the fulfilment of a particular project or purpose in the lives of men. For instance Abraham called the place of provision 'Jehovah Jireh' and this list goes on and on. It's not a myth, I discovered that you cannot number or count the names of God because he is the beginning and the end and from everlasting to everlasting. No wonder God used the Lord Jesus to make arguably his 'first or birth name' available to us because it is the only name that is highly exalted above every other name [Philippians 2:9-11]. This is the name that has given us access to the privilege of royal priesthood in Christ Jesus to which Apostle Peter testified to in [1 Peter 2:9] – "But ye are a chosen generation, a royal priesthood, an holy nation, a peculiar people; that ye should shew forth the praises of him who hath called you out of darkness into his marvellous light." We are a chosen generation because God chose us before the world began. We are a royal priesthood because we come from Christ, through Christ and are made and named by the royal authority in the name of Jesus the Christ to spread the gospel for the glory of the Father. We are a holy nation because we were created by a holy God. We are a peculiar people because we are endowed with supernatural ideas, abilities and capabilities from God through the recreated spirit in us and then [Philippians 3:10a] says – "That I may know him, and the power of his resurrection…" The only way we would ever know him is through his words and by a clear understanding of our brand new identity and name in Christ which is 'Jesus'. The Scripture says in the book of [Romans 8:11 and verse 14] "But if the Spirit of him that raised up Jesus from the dead dwell in you, he that raised up Christ from the dead shall also quicken your mortal bodies by his Spirit that dwelleth in you. {Verse 14} For as many as are led by the Spirit of God, they are the sons of God." This later verse paints a clear picture of my message thus:

for as many as get the revelation of functioning '*in the name of Jesus*', they become like 'Jesus – sons of God'. Then what happens to the daughters of God? Well if only they believe the word, that promise is entirely for all the children of God.

Going further in [Romans 8:16-17] "The Spirit itself beareth witness with our spirit, that we are the children of God: {Verse 17} And if children, then heirs; **heirs of God**, and **joint-heirs <u>with Christ</u>**; if so be that we suffer with him, that we may be also glorified together." Here we are called 'heirs of God' just what Jesus was. Jesus was an heir of God, then the Bible calls us 'joint heirs with Christ'. Christ here means the glorified and exalted Jesus. Notice that it did not say 'joint heirs with Jesus' because we now function and operate in his name – Jesus, while he remains the Lord and Christ in heaven sitting at the right hand of God the Father. We are one with Christ because Christ was in Jesus and one with Jesus and is in us today hence "Christ in us the hope of glory [Colossians 1:27b]". If whatever that is in me belongs to me for instance my organs belong to me because they were given to me by God, this therefore goes to confirm that if I have Christ in me then I am Christ's and Christ is mine. Also the Spirit bears witness with our spirit the same way that the Father bore witness of Jesus 'because they were and are still one' [John 8:18, John 10:30 and John 14:20]. What this further explains is that if Jesus is one with the Father, then we are equally one with Jesus (our father) since it is the same Spirit that was in Jesus that dwells in us today and has quickened us…just like Jesus. It is therefore that sinless Spirit that we invite to dwell in us by (us) being sinless, the same Spirit causes us to triumph in the name of Jesus. This is particularly sensitive knowledge rather than crass. Think about this – '*in*' the name of Jesus. What does it tell us? He in us and we in him [1 John 4:13 and verse 15]. Therefore the name of Jesus indemnifies the believer against any loses, calamities or weapons being formed against the believer. In this regard the blood of Jesus as such becomes our insurance policy as often as we partake in the Holy Communion instituted by our Lord and Messiah Jesus the Christ. This automatically transfers any risks and consequences that may arise against us in any form of peril to the name of Jesus and that name is the place of Christ spiritually. We are anointed to be Jesus yet not Christ the Messiah because Jesus more than any other name often addressed himself as the *Son of Man* and we are sons and children of men and of God. Jesus was also the Son of God and the New International Version puts it this way in [Galatians 3:26] – "You are all sons of God through faith in Christ Jesus" which I'd then summarise as *'through Christ but as Jesus'* because Jesus gave us that power and the authority to become like him through the same Spirit in us that also raised up Christ from the dead.

God used the name of Jesus to work through Jesus and exalt Jesus. The book of [Hebrews 2:11a] tells us this – "For both he that sanctifieth and they who are sanctified [are] all of one..." If truly we are one with him who has sanctified us and he who has sanctified us is called by the name of Jesus (that became the Christ), then also we shall be equally called by the name of Jesus because we are one with him that sanctified us. Today as the 'body of Christ', God is using the same name to work through us and exalt us over situations and circumstances, just like Jesus (the Christ) was exalted. It's as simple as that. It is not a mystery then that the power of God in us (which is Christ) has given us the privilege to use the same name he used while he was on earth. This explains why all prayers must be made to God, by the power of the Holy Ghost and ***in the name of Jesus***. The same Spirit makes intercessions for us as is written in [Romans 8:26-27] - "Likewise the Spirit also helpeth our infirmities: for we know not what we should pray for as we ought: but the Spirit itself maketh intercession for us with groanings which cannot be uttered. {Verse 27} And he that searcheth the hearts knoweth what is the mind of the Spirit, because he maketh intercession for the saints *according to the **will of God***." In {Verse 34} of the same chapter the Scripture gives a slightly different account of this intercessory role – "Who is he that condemneth? It is Christ that died, yea rather, that is risen again, who is even at the right hand of God, who also maketh intercession for us." In the later Verse, Apostle Paul stated that Christ died (as Jesus) and rose (as Lord and Christ), therefore Apostle Paul also used the name of 'Christ' as our intercessor because the same is the Holy Spirit of God. He it is that is in us and intercedes with us, through us and for us (when we speak in other tongues) to God the Father. Apostle Peter was one of the twelve who witnessed Jesus transcend to the Christ, no wonder he had the audacity to perform miracles *in the* *name of Jesus Christ* (because he knew him personally) rather than *in the name of Jesus* as we were instructed in the written and infallible word of God. They (the Apostles) had a first class encounter of the transformation and experienced it live in action. It's no wonder then that this encounter occurred in [Acts 3:6] as recorded thus – "Then Peter said, Silver and gold have I none; but such as I have give I thee: In the name of Jesus Christ of Nazareth rise up and walk." Remarkably it was Jesus that was of Nazareth, Christ was not but the apostles saw Jesus become the Christ. It was a rare privilege for the apostles hence Peter said '…*such as 'I' have…'* This explains to me that the apostles were later able to understand that *they became Jesus by having Christ* and they had every right to emulate Jesus and to be like Jesus in every meaning of it because Jesus was more than a *pastor, prophet or evangelist* to the apostles and the other disciples. As such pastors, prophets and evangelists were irrelevant in the days of Jesus because his disciples eventually became even more honourable than the pastors of this day. Why? They knew the real person of Jesus. They had a knowledge (a knowing) and an experience, they saw who Jesus really was. Today what the Church has is an awareness and an experience of Jesus (the Christ), not an immediate physical knowledge. The disciples knew his physical presence, the Church today knows his spiritual presence. The physical presence had limits, the spiritual presence does not, yet the Church has entertained hindrances. We can't see Jesus today because we became Jesus when Jesus became Christ, by his Spirit.

Prior to this miracle, the man who was at the beautiful gate was expecting to receive '*something*' from them, and he received that something. Hunger gives birth to desperation and desperation attracts the miraculous. Later in [Acts 3:13] the Bible says that - "God glorified his son Jesus", but it was Peter and John who performed the miracle '*in the name of Jesus*'. So God glorified himself through Peter and John but the Scripture said that *God glorified Jesus*; that tells anybody that Peter and John became Jesus (not the Christ) in the *absence* of Jesus, but in the *presence* of Christ which is the Spirit of God that they carried. The following third verse made this clearer [Acts 3:16] – "And *his name through faith in his name* hath made this man strong, whom ye see and know: yea, the faith which is by him hath given him this perfect soundness in the presence of you all." After

Jesus's ascension, we henceforth believe *in his name* and therefore occupy his name in the faith that was written (authored) and published (finished) in the name of Jesus which is our model or framework. There is therefore such guaranteed assurance that we can throw our names in the garbage and walk tall like Jesus walked [1 John 2:6] in the name of Jesus because Jesus is life in us, Jesus is live for us and Jesus is alive through us. The name of Jesus is our right, not just for believers but for unbelievers alike, but *in life the right you fail to exercise automatically becomes a wrong*. Apostle Paul understood that it was faith (in) 'the name of Jesus' (not an image of a man called Jesus) that got the lame man at the gate of the temple called '*Beautiful*' his healing, hence the repetition "And *his name* through faith in *his name*..." For example when I got the "JESUS" tattoo on my back, from my understanding now I can say that I was totally ignorant of whatever it meant or whatever it would later mean to me and this was regardless of what it meant or would ever mean to anyone. One mind told me it was a huge error and another voice said to me '*you've just helped yourself forever because I'd defend you every day*'. I was ignorant that the word of God was against marks, tattoos or any inscriptions on our bodies. My ignorance may have turned to some wisdom of some sort because that name Jesus has repeatedly and undeniably backed me up through it all and I don't say this to encourage anyone to go garner some "JESUS" tattoos on their bodies because having the knowledge of the written word of God now, I wouldn't do any tattoos today. Sometimes I reflect on my past experiences, encounters, challenges and triumphs and I can't help but believe what God has spoken to me severally that I'm like the very '*foolish things*' that he'd in this generation to confound the wisdom of the world - [1 Corinthians 1:27]. My life became an epitome of survival from incessant afflictions of death and dearth. It's been like a movie and in this movie, I've played that character Jesus (in his name) while Jesus is God 'in' me (in the name of Christ and in the person of the Holy Spirit). It's a movie once plagued with doom and gloom but now being powered in light. It's been a movie full of fun, drama, victories and triumphs won because the actor (as Jesus) is being backed by deity so even '*we*' (the audience) know that I'd never lose any battle in this life of the movie as much as I wouldn't lose any battle in the movie of my life which I watch me act. The name of Jesus is making this drama turn into more than a block-buster thriller of an action-packed movie just because Scripture has declared it that I am more than a conqueror [Romans 8:37].

Going further with this I discovered that the vast majority of the people living in the United Kingdom (for instance) claim to live in London. Most of them don't actually have any business whatsoever with London and it's not because they don't have access to London. A smaller fraction of them actually work in London but don't live in London but all lay claims to living in London just the same way majority of the born-Nigerians living abroad lay claims to being born in the Lagos State of Nigeria. The reason is this, as human beings we take pride in huge names but we don't want the enormous responsibilities and/or challenges attached to those huge names. That's how it is for most believers (Christians). They love, adore, worship, preach and teach Jesus but they never want the responsibilities attached to laying claims to the name of Jesus. Real believing (Christianity) may not be very easy and the moment you identify with Jesus the assignments and challenges ahead of you naturally seem to outweigh your natural strength and ability. This is all recorded in the Holy Bible but we skip those bits and read only the bits that give us joy with promises of good tidings not realising that it may not be all green. This is why we need the special name of Jesus because it is the power of God for salvation and whatever name you bear naturally becomes a force in your life, either for a light or for a darkness but Jesus is the light. In the name of Jesus means in a crown of glory and this explains that there is maybe not exactly a ginormous but a grandeur crown of glory on our heads as believers and our head is Christ the head of the Church. The name of Jesus is our evidence as believers and every evidence seeks to and should be a voice to any and every doubter. The source of every evidence is a clear and precise information or detail and without information there's no revelation and without revelation there's no transformation. Names affect destinies supernaturally (spiritually) and naturally (physically), and I did a personal analysis regarding individual names where I concluded that – "*if you have the letter (i) in your name, sometimes you will get selfish. Don't worry, it's only natural. People don't have to understand why. Every letter in your name will have a very strong influence over your life. This is my 'personal' opinion, so you don't have to believe it. My argument is that when Jesus walked*

the earth, it was all about others because he became selfless; however immediately Jesus rose from the dead and became Chr(i)st, it became all about him because of that single letter 'i'." This is why it is a great spiritual exercise when we (as believers) study the Holy Bible, the Holy Spirit will always show us things that others could not see; and as much as I love the name the Lord has given my three children (Kingdom, Freedom and Wisdom) because for a name to be found in the Scriptures of God and also in the dictionary of men at the same time, such names surely do not come cheaply. However the name of Jesus is exalted above all other names and it is the seal of our eternal covenant with God. While Jesus is the exalted name, the exalted one is Christ. Names carry a more treasured weight of glory than *titles* do. Names are prophecies that identify you anywhere on earth. A title is equivalent to death because when people die what they leave behind is their name, their titles go with their dust. Your children take up your name, not your titles. Names are permanent adventures that are intended to last a lifetime while titles easily fade away because they are temporary in nature. Although names can be changed by the holder at will, they cannot however be withdrawn, but, titles can be withdrawn against the holder's will by the issuing authority. A name is like a big tree while titles are like the leaves of the tree, during the course of life the tree loses its leaves and a good instance is during the change of seasons. This is how easy it is for titles to be lost. For instance God used Jesus to show us this example by giving him a name which we (as believers) have carried on today, but his titles are Lord, Master, Saviour, Messiah, King and so on. Regardless of these titles of our Lord Jesus, the saving grace is in his name (Jesus) hence the effectiveness of our prayers dwell on his name (Jesus) for the expected results, not on his titles. **Titles represent one's office while names represent one's personality.** What makes people popular is their names, not their titles. This is why your name is your identity and a transferable one at that just like the name of Jesus, not his titles. As such we only remain Jesus until Jesus returns to sieve the earth and the centre of my argument drawing on [John 12:45] – "And he that seeth me seeth him that sent me." If then seeing Jesus meant seeing God, then seeing us must mean seeing Jesus because God sent Jesus **as God** and Jesus sent us **as Jesus** [John 15:16]. Hence we are sent to **preach the**

Kingdom of God and to **teach the gospel of Jesus** [Acts 28:31] with the boldness of being Jesus.

The place of Christianity:

Here's a very complex and quite inconclusive one, and have remained incomprehensible to many believers as well as arguably all unbelievers. Many of our Holy Bible teachers have argued that '*Christianity is a living person and his name is Jesus*', while some say that '*Christianity is a relationship with Jesus*'. However we may try to understand this even further. I have always wondered why Jesus never referred to himself as a Christian, yet we believe in him and call ourselves Christians. The argument of many is that Christianity means *Christ-like* but I'd think that is the mental definition given by the believers (Christians) themselves since the word '*Christian*' begins with the word '*Christ*'. We'd also notice that even the disciples of Jesus were never called Christians originally (not even in the upper room) until they arrived at Antioch alternatively referred to as *Syrian Antioch* today, located in Turkey and bordered by Syria. This makes it reasonably possible and quite concretely arguable that the terminology called Christianity may have originally been coined by unbelievers for believers as recorded in [Acts 11:26] – "And when he had found him, he brought him unto Antioch. And it came to pass, that a whole year they assembled themselves with the church, and taught much people. **And the disciples were called Christians first in Antioch**." Even Apostle Paul preferred to address himself as a Pharisee rather than as a Christian as chronicled in [Acts 23:6] – "But when Paul perceived that the one part were Sadducees, and the other Pharisees, he cried out in the council, Men [and] brethren, **I am a Pharisee**, the son of a Pharisee: of the hope and resurrection of the dead I am called in question." So do we really believe in what the Apostles of Jesus believed in? I sometimes call the term Christianity into question, however I never doubt my relationship with the resurrected Jesus (the Christ) as I acknowledge his Lordship. I believe in the gospel and I have received the Holy Ghost, however sometimes I argue in my mind on the word called *Christianity* if it has no strong Biblical backing although I still refer to myself as a Christian just to satisfy the world, but better together we're the Church which is what Jesus built. At the same time I don't want to see myself as over-thinking and in [Acts 23:8] Scripture tells us that – "For the Sadducees say that there is no resurrection, neither angel, not spirit: **but the Pharisees confess both.**" Therefore I'd humbly ask the question – "why would the Pharisees confess what we believe in if we're not Pharisees?" and "do we not really think or maybe consider that we should be referred to as believers or simply just as the Church as already stated?" I believe these things are the reasons why we (as a Church) should focus more on preaching and teaching the *verbatim* gospel of Jesus, rather than merely preaching or teaching the word of God because you can preach or teach the word of God without preaching or teaching the true gospel of Jesus thereby focusing on the Old Testament, but you cannot preach or teach the gospel of Jesus without preaching or teaching the word of God because the New Testament is the continuation of the Old Testament. Could the doctrine of Christianity be the reason for the divisions among the Churches today because maybe we could dig deeper to understand the motive behind this title arguably given by unbelievers and we easily adopted it without any further references of this notion being made in the Holy Scriptures?

Although I reluctantly call myself a Christian since Jesus never called us that, however I may also conclude that this could be why Christianity is considered a religion by the world today because the religious unbelievers coined that terminology. In [2 Corinthians 6:15] the Apostle Paul refers to us as believers but if we considered the day of Pentecost, our Pentecostal doctrine would then be a strong argument for us to probably be called Pentecostals, although not every Bible believing Church attaches it's systems with this Pentecostal phenomenon; thereby making the Church our universal unit. The denominational foundation in the different Churches today have led our Churches to battle to trace the history of the plague of religion even as the religion of a plagued history trails the current Church, thereby diverting our focus from preaching the true gospel. In [Ephesians 2:6] the Scripture says – "And hath raised [us] up together, and made [us] sit together in heavenly [places] in Christ Jesus." This Scripture says that the Church (as believers) are seated with Christ, not in a museum, not in a park, not even in a building called 'the Church', not in a believers conference, not in a movie theatre, not on the train or bus but on the throne of glory '*in heavenly places*' but this seems not to be the case today as the Church subconsciously seeks to be seated in religious places and thereby being compared with the religions of the world yet we seem unaware with our current place or position in the relevant matters that affect the Church today. Christianity has put the Church in a box of limitation. The Church was intended to function without walls and be the school where moral standards are taught and learnt, a place of constant movement, growth and advancement however we've made the Church seem more like a destination or a permanent residence permit/status that allows one to live permanently in a particular country but does not guarantee progress in living standards within those walls where it has been issued. It seems as though that once we achieved this status, we remained static enjoying this single victory without making any further attempts of progress or improvement because we have accepted a tag that gives us a false sense of fulfilment or accomplishment. We tend to restrict or stall our growth in Christ once we identified ourselves as Christians because we're of the sense that we've come to the climax of our association with Christ and therefore nothing could be improved any further. Religion!!! Apostle Paul said as quoted in [Acts 26:5] – "They have known me for a long time and can testify, if they are willing, that according to the straitest sect of our religion, I lived a Pharisee." This was Apostle Paul as recorded by Luke in the Acts of the Apostles indirectly referring to Christianity as a religion, even though he calls himself a Pharisee. Following this [Acts 26:28-29] says this – "Then Agrippa said unto Paul, Almost thou persuades me to be a Christian. {Verse 29} And Paul said, I would to God, that only thou, but also all that hear me this day, were both almost, and altogether such as I am, except these bonds." From this we can understand that Apostle Paul fell short of accepting the tag of Christianity, rather he insisted that he wished Agrippa and all that heard him '*became what he was*' (regardless what they called it). The main point being that they understood what he was regardless what they tagged it. Then going further in the New Living Translation, [Matthew 6:7] tells us this – "When you pray, don't babble on and on as **other religions** do. They think their prayers are answered only by repeating their words again and again." If this Scripture made reference to '*other religions*', then it means that what we call Christianity must be a religion except then we come to the conclusion that the New Living Translation is not a good translation of the original words of the Bible that this version was translated from. The curriculum of the present Church has been enormously edited from origin and currently seems to be in a chronically incompatible state with the charismatic orientation that the Church was originally established on and the New Living Translation also made a notable comparison between *real authority* which Jesus had and the *religious law* which then contradicts its original stance that Christianity is religious in [Matthew 7:28-29] – "After Jesus finished speaking, the crowds were amazed at his teaching, {Verse 29} for he taught as one who had real authority – quite unlike the teachers of religious law." A very controversial thought regarding Christianity came from Peter in [1 Peter 4:16-17] – "Yet if [any man suffer] as a Christian, let him not be ashamed; but let him glorify God on this behalf. {Verse 17} For the time [is come] that judgement must begin at the house of God: and if [it] first [begin] at us, what shall the end [be] of them that obey not the gospel of God?" I want to believe that Peter was addressing believers as Christians being a language that was coined and therefore understandable or identifiable to any unbelievers that cared to listen to his message.

The Church is currently so much disfigured at the moment in my opinion (which will be dealt with in detail later in this book) and although [1 Corinthians 12:20] speaks thus – "But now *are they* many members, yet but one body", still there seems to be not one body in the Church today. Then I ask whose voice do all these sects hear from, because Catholics have their own rules, beliefs, and doctrines; Anglicans have their own rules, beliefs and doctrines; Pentecostals have their own rules and beliefs; and the rest of the numerous '*units*' or denominations under the **Christian** Church have their own different rules, beliefs and doctrines but all use and lay claims to the Holy Bible. In contrast all other religions celebrate themselves as one in every part of the world. For instance Jews are Jews and believe the same everywhere, Muslims used to be Muslims and believed the same everywhere until the sect that tagged themselves '*the extremists*' arrived. Only the Christian Church appears to be really broken, disintegrated and totally divided at the moment. It'd be days like this but it is really important that we desist from being more loyal to a denomination than we are to God's kingdom and the gospel. There is a world of difference between the two commitments because there is only one Church in the eyes of God and therefore the walls built by the different denominations of Christianity must come crumbling down. Apostle Paul referring to the Christian doctrine and their different divisions and preaching methods said in [Philippians 1:15-17] – "Some indeed preach Christ even of envy and strife; and some also of good will: {Verse 16} The one preach Christ of contention, not sincerely, supposing to add affliction to my bonds: {Verse 17} But the other of love, knowing that I am set for the defence of the gospel." The New Living Translation renders it thus [Philippians 1:15-17] – "Some are preaching out of jealousy and rivalry. But others preach about Christ with pure motives. {Verse 16} They preach because they love me, for they know the Lord brought me here to defend the Good News. {Verse 17} Those others do not have pure motives as they preach about Christ. They preach with selfish ambition, not sincerely, intending to make my chains more painful to me." The idea of Christianity therefore needs to be really identified in detail to ascertain if this was really the intention of Christ lest we tag ourselves by some *unbelieving twig*. Hence religious delusions have eventually cornered our belief systems in the Church and instead of the Church changing the world, the world begins to change the Church, giving birth to a seemingly irretrievable state of unconsciousness and possibly eternal coma with no hope of eventual resuscitation (until the return of Christ) if the Church will just keep standing there looking while it's being changed and forced to accept and adopt the dictating of the unbelieving world. The religion of the unknown god seems to have intentionally or unintentionally assassinated the future of the gospel of Jesus and of our Churches as they constantly devise strategies to forcefully but diplomatically indulge or engage alien religion (in our Churches) laced with toxic spices and laden with spurious falsehood and this is the reason why the world seems to be currently stuck with terrorism unfortunately. We cannot just excel on a template in a foreign vault designed and dictated by a foreign god and orchestrated with premeditated intention to kill indiscriminately. The Church needs to prioritise our focus strong enough to boldly reject and eject the devices of the world and wiggle out of this very chaotic religious state by emphasizing our own doctrines and values, channelling and injecting them back into the society.

The place of Taking-Nothing:

Taking-nothing seems incomprehensible and impossible but I've often heard that the undisguised, real and true meaning of the word '*impossible*' is clearly '*I'm possible*' and how true this knowledge really is. The words of God are more than just the Holy Bible because God is constantly speaking through different mediums every day. All through my afflictions it was the deep and vast words of God that kept me strong and alive. These were words spoken through varying mediums which include:

*The Holy Bible – These are promises of God that can never fail regardless the strength and wealth of the challenges one may be facing.

*The blood of the Lamb – The claim to the blood of Jesus gave me guaranteed access to the grace of the Cross of Calvary as I confessed it daily as a weapon to overcome the enemy - [Revelation 12:11].

*The word of our Testimony – This involved speaking forth my healing into existence with my mouth regardless the symptoms I felt in my body. At that point when my health was at its lowest ebbs I always spoke spirit and life to myself - [Revelation 12:11 and John 6:63].

*The Prophecies – These were words spoken by God through his servants over or into my life during my Egyptian experience of plagues. I'd discuss '*prophecies*' in detail later in this book.

*The personal accounts and encounters – These are situations where God had personally given me specific words of encouragement and sound health through dreams and visions. I'd equally expound on this later through the cause of this book.

The fulfilment of all these words and actions will be founded on this principle and sub-head titled '*Taking-Nothing*'. You take nothing but faith into the path of destiny and [Matthew 10:5-10] clarifies this in detail but for the purposes of precision we'd only look at [Matthew 10:9-10] – "Provide neither gold, nor silver, nor brass in your purses, {Verse 10} Nor scrip for *your* journey, neither two coats, neither shoes, nor yet staves: for the workman is worthy of his meat." When Jesus sent his disciples to go and wrought diverse kinds of miracles, he warned them to take nothing with them because being the work of God the disciples could not have helped God finish his work by providing for anything they may have thought that they required. In the gospel according to [Mark 6:7-13] a similar account was rendered, however specifically in [Mark 6:7-9] the Scripture records this – "And he called *unto him* the twelve, and began to send them forth by two and two; and gave them power over unclean spirits; {Verse 8} And commanded them that they should take nothing for *their* journey, save a staff only; no scrip, no bread, no money in *their* purse: {Verse 9} But *be* shod with sandals; and not put on two coats." Taking-Nothing I've often heard is a major phase in the establishment of a divine ministry. You take nothing not because you have nothing, you take nothing because God provides in his service. Here is also the mystery for those that doubt the power of God in Jesus and it may be relevant to share this testimony. Growing up I hated pastors, reverends and other ministers of God or clergy men. I had this impression that they were so broke and unbelievably weird. Incomprehensible was the word! Not because they were bad, but they were just misunderstood and unfortunately I was one of those who misunderstood them. Whilst growing up my late Dad was a core heathen who would flog me and my sister with the cane for attending Church services on Sundays with our mum. My Dad would later go on a live TV broadcast and announce that "Jesus Christ is a mere concept." Those were his words before the world. That was the venomous anger he took from the knowledge that his late Dad (my late grand-dad who I never met) who was one of those who had brought the Anglican Church to our village and still (his Dad) was involved in a lot of traditional and customary activities. He could not reconcile this knowledge, therefore *innocent* Jesus had to pay for his experiences, thoughts and frustrations. His ideas about Jesus turned really sour and my late Dad psychologically and verbally started what could be referred to as the '*fight-Jesus campaign*'. But it wouldn't last forever because one day eventually came when dramatically he started studying the Holy Bible, singing hymns, psalms and other spiritual songs, also fasting and praying. He would start waking us up on Sunday mornings to prepare to attend Church services and by then I did not want to go to Church services anymore and sometimes we argued over this. At which point I started questioning God myself as already testified herein. Eventually I had encounters that got me where I am today but my point is that it's better to take nothing than to take the wrong thing(s) or carry along wrong or terrible ideologies and information with you. My Dad took the hatred of Jesus from the part of his background that gave reverence to idols and diabolical things, then he tried to force the same ideologies on us which culminated in me not feeling very attracted to the things of God. But the Scripture says in [2 Corinthians 12:9-10] that – "And he said unto me, My grace is sufficient for thee: for my strength is made perfect in weakness. Most gladly therefore will I rather glory in my infirmities, that the power of Christ may rest upon me. {Verse 10} Therefore I take pleasure in infirmities, in reproaches, in necessities, in persecutions, in distresses for Christ's sake: for when I am weak, then am I strong." It was grace that brought my Dad through the dialogue his mind had presented him with about Jesus but I also believe that he had a personal encounter with Jesus that he may not have revealed to anybody which would eventually go on to change that mind-set of destruction that he had at the time. So for people out there who doubt the authenticity of Jesus, they are yet to have an encounter with Jesus which could be through healing from a chronic or terminal health challenge or some other sort of very strong and personal encounter, and until then I'd advise you not to rest on your laurels just yet.

The Scripture in [Luke 9:1-5 and Luke 10:1-12] also gives quite similar accounts of the reason why we *take nothing*. In [Luke 9:3] it is written – "And he said unto them, Take nothing for your journey, neither staves, nor scrip, neither bread, neither money; neither have two coats apiece." Although they took nothing, in [Luke 22:35] Scripture records this – "And he said unto them, When I sent you without purse, and scrip, and shoes, lacked ye any thing? And they said, Nothing." ***So they took nothing yet they lacked nothing.*** They experienced manifold supernatural provision because they went out with nothing but in the authority of the name of Jesus. That authority activated the faith thy needed to create something out of nothing. The apostles took faith into ministry and thereby pleasing God [Hebrews 11:6] they activated and reaped excellent harvests, acquiring wealth that they had not laboured for as recorded thus in [Acts 4:33-37] - "And with great power gave the apostles witness of the resurrection of the Lord Jesus: and great grace was upon them all. {Verse 34} Neither was there any among them that lacked: for as many as were possessors of lands or horses sold them, and brought the prices of the things that were sold, {Verse 35} And laid *them* down at the apostles' feet: and distribution was made unto every man according as he had need. {Verse 36} And Joses, who by the apostles was surnamed Barnabas, (which is, being interpreted, The son of consolation,) a Levite, *and* of the country of Cyprus, {Verse 37} Having land, sold *it*, and brought the money, and laid *it* at the apostles' feet." This Scripture justifies the wealth of ministers of the gospel as long as the funds are invested back into the Church or in those who need it and in the things they are needed for. A good number of these ministers went into ministry empty, without hope and sometimes even without faith yet they dared to obey the voice of God. They may have acted out of having no alternative choice(s) and got rewarded. There is a saying that *you never know how strong you are until being strong is the only choice you have.* That unknown strength amounts to faith in the supernatural God and wherever faith is exercised becomes the sweetest part of any story.

For instance I attended the evening service on Friday 06 February 2015 at a particular Church with my first son and during the service my son slept off. But before we left for that service I had only seven pounds (£7) and had intended to give six pounds (£6) for an offering (because it was the sixth day of the month) but some gut instinct pushed me to take the entire amount, so I had determined that I'd be giving five pounds (£5) as my offering and let my son give the two pound (£2) coin as his offering. By the time the message was over and it was time for the offering my son continued sleeping and I tried to wake him up and he just would not wake up from sleep. So I just pulled him up and dragged him along to the front of the Church for us to drop the offering seeds and he started walking by himself (just sleep walking though). I got to the offering *basket* and dropped my *fiver* (£5) and was walking back to my seat and noticed that my son did not drop his seed because the boy was still sleeping even though he was walking. I tried to get his attention but this was to no avail, so on getting back to our seat I ordered him to go to the front of the Church (again) and drop his offering (because I was too shy to give coin offerings).

The boy left the seat again, got to the front and just would not drop this offering for some reason, then he walked back to his seat with the money still in his hands, still sleeping. I went quite berserk and got thinking how I could drop that seed. I eventually made up my mind that no matter what happened I'd not take that money out of that Church environment, worst case scenario I'd just drop it on the Church floor and leave. So while I was waiting for that to happen because I would have needed some courage to drop it on the floor bearing in mind that anybody could pick it up and while I was battling with my mind people were already leaving for their homes. Then suddenly my son woke up very alert still clutching onto his offering seed and from nowhere a second offering was called by another pastor in the Church to support the prophet who had just delivered the message of the gospel. I thought what a good favour this must be but what I did not realise was that my little radical faith of persistence and my son's sleeping session(s) was masterminded by God and had just opened a better door to give. Then after praying over the seeds the pastor instructed that they would be laid at the Lord's altar. I could not believe it and in excitement I sent my son to rush and drop his two pound (£2) seed coin on the altar and he did. I just went home thinking how truly God used the *foolish things* to confound me. My son's sleep turned out even a better blessing because I dropped my *fiver* (£5) in the offering basket but he dropped his coin offering on the altar of the living God. Which means that God knew that the second offering would be called for his prophet and God wanted us to be a part of it so he caused my son to fall into a deep sleep and I've not known my son to be such a deep sleeper particularly in such an open place with all eyes glowing on everybody with such intent. I left that service feeling very fulfilled knowing that I was taking-nothing but my multitude of miracles back home.

Taking-nothing seems to connote or seems to build a mind-set of incompleteness, however nothing is complete except in Jesus as seen in [Colossians 2:10] – "And ye are complete in him, which is the head of all principality and power." For instance as daring as this book you are reading right now is, yet it is incomplete. It is quite daring because of the topic being addressed herein, and it is incomplete because no book is complete and I can prove this from the Holy Bible from [John 20:30-31] – "And many other signs truly did Jesus in the presence of his disciples, which are not written in this book: {Verse 31} But these are written, that ye might believe that Jesus is the Christ, the Son of God; and that believing ye might have life through his name." This Scripture gives the impression that the Holy Bible is not complete because the entirety of the miracles that Jesus performed were not recorded in the Holy Bible. The book of [John 21:25] also confirms this truth – "And there are many other things which Jesus did, the which, if they should be written every one, I suppose that even the world itself could not contain the books that should be written. Amen." Then [Hebrews 11:32] gives us a similar impression. Yet what our physical eyes as human beings call incompleteness are complete in the eyes of God if they are able to fulfil the main purposes why they have been made, because [2 Timothy 3:16-17] tells us this – "All scripture *is* given by inspiration of God, and *is* profitable for doctrine, for reproof, for correction, for instruction in righteousness: {Verse 17} That the man of God may be perfect, thoroughly furnished unto all good works." This means that the Holy Bible is therefore complete if it is complete enough to achieve what it is intended to achieve. This also means that *taking-nothing* does not therefore signify incompleteness because Jesus made us complete. It's like having children with very unique gifts and talents and comparing their individual strengths and abilities as though they were incomplete or in this context as though they '*took nothing*'. What we may not realise is that we have all been made complete in Jesus with our individual strengths and the only way we acknowledge that we're complete in him is when we submit to his leadership. The Scripture says in [2 Corinthians 10:12] that – "For we dare not make ourselves of the number, or compare ourselves with some that commend themselves: but they measuring themselves by themselves, and comparing themselves among themselves, are not wise." From the foregoing therefore it means that the concept of taking-nothing does not mean that we're going empty because our commission is a spiritual one to be manifested and completed in the physical. Therefore our provision for its fulfilment is a spiritual provision being a spiritual assignment because the commission is often given or revealed to men *spiritually* (through a vision or a dream), which is the work of the Holy Spirit.

The place of Persecutions and Tribulations:

In [Acts 9:15-16] Jesus (as recorded by Luke) talking about the conversion of Apostle Paul made revealing comments thus – "But the Lord said unto him, Go thy way: for he is a chosen vessel unto me, **to bear my name** before the Gentiles, and kings, and the children of Israel: {Verse 16} For I will shew him how great things he must suffer for my name's sake." Jesus confirms that Paul (who was a sinner and the persecutor of the early Church) known as Saul was his chosen vessel and will *bear his name* and then bearing his name means that Paul must suffer greatly almost like Jesus suffered. But the gospel reassures us in [1 Corinthians 10:13] that – "There hath no temptation taken you but such as is common to man: but God *is* faithful, who will not suffer you to be tempted above that ye are able; but will with the temptation also make a way to escape, that ye may be able to bear it." As much as there is a guarantee of impending challenges, there is equally an assurance of subsequently guaranteed escape. To this effect [Acts 14:22] writes – "Confirming the souls of the disciples, [and] exhorting them to continue in the faith, **and we through much tribulation enter into the kingdom of God**." The apostles and other disciples of Jesus suffered a great deal. In [Acts 14:19] it was recorded that Apostle Paul got stoned almost to death and in some other accounts the rest of the apostles and disciples had life-threatening incidents on numerous occasions. Some got killed, some stoned, some beaten whilst preaching the gospel but in all these challenges were they encouraged. It's the most daunting challenge on earth but it is the work of God so it will not come so easy. 'We must through much tribulation enter the kingdom of God.' So if you think your challenges are over in life, better think again because they may have actually just started. It's not a prophecy and surely not a prayer...it is just the reality from these Scriptures above, yet there is an assured victory in them all. A man without challenges (not problems) is a dead man and challenges in life come like the rain. When they feel heavy, you don't wish or pray for them to be more bearable, however you may then ask the Lord for a stronger or more reliable protection (spiritual umbrella) to protect you from the seemingly heavy rain. The rain is for our good because it takes us to our destiny. It's somewhat like shedding tears when someone is *lost*, we don't shed tears for the dead. Those tears are intended to satisfy our appetite that longs to remember and celebrate them because we miss them. The tears we shed are not problems to us, they are emotional challenges for us. Problems are from the enemy, challenges are tests from God. Regarding this Jesus said in [John 15:20] – "Remember the word that I said unto you, The servant is not greater than his lord. If they have persecuted me, they will also persecute you; if they have kept my saying, they will keep yours too." But the promise stands sure as chronicled in [Revelation 3:12] that – "Him that overcometh will I make a pillar in the temple of my God, and he shall go no more out: ***and I will write upon him the name of my God***, and the name of the city of my God, [which is] new Jerusalem, which cometh down out of heaven from my God: and [I will write upon him] my new name." That new name could easily and strongly argued to be *Jesus* because it is the only name given **among men** whereby we must be saved; and that name could be borne by both man and God.

With regards to persecutions and tribulations I recently reviewed and analysed the relationship I lead with my siblings and discovered that I was a brother to them but on the contrary they were not necessarily brother(s) and/or sister(s) to me without a purpose which sometimes strangely included attempting to take God's glory for what they have not done in my life and I found this really appalling. I realised that our issue(s) and grievances were not necessarily a case of agreeing to agree or agreeing to disagree. Their act(s)/habit(s) overtime seemed really made-up or falsified and biased towards me, eventually prompting the relationship to break down uncontrollably, particularly after our late Dad got murdered by cancer. I use the word '*murdered*' intentionally, also upset because cancer was not arrested. Had a man murdered our late Dad they will probably be in jail right now. Considering these events that unfolded and the '*persecutions*' that ensued afterwards, I pondered the words in the book of [Micah 7:5-8] – "Trust ye not in a friend, put ye not confidence in a guide: keep the doors of thy mouth from her that lieth in thy bosom. {Verse 6} For the son dishonoureth the father, the daughter riseth up against her mother, the daughter in law against her mother in law; ***a man's enemies are the men of his own house***. {Verse 7} Therefore I will look unto the LORD; I will wait for the God of my salvation: my God will hear me. {Verse 8} Rejoice not against me, O mine enemy: when I fall, I shall arise;

when I sit in darkness, the LORD shall be a light unto me." I searched the Scriptures again and meditated on a similar Scripture in [Matthew 10:34-36] – "Think not that I am come to send peace on earth: *I came not to send peace, but a sword.* {Verse 35} For I am come to set a man at variance against his father, and the daughter against her mother, and the daughter in law against her mother in law. {Verse 36} *And a man's foes shall be they of his own household.*" Jesus said that he came to send a sword and [Ephesians 6] talks about this sword in depth which is the sword of warfare (the word of God) whilst also warning of our inevitable foes from the family-line and abroad as published in [Ephesians 6:16-18] – "Above all, taking the shield of faith, wherewith ye shall be able to quench all the fiery darts of the enemy. {Verse 17} And take the helmet of salvation, *and the sword of the Spirit, which is the word of God*: {Verse 18} Praying always with all prayer and supplication in the Spirit, and watching thereunto with all perseverance and supplication for all saints." Jesus came to send a sword of warfare and vengeance having pre-warned us of the enormous battles, challenges, persecutions and tribulations that lay ahead of us, also having been given the right to dwell, to war and to finish well in the name of Jesus. This equipment or forewarning is detailed further in [Ephesians 6:11-13] and expatiates on this – "Put on the whole armour of God, that ye may be able to stand against all the wiles of the devil. {Verse 12} For we wrestle not against flesh and blood, but against principalities, against powers, against the rulers of the darkness of this world, against spiritual wickedness in high places. {Verse 13} Wherefore take unto you the whole armour of God, that ye may be able to withstand in the evil day, and having done all, to stand." Henceforth are we established in the truth and enormity of the tasks ahead, however being also persuaded by the awareness that we are equipped for them.

For every chaotic challenge there is a purpose and when we run from the pain of that challenge, the outcome or our testimony is either foiled or further extended. Jesus told his disciples in [John 16:20-22] – "Verily, verily, I say unto you, That ye shall weep and lament, but the world shall rejoice: and ye shall be sorrowful, but your sorrow shall be turned into joy. {Verse 21} A woman when she is in travail hath sorrow, because her hour is come: but as soon as she is delivered of the child, she remembereth no more the anguish, for joy that a man is born into the world. {Verse 22} And ye now therefore have sorrow: but I will see you again, and your heart shall rejoice, and your joy no man taketh from you." From the natural mind this line '…*ye shall weep and lament, but the world shall rejoice…*' seems like the psychological argument the terrorists make for their mass murders, claiming that they please their (god) by their killings and that their grievous acts will make them martyrs; however from the spiritual mind this promise is made to the believer with a secure and guaranteed hope for a joyful (not sorrowful) end. This promise does not encourage killings or mass murders in any way, but rather it assures the believer that in the name of Jesus we could be persecuted and some may face gruesome tribulations but that at the end comes sweet victory and *shalom*-peace. Also imagine the narrative that Jesus used here – 'the sorrowful birth of a child' which eventually brings great joy and utmost fulfilment. In the midst of all these regardless we must first of all always strive to make our world different before endearing to make a difference in the world. We tend to mix these up by chasing a better world before a better self, yet without a better self a better world is unachievable and always remember that charity they say begins at home through our well doing. Our good works cannot however stop the persecutions and tribulations that we may face even from the family line since these are inevitable, yet we remember that even in the time of death, Jesus was still doing good things for believers and unbelievers alike because at the time of his crucifixion he saved a criminal for his paradise [Luke 23:43]. Jesus is our role model as believers so we must persevere like he did in times of trouble.

The place of Fear of God:

I normally get as radical as king David (sometimes) who ate the hallowed bread or shewbread kept for only Priests in the House of God 'because he was hungry' - [1 Samuel 21:3-6] and [Matthew 12:3-4], but that's not what I did. As I entered my thirty-fifth (35th) birthday on 20th February 2014, I needed God to put something in my hand desperately so I took a desperate action. Please *do not try this at home* but I entered my thirty-fifth (35) birthday standing barefooted (ten toes) on the words and pages of the

Holy Bible and then standing on these promises I prayed earnestly and fervently in tongues. The main reason why I made that desperate move, God performed it exactly three months after and I did not qualify for what I sought God for in any way. But from 20th February 2014 until much later in 2014 I had been battling with severe trauma or what could be tagged *psychological bondage*. I have been scared of God for what I did, worried that God may be upset with me or even kill me. But nine (9) months after on the 30th of November 2014 I had a dream where one of my pastors was telling me that *'because I had actually stood on the word of God in faith, that God accepted my radical act of faith and granted my heart's desire; and that I should glorify God and be very careful not to turn that single act of trust on the word of God to a ritual or tradition.'* I woke up that day feeling satisfied and quite happy, then I forgot about that dream again and only remembered it two days later. For me this was a clear indication that I had a conscience that feared and reverenced God and the best conscience in the world is a genuine and original fear of God. It controls me and keeps me from getting into silly habits that I may regret because I always ponder on how God will or may react in certain situations and then I'm suddenly overwhelmed with fear. If I had to rewind the months back, I'd not have the courage to literally stand on the Holy Bible again. I fear God that much but regarding this particular challenge I was desperate enough to take that one-off chance and it's a chance that I've never heard that any other person took it before. I never told a soul what I did, not even my lovely wife and surely not my beloved pastors but just one dream justified me. In the book of [Job 32:8-9] it was written – "But there is a spirit in man: and the inspiration of the Almighty giveth them understanding. {Verse 9} Great men are not always wise: neither do the aged understand judgement." The same Spirit teaches us godliness, righteousness, holiness and surely faithfulness (which when summarised entails the fear of God) thereby ensuring that we put on the new man 'Jesus' [Ephesians 4:24]. It is this same Spirit that expounds and unearths the surreptitious knowledge of this complex truth that we are able to believe, proclaim and conquer in the name of Jesus and as such every child of God's idiosyncrasy must be conformed and established upon and by this truth hinged on an undying fear of the deity. This knowledge therefore enables us to do things differently (in our new spiritual name and authority), rather than doing different things (in our old natural names).

It is the same Spirit that instructs us both to will and to do [Philippians 2:13]; to do things right and to do the right things but I'd rather that we did things right. It is the fear of God and awareness of eternity that causes us to do right because the Holy Bible says that the wages of sin is death [Romans 6:23] and that death connotes total destruction in hell. Although the word of God also confirms that it is not all sins that end in death [1 John 5:17] which will be quite unbelievable to the eternity-conscious mind. I'd further explain that '*doing things right*' involves a natural consciousness to always be in the right attitude, whereas '*doing the right things*' is not natural but also involves a conscious effort to try to be in the right attitude but in this instance during your unguarded moments you'd revert to the real you (flesh).

After Jesus healed the man sick of the palsy, the Scripture says in [Matthew 9:8] – "But when the multitudes saw [it], they marvelled, and glorified God, which had given such power unto **men**." Although they did not use the name 'Jesus', rather they used '*men*'; in this Scripture I believe 'men' was clearly intended to mean '*Jesus - the man and the servant of God*' because it was Jesus who had performed the miracle and Jesus is the power of God invested in men. It is evident that God had given such power for men to become exactly like 'Jesus', hence the use of the word 'men'. But it did not however say they were marvelled because of the power God had given to 'believers only' neither did it say to 'Christians only', it said to *men*. Now the irony is that even the multitude were men, so why were they marvelled then? They should equally have the same power if it was given to 'men' by God. I believe the multitude were possibly staunch unbelievers and in its literal meaning '*did not believe*', otherwise they may have marvelled at the power God will later give (through Christ after resurrection) to men (the would-be believers or Christians) if you may. Where unbelievers don't believe and won't use the name of Jesus at all, they tend to suffer. However there are still unbelievers that would daily shout the name of Jesus when faced with trouble as already discussed earlier in this book and they're saved from destruction. This argument continues in [1 Corinthians 15:45] where Jesus was addressed as 'Adam' the name of the first man – "And so it is written, The first man Adam was made a living soul; the last Adam [was made] a quickening spirit." It is the function of that same power and privilege from God attracted by an undying knowledge and fear of God that made God to let the first man Adam name every living thing God created [Genesis 2:19-20] because Adam was *probably* intended to be the first Jesus in human form because the Bible addressed Adam as 'the son of God' in [Luke 3:38]. However I believe that Adam could not live up to that high calling after he lost the fear of God as a result of man's sudden and intentional fall to sin. If Adam was then called 'the' (not 'a') son of God, how come Jesus became *the* 'only' *begotten* son of God [John 3:16]? For this to be possible, that means Jesus is arguably the rejuvenated Adam because one was '*made or created*' and the other was '*begotten*'. Adam (arguably the first Jesus) was made/created and Jesus (the last Adam) was begotten. If Jesus was not the new Adam, how come he became the first and only son of God if Adam was also the son of God and according to the Holy Bible the physical role of Adam was played before the physical role of Jesus? Could it be why God had to change the name from 'Adam' in the Old Testament to 'Jesus' in the New Testament and then went on to '*highly exalt*' (which was what the first Adam lacked – that high exaltation) the personality of Jesus and given Jesus a name that is above every other name so that the last Adam (Jesus) could not have failed again like the first one?! As believers called Christians, sometimes we interpret the Holy Bible literally and alas destructively without the divine revelation that the Holy Bible is not for literature but a spiritual book for our growth and uplifting. The fear of God is not an occasion of sudden terror, embarrassment or ridicule, rather it's simply honouring God's will voluntarily and consciously in every situation that we encounter.

The place of Obedience:

The Holy Bible testifies against Saul in [1 Samuel 15:22-23] – "And Samuel said, Hath the LORD *as great* delight in burnt offerings and sacrifices, as in obeying the voice of the LORD? Behold, to obey *is* better than sacrifice, *and* to hearken than the fat of rams. {Verse 23} For rebellion *is as* the sin of witchcraft, and stubbornness *is as* iniquity and idolatry. Because thou hast rejected the word of the LORD, he hath also rejected thee from *being* king." Disobedience does not just constitute a sin, it is considered as witchcraft before God. The great commission is a testimony of and therefore encourages *'obedience'*. In [Acts 3:16] we're told – "And his name through faith in his name hath made this man strong, whom ye see and know: yea, the faith which is by him hath given him this perfect soundness in the presence of you all." It said through faith *'in his name'*, not faith 'on' or 'through' his name. In his name all manner of miracles happen, however we cannot access God (*on*) his name neither can we access God (*through*) his name. It all happens (in) his name. That means we actually enter his name and dwell inside his name because our peace resides *in his name*, therefore taking his earthly place we subdue the enemy. Well as a student of the word of God (which is my school) being taught by the Holy Ghost (who is my teacher) this is what I understood from the Scripture and Jesus tried to make his disciples understand this in every way and he successfully did. More than anything else Jesus was a very dedicated teacher and this is why I study so that I can learn (because a teachable spirit is usually an obedient spirit) and hopefully teach someday by the grace of God. The New King James Version of the Holy Bible always showed Jesus as the teacher, other versions addressed him in different ways and some called him the master or then usually as the Lord that he is. In [Mark 10:1 – NKJV] we learn this – "Then He arose from there and came to the region of Judea by the other side of the Jordan. And multitudes gathered to Him again, ***and as He was accustomed, He taught them again.***" Jesus's primary assignment was to teach (witness) and fulfil the will of God through obedience; this is his motive for us as well. In the following Scriptures, Jesus commanded his disciples (us) to preach, teach and publish the gospel:

[Matthew 24:14] - "And this gospel shall be preached in all the world for a witness unto all nations; and then shall the end come."

*Jesus made clear his intention of *world-evangelism* for the gospel to be preached everywhere on earth.

[Matthew 28:19-20] – "Go ye therefore, and teach all nations, baptizing them in the name of the Father, and of the Son, and of the Holy Ghost: {Verse 20} Teaching them to observe all things whatsoever I have commanded you: and, lo, I am with you always, even unto the end of the world. Amen."

*Jesus commanded every believer to teach and baptise *all nations*.

[Mark 13:10] – "And the gospel must first be **published** among all nations."

*Jesus emphasized the *publication of the gospel world-over*. Publication here represents teaching, preaching or actually authoring books (like this one) or magazines intended to spread the gospel of the kingdom of God through personal testimonies, encounters and experiences.

[Mark 16:15-18] – "And he said unto them, Go ye into all the world, and preach the gospel to **every creature**. {Verse 16} He that believeth and is baptised shall be saved; but he that believeth not shall be damned. {Verse 17} And these signs shall follow them that believe; In my name shall they cast out devils; they shall speak with new tongues; {Verse 18} They shall take up serpents; and if they drink any deadly thing, it shall not hurt them; they shall lay hands on the sick, and they shall recover."

*Jesus instructed us (his disciples) to *preach the gospel to every creature* with miracles, signs, wonders and the results of these being expected testimonies. This seems quite daunting, particularly preaching to '*every creature*' may not necessarily include wild animals or insects (many would argue since this may constitute self-destruction), and however, it was Jesus's way of emphasizing the necessity to reach the world in every detail of it through the spread of the gospel.

[Luke 9:1-2] – "THEN he called his twelve disciples together, and gave them power and authority over all devils, and to cure diseases. {Verse 2} And he sent them to preach the kingdom of God, and to heal the sick."

*Here the instruction was geared towards preaching the kingdom of God. Prior to this time the disciples were too familiar with Jesus and as long as he remained with them, they could not *perform any miracles*.

[Luke 21:12-18] - "But before all these, they shall lay their hands on you, and persecute you, delivering you up to the synagogues, and into prisons, being brought before kings and rulers for my name's sake. {Verse 13} And it shall turn to you for a testimony. {Verse 14} Settle it therefore in your hearts, not to meditate before what ye shall answer: {Verse 15} For I will give you a mouth and wisdom, which all your adversaries shall not be able to gainsay nor resist. {Verse 16} And ye shall be betrayed both by parents, and brethren, and kinsfolks, and friends; and some of you shall they cause to be put to death. {Verse 17} And ye shall be hated of all men for my name's sake. {Verse 18} But there shall not an heir of your head perish."

*Jesus herein reassured us of the need to *testify the gospel* with miracles that will be apparent to our adversaries, although we may experience trials and betrayals yet our lives remain insured.

[Luke 24:47-49] – "And that repentance and remission of sins should be preached in his name among all nations, beginning at Jerusalem. {Verse 48} And ye are witnesses of these things. {Verse 49} And, behold, I send the promise of my Father upon you: but tarry ye in the city of Jerusalem, until ye be endued with power from on high."

*Jesus emphasized the need for the gospel of forgiveness of sins to be preached *bearing witness* of the promise all over the earth in the name of Jesus (not through the name of Jesus) starting from Jerusalem where his apostles and disciples were to be endued with power from heaven.

[John 15:16] – "Ye have not chosen me, but I have chosen you, and ordained you, that ye should go and bring forth fruit, and [that] your fruit should remain: that whatsoever ye shall ask the Father in my name, he may give you."

*This is a direct gospel-call to every believer to spread across the globe and take territories in the name of Jesus.

[John 20:21-23] – "Then said Jesus to them again, Peace be unto you: as my Father hath sent me, even so send I you. {Verse 22} And when he had said this, he breathed on them, and saith unto them, Receive ye the Holy

Ghost: {Verse 23} Whose soever sins ye remit, they are remitted unto them; and whose soever sins ye retain, they are retained."

*Jesus sent us just as he was sent and empowered us just as he was empowered by the Holy Ghost with *authority to decree a thing and it is established* unto us.

[Acts 1:8] – "But ye shall receive power, after that the Holy Ghost is come upon you: and ye shall be witnesses unto me both in Jerusalem, and in Judaea, and in Samaria, and unto the uttermost part of the earth."

*Jesus was only emphasizing the exploits we will make in his name by the power of the Holy Ghost beginning (again) from Jerusalem and *reaching even the ends of the earth.*

Therefore it was a commission meant for every believer to obey rather than just for preachers and/or pastors only. However I still believe in hearing the call of God before we embark on this great commission. As an academic professor my late Dad used to joke saying – "Chuka Okonkwo will be the last teacher in his family!!" Well now I think about it and I can see how wrong he was. He was an academic lecturer/teacher whereas I am currently studying the word of God so that I can fulfil the great commission by becoming a witness of the gospel and a *word student-teacher* because I'd have to keep studying the Scriptures for the rest of my life being surely persuaded that the rest of my life will be the best of my life through this life-time Scriptural-journey. So the teaching profession in my family lineage that was instituted by God (from my late Dad) continues on an elevated platform by the grace and power and to the glory and majesty of God. My late Dad greatly explored and made the most of his academic prowess in the teaching profession, authoring over twenty academic books in education during his lifetime. I saw the need to take that family gift from the academic line back to the Biblical line where it all started because of the call of God on my life. This is why I study and learn from the Holy Bible daily, from every preacher/pastor that I'd ever listen to and from every book that I will ever read or even write.

In [Acts 4:10-12] Scripture says – "Be it known unto you all, and to all the people of Israel, that by the name of Jesus Christ of Nazareth, whom ye crucified, whom God raised from the dead, even by him doth this man stand here before you whole. {Verse 11} This is the stone which was set at nought of you builders, which is become the head of the corner. {Verse 12} Neither is there salvation in any other: for there is none other name under heaven given among men, whereby we must be saved." The name of Jesus has been given among '*men*' on earth today through the power of the Holy Spirit only because Jesus obeyed to be used by God and is in Heaven with the Father having been exalted due to his obedience. The main purpose is that the name was established for believers, however non-believers would sometimes call on Jesus and the saving grace would be made available at that moment. This does not encourage unbelief, however it happens to create some consciousness in the unbeliever that the name of Jesus saves because our Lord did not intend to lose any soul and this was why Jesus died…for all souls. As also seen in [Deuteronomy 28:10] – "And all people of the earth *shall **see that** **thou art called by the name of the LORD**; and they shall be afraid of thee.*" The Bible says they shall 'see', not 'hear' that thou (you and I) are called by the name of the Lord. Then what happens next? They shall fear us. The name of the LORD that men are called by is Jesus and it is the name that threatens the enemy and his gang! In [2 Corinthians 2:10] Apostle Paul testifies - "To whom ye forgive any thing, I [forgive] also: for if I forgave any thing, to whom I forgave [it], for your sakes [forgave I it] *in the person of Christ*." This is quite daring to believe but Apostle Paul was speaking about the person of the resurrected Jesus. This is because it is the name of Jesus that over-rides the sins, persecutions and accusations of the enemy having humbled himself in obedience. As the apostles of Jesus, they automatically became the Jesus of those days immediately Jesus ascended into Heaven to be with the Father. Jesus empowered them with the breath of life saying '*receive ye the Holy Ghost*' [John 20:22], because '*I go to my Father*' – [John 14:12] and [John 16:10]. Jesus was a man and somebody had to take his position here on earth in the body of a man, so he asked the Father to send his Spirit but because the Holy Spirit is not flesh he had to reside in bodies like ours to enable us to be what Jesus was and to do what Jesus did in human form. This is similar to the creation of man because if man is the light of the world

[Matthew 5:14], that means that man was ***spoken** into being* by God in [Genesis 1:3] – "And God said, Let there be light: and there was light." The Lord revealed to me that this Scripture was the beginning of man (light) and that man (light) was only put in a body at a later stage during the creation. This is why we are Jesus the man (not the Lord and not the Christ, I reemphasize) on earth today.

The word of God tells us in [2 Corinthians 2:15] – "For we are unto God a sweet savour of Christ, in them that are saved, and in them that perish." This was probably referring to the ministers of the gospel witnessing in Christ and for Christ, but in the obedient and humble spirit as Jesus. Why would God smell us and perceive Christ? It is because our aroma comes from the name, relationship and loyalty we have with the name of Jesus. The argument may then be that since he is the God of *all flesh* (believers and unbelievers alike) and perceives us all as Jesus, how come the world is full of evil atrocities being committed by the religionists in the world? Well this question was predicted and answered by Jesus as recorded by the disciple John in [John 16:1-4] – "These things have I spoken unto you, that ye should not be offended. {Verse 2} They shall put you out of the synagogues: yea, ***the time cometh, that whosoever killeth you will think that he doeth God service***, {Verse 3} And these things will they do unto you, because they have not known the Father, nor me. {Verse 4} But these things have I told you, that when the time shall come, ye may remember that I told you of them. And these things I said not unto you at the beginning, because I was with you." So it is not a surprise that the Islamic terrorists today surely think and claim that they are doing God service by killing people because this is what they believe in as a result of their ignorance of the truth. Therefore acting on ignorance is not obedience, acting on the truth is. Jesus predicted these occurrences multiple times as also seen in [Mark 10:29-30] – "And Jesus answered and said, Verily I say unto you, There is no man that hath left house, or brethren, or sisters, or father, or mother, or wife, or children, or lands, for my sake, and the gospel's, {Verse 30} But he shall receive an hundredfold now in this time, houses, and brethren, and sisters, and mothers, and children, and lands, ***with persecutions***; and in the world to come eternal life." So it was predicted by Jesus that we will receive and have all, however not without persecutions. Even so and regardless the persecutions in whatever form they come, we overcome all in the name of Jesus. It is the name, power and authority given by God for us to oppress, suppress, compress and depress the enemy and his hosts of darkness. This is possible because obedience naturally builds in us the mind and nature of Christ as seen in [1 Corinthians 2:16] and [2 Peter 1:4] respectively. Regarding this I realised that to emulate Jesus, our three most important prayer points must be:

- Abba Father let your will be done in my life in Jesus name Amen [Mark 14:36].

(Even Jesus prayed thus and God has already reassured us that the plans he has for us are plans of good and not of evil)

- I plead the blood of Jesus over my life and family in Jesus name Amen [Revelation 12:11]

(The Holy Bible clearly spells out that the blood of Jesus defeats the enemy, even as we testify)

- Holy Ghost I need your presence, fresh breath, power and anointing to evangelise the gospel in Jesus name Amen [Acts 1:8 and Acts 10:38].

(In [John 20:21-22] Jesus imparted the same into his disciples and it ensures that we remain relevant in every of our ministry endeavours)

Most of whatever we may want to ask God for in prayer has already been given to us and as a result some prayers could be considered as vanity or vain repetitions. I discovered that anytime I asked God for wisdom and grace, I hear the Lord telling me - "I have already given them to you, use them!" Even when I'm still confused I hear his voice say again - "Spiritually you received them once you received the Holy Ghost; physically I gave you a daughter and called her Wisdom, so you have the wisdom you need; and then I gave you a complete family of five people (yourself, your wife and your three children) and if five is the number of grace, then together you all are grace." In summary the commission is not to go and pray for sick people or to go and bury the dead, the commission is obedience to go and '*heal*' sick people and the sick person must first have hope that they will be healed and this hope is evident in their faith. Also the commission is obedience to go and raise the dead, but where is the faith of a dead man to be able to get raised from his death? This analogy will therefore conclude that to be Jesus, our faith as believers (first) then as ministers (next) is what matters most during the healing process because when Lazarus was dead, Jesus never asked the dead man if he had faith to be raised from the dead. Jesus simply commanded the dead body to rise up as recorded in [John 11:43] thus – "And when he thus had spoken, he cried with a loud voice, Lazarus, come forth", and the dead man simply obeyed him. This tells me that *sometimes our obedience as witnesses of the kingdom and as today's Jesus may just have to override the natural circumstances*, for instance in cases as seemingly impossible as the dead Lazarus.

Many times I've had to empty my pocket in Church immediately I hear the voice of God and shortly after I'd overcome a challenge supernaturally or encounter victory in some way. I got to Church one Sunday morning during the winter of 2014, it was in December 2014 to be precise and I was wearing a new shirt my wife had just bought for me as a gift and towards the end of the service I heard the Lord speak to me saying - "remove this shirt now and give it to the homeless man sitting in front of you now." This was in my human mind an embarrassing request at possibly the most unlikely environment. So I meditated to the Lord in my heart asking - "my new shirt?", whilst muttering slowly to the homeless man clearly of Asian origin – "excuse me sir, do you like this shirt?" He gasped "yes" in excitement, but I wasn't even instructed to ask if he liked it. I was instructed to 'remove the shirt *now* and give it to the homeless man *now*'. At that point it dawned on me that I had already disobeyed the voice of God. So I told the man to wait while I went to the toilet to get the shirt off because it would be even more embarrassing for me to remove my shirt in Church, although I had a decent inner wear and then I also had my winter jacket for the freezing weather outside. But then I heard the voice again very firmly this time say to me – "remove the shirt right here and right now and hand it over to the homeless man!" I couldn't go any further with my argument in my heart so reluctantly I just got my shirt off and handed it over to the man. This was in Church and the man was very excited but I wasn't. I just managed to obey but he wasn't hearing the voice I heard speaking to me on his behalf. So I got my jacket on and left the Church building and headed home after the service. The very next Sunday the same homeless man rushed and sat right next to me and I wasn't really happy about it first because the man being homeless had an indecent look and some strong body odour and secondly because I didn't want the Lord to speak to me on his behalf and in his favour again. So I kept frowning my face at him hoping that he'd leave from my side, but he cared less what I was battling with in my mind and stayed put seated next to me. I had just over seventeen pounds sterling (£17) for my Church offering on this day and when it was time to give our offering, I heard the Lord speak very audaciously to me – "give *my* offering to him." I just thought - "Lord not again!" I heard him again – "give him every penny you have in your pocket which you intended for my offering". Well I wasn't going into any further arguments with the Lord at the start of the week, so I handed over every penny I had which was just seventeen pounds sterling (£17) and some change. The man was excited again, hardly said a 'thank you' and just jumped off with my Church offering as though I was going to change my mind the next second. Although I wish I could but I couldn't because it would have been my Church offering anyway, so I had intended to give all away. By the next Sunday I just concluded in my heart – "Lord whatever you want." The man came to Church on this third (straight) Sunday and walked directly to me for a hand shake and I maintained my stern face though. He sat behind me this time around, and just shortly after, the Lord must have ministered to him or something and he suddenly stood up and moved to another seat away from me. I felt some air of freedom around me otherwise this could have been the third Sunday in a row that I could have been led to bless him, regardless of the fact that I needed a blessing myself. Above all, within one month from December 2014 (when these tests occurred) the Lord called me into the ministry. I don't know if these tests has anything to do with my calling, however I remember these events and some other incidents and I'm pondering whether I failed or passed the tests that were thrown at me because I obeyed (during these instances) by fulfilling the demands placed on me in my spirit, however I did these reluctantly. I may have passed some of them, but it would have been unenthusiastic passes. But God adores and rewards obedience somehow by crowning the obedient someway. Matter of truth, obedience is *disguised faith* because it is an act of faith, but sometimes the request by God may seem ridiculous.

The place of Dreams and Visions:

The only difference between a dream and a vision is that one (dream) involves sleep although both involves sight. When you're awake you see physical things and when you're asleep you see spiritual things; but a vision involves seeing beyond the physical. Scripture says in [Job 33:14-16] that – "For God speaketh once, yea twice, *yet* man perceiveth it not. {Verse 15} In a dream, in a vision of the night, when deep sleep falleth upon men, in slumberings upon the bed; {Verse 16} Then he openeth the ears of men, and sealeth their instruction." The work of the Spirit of God in us is wide and vast, but all hinges primarily on discernment through dreams or through some supernatural encounter. This is primarily because of what Jesus accomplished and I'd give a few instances of how this Spirit helps us. In my dream on the night of 21 July 2012 I was in an aeroplane that was about to crash and the blood of Jesus delivered me. By the time I'd woken up the LORD revealed to me that it was regarding my immigration status in the United Kingdom. Truly God delivered me somehow and I eventually became a citizen of this great nation, however it never came through without the daunting challenges that it presented with it initially. Although the dreams and visions of Jesus goes beyond immigration issues, Jesus however became an immigrant (legal or illegal) with his parents when they fled from king Herod to Egypt [Matthew 2:13-14]. The decision to flee to Egypt was revealed to Joseph by the angel of the Lord in a dream because Herod sought Jesus to destroy him. After my late Dad got admitted in the hospital for a surgery, I always had strange dreams during this period and would often tell my late Dad those dreams. They were signs and because of them I never supported him going for surgery, neither did he like the idea but my siblings tried to persuade him through it against his desire. Although they were hoping to get the best for him, however what they intended to achieve was greatly foiled by the spirit of death. In one of those dreams I saw myself alive yet visiting the mortuary to see a relative that had died but I didn't know who it was. I always woke up very confused and unable to comprehend those dreams. The first time I had it, after I'd told my late Dad (who was still on the hospital bed at the time), he said "Eziokwu?" meaning "is it true?" I responded "Yes" and he then said "that's very serious you know, keep praying." Also anytime I rang to encourage him, he always reassured me with these words - "I'm trying my best. When I get better I'd come to London to see you and your family because I have so many things to tell you but I can't discuss them over the telephone. They are for your ears only!!!" Unfortunately he never made it and that means I was not able to learn whatever he had intended to inform me. Once during the same period, in a dream of the night I saw two caskets lying side by side. I equally told my Dad at the time and he said "keep praying!" By telling him my dreams I did not intend to frighten or scare him to death and my Dad knew better than that. My late Dad was a Biafra Soldier who dedicatedly fought in the Nigeria-Biafra war and a very strong man naturally. It could have been God preparing him for the worst through my repeated dreams. He remained resilient and confident in God until death.

However a day before my late Dad's funeral in Nigeria, my wife rang me from London UK to inform me that our very lovely daughter had suddenly taken ill and was admitted in hospital on a life support machine (in a coma state). It was an unexpected attack from the enemy and the timing was incredibly impromptu. This was on Thursday 3rd July 2014, my late Dad's funeral was scheduled for the next day Friday 4th July 2014. I prayed with my wife for our daughter over the telephone and encouraged her to call our pastor at the time to pray for our daughter as well, which she undoubtedly did. Through this period of my late Dad's funeral our daughter remained in coma. After the funeral which was on the Friday, the Saturday was a free day and then the Sunday 6th July 2014 was the *'outing'* or thanksgiving service for a successful funeral ceremony for my late Dad. By my daughter being in the hospital, the devil's plans was clearly to get me destabilised at this critical time but by the help of the Holy Spirit I remained very positive, sound, active and helpful through my late Dad's funeral. I refused to tell anybody (not even my siblings because you never know who the devil's cohorts are) until Monday 7th July 2014 after my daughter was discharged from hospital. That means practically my daughter was admitted in hospital a day before my late Dad's funeral on Thursday 3rd July 2014 and was discharged home a day after my late Dad's funeral thanksgiving on Monday 7th July 2014. Meanwhile the funeral ceremony itself lasted from Friday 4th July 2014 until Sunday 6th July 2014 which was exactly three months after my Dad died on Sunday 6th April 2014. It took another three months after I'd returned home to the United Kingdom from the funeral that took place in Nigeria for the Lord to show me what I could not initially see. I was having my bath in the bathroom when it suddenly struck my mind through a revelation that the second casket I had seen in my dream while my late Dad was still lying on his hospital bed was intended for our lovely daughter's enemy (not for our lovely daughter). I was really shocked because I would never have seen that revelation coming if the Holy Ghost did not show it to me.

Also shortly after I returned from my late Dad's funeral, in August 2014 I had another strange dream. In that dream a former colleague of mine rang me and during our conversation he invited me over to his sister's house. So I went and on getting there he welcomed me in, ushered me to a seat and then he said - "I know you have just returned from your Dad's funeral and must need some money before you get back fully on your feet financially because funerals in the part of Nigeria where we come from require a lot of money. So I want to support you with this." Then he handed me a white bag and told me to open it. So reluctantly I did and saw cash of about ten thousand pounds sterling (£10,000) in fifty pound (£50) notes. I was so shocked and for a minute I could hardly mutter a word. As shocked and as confused as I was I managed to utter these words – "so you gave me all this money and I need money now?" He just smiled. Then I shook my head and was putting the cash back into the white bag when he started screaming - "So you came here to rob me? You came to my sister's house to rob me before my own eyes? Call the police, call this, call that..." Meanwhile his sister was equally shouting from the other end of her living room. I was down and shocked again by the sudden eruptions and developments. Then I asked – "so this is a set up? So you told me to come to your sister's house just to get me in trouble?" In the middle of that storm I woke up from that dream, saw it was day break already and said – "Lord I do not understand this dream but Holy Ghost over to you". Surprisingly later that same evening about 11pm at night, another friend of mine rang me and during our conversation he said - "Take a leave from work for a few days because I want us to go somewhere and relax." I said to him that it'd not be possible because I've just returned from my late Dad's funeral in Nigeria and I don't even have a *dime* in my account. He replied - "Don't worry because I will pay for the entire trip – flights, hotel and everything we'd eat. Let's go to Spain or Poland, but I'd prefer Spain." I told him to give me a few days to be able to confirm from work if my holiday will be authorised. This conversation was happening on a Friday night so I told him to give me until Monday morning for a feedback. Meanwhile during this time I did not even remember that I'd had a similar dream earlier that day in my sleep giving me an offer that almost got me in trouble, however I was convinced that I will not be going on that trip. It was too sudden and unexpected, very enticing and maybe very dangerous too. So I was still thinking through it during the weekend and after the Sunday service I was already assured and reassured that I was not going anywhere but I waited until the Monday (as promised) to land him my feedback. On Monday morning I told him that my work had not authorised the *sudden* holiday. He then responded thus - "It is okay, maybe we'd leave it until October so that you can plan a few days off from work by then." I said it was a fine idea though but I knew in my heart that it was never going to happen because within my spirit I was convinced although I had still not realised why I was adamant on not going for it. Meanwhile I got discussing with my wife about this (the dream of a free cash of £10,000 and the reality of a free fully-funded holiday to Spain) a few days later and was then able to see the interpretation of that dream. From the revelation I got regarding this dream, the white bag that contained cash in it could easily have been cocaine wrapped up for distribution or sale. Again it was an offer in my dream and an offer came later the same day. I believe it was God showing me what to avoid and how to avoid it.

About a month after this I had a second dream that I had visited the friend that had made the free travel offer to me at his residence somewhere in England and in that dream some of his friends suggested that we got into town to '*have some fun*'. On our way we got stopped by the police and they found some cocaine stacked at different areas in his vehicle. I was scared stiff in that dream and I remember saying to God while I was sitting in that car - "Lord you know my hand is clean, Lord save me because you know I am not involved in this." Then the police also made calls for more back-up officers because of the amount of cocaine that was recovered in that vehicle and also requesting that my friends' homes/residential addresses be searched. While this search was still going on I woke up from that dream and could not believe these back to back dreams on the same issue. Although I summoned up some courage and told this particular friend of mine about this later dream and he just dismissed it as a mere dream. By writing these dreams here I am in no way insinuating that I have friends that deal on class 'A' or restricted drugs. These are just dreams I believe that God was using to keep me away from trouble, nothing else intended. Hence in [John 16:13] it is written – "Howbeit when he, the Spirit of truth, is come, he will guide you into all truth: for he shall not speak of himself; but whatsoever he shall hear, that shall he speak; ***and he will shew you things to come***." I wouldn't dare to imagine what could have happened to me now if I did not have the dreams I had through the active inspiration of the Spirit of God in us. In [Job 32:8] we see – "But there is a spirit in man: and the inspiration of the almighty giveth them understanding." It is the same Spirit that shows us those things to come through dreams, visions and other encounters with God; the same Spirit gives us the revelation or understanding of those dreams and we receive it in the name of Jesus. Above all in the early hours of Wednesday 21 January 2015 I had a dream that Pastor Benny Hinn laid his hands on my head and prayed for me. I spoke to the Right Reverend Bishop Ngozi Durueke a few days later about it and he told me that it meant 'commissioning' because prior to this time I'd had dreams that signified that God was calling me into the ministry. Exactly two days after that encounter in my dream, on Friday 23 January 2015 I was sitting in my living room and the Lord was speaking to me in detail about starting his ministry and I wrote every vision down. A couple of hours later on same evening I was led to visit a Church here in London UK for the very first time and whilst the service was going on the Lord spoke to the pastor (Pastor Abbeam Danso) about me, clearly confirming the visions that the Lord had revealed to me few hours earlier in my living room. I was startled and I'd yet go into the details of these dreams, visions and prophesies of my divine-calling later in this book, however shortly after this I had another dream in the early hours of 14 March 2015 that Pastor Alex Omokudu laid hands on my head and prayed for me. Some dreams repeat events that have already taken place in our lives while some reveal to us what is yet going to occur and then others show us what we must endeavour to do or overcome through fervent prayers. For instance on the night of the 28th to the early hours of the 29th December 2014 I had a dream that I visited the United States of America and while I was there on vacation, it was being attacked with *heavily armoured 'flying' ships*. I could not clearly understand this dream, particularly the 'flying ships' bit; however what I remembered was that just a couple of nights earlier I had exactly the same dream but I'd ignored it. Well I just got up after this second dream and prayed against it in the name of Jesus. Also having recently started the ministry on the Easter (resurrection) Sunday 05th April 2015, I had a dream in the early hours of 12th April 2015 where I was anointing the sick with oil by laying hands on them. I saw a man and his young daughter being healed by Jesus in that dream during one of our Church meetings. Then after praying for them the Holy Spirit reminded me of the following Scripture in [1 Timothy 5:22] – "Lay hands suddenly on no man, neither be partaker of other men's sins: keep thyself pure." So as the next lady was coming for prayers, I refused to lay hands on her and instead I held her hands and prayed for her. Dreams and visions therefore disclose a lot about our future and destiny; they also reveal things about others and warn against impending danger as much as it shows us good tidings about to come our way so that we'd be readily prepared to receive them. A man without dreams is disabled spiritually and a man without visions is disabled physically. The Lord uses dreams and visions concurrently to speak.

The place of Pilgrimage:

The use of that name *Jesus* is the purpose of this book titled 'I am Jesus (not the Christ)…so are you the saved. Being 'Jesus' does not make us Jesus Christ. We (the children of God) are Jesus; however we are not the

Lord, not the Christ, not the Saviour and definitely not the Messiah. Please understand this truth that I am just a child of God (my Father) bearing my father's name as his son and his heritage. Remarkably in the past few years I've been learning from the Lord Jesus and his apostles in different ways. A few years ago I told God to grant me the *grace to be* and the *ability to do* because I want to visit most of the relatively risk-free *Christian* pilgrimage sites, particularly the Holy Land which I intend to see every year for the rest of my life by the grace of God and I'd explain the relevance of pilgrimage in this book. God has been very faithful because in between very tight schedules I've somehow managed to be in the following places for Holy Pilgrimage and have returned home to encounter major testimonies:

*Jerusalem, ISRAEL: 14 May 2012 – 23 May 2012 (On this trip we toured through numerous cities of Israel and places like Galilee, Dead Sea and so on in the land of Israel, walking on places where Jesus walked; we also passed by land through the Red Sea like the children of Israel into Egypt and stayed at the St Catherine's monastery from where we went to *see* Mount Sanai, Moses's well and the site of the Burning bush). Going *'up'* to Jerusalem was also a command in the Holy Bible [Zechariah 8:21-22] and [Zechariah 14:16-17]. God has an eternal covenant with Jerusalem and this is why in the Scriptures it always makes reference to going *UP* to Jerusalem because it signifies going up to the mountain of God. A symbol of supernatural lifting, divine elevation, arising, building and ascension. This is without doubt my most favourite place in the world.

*Rome, ITALY: 28 October 2013 – 01 November 2013 (On this trip we stayed right within the walls of the Vatican City and we saw a serving Pope live. It was an exceptional experience with my family. This was a very remarkable trip because it is the headquarters of the Roman Catholic Church and my wife was originally a Roman Catholic from Poland which is the home of the Late Pope John Paul the second, before I turned my wife towards Pentecostalism). Apostle Paul intended to go to Rome and Jesus also instructed him to do the same as seen in [Acts 19:21] and [Acts 23:11]. This is why this trip was so pertinent to me since I became a huge fan of this very controversial Apostle of Jesus Christ named Paul.

*Canterbury, UK: 25 December 2014 (This is the headquarters of the Church of England and it was another amazing and uplifting experience; an encounter with the living God). This was a one-day pilgrimage on Christmas Day 2014 which I had attended with my sons and some friends. While we were enjoying our time here, I heard the Lord speak to me saying that my next pilgrimage tour will be somewhere around Athens, GREECE in 2015.

Each of these encounters had a very major impact in my life and I decided to take pilgrimage as a priority in my life-time because Jesus's parents always took him up to Jerusalem yearly for the Feast of Passover [Luke 2:41-43]. I thought that was some sort of annual pilgrimage and I've always hoped to get into the same kind of Godly and divinely-spiritual habit of going up to Jerusalem every year. They are equally times to reflect on the realities of the Scripture and how the journey of the Church has panned out so far with a raw feel of how and where it all started. The New International Version in [Psalm 84:5] says – "Blessed are those whose strength is in you, who have set their hearts on pilgrimage." Pilgrimage also gives a direct feel or experience of what these pioneers of the faith went through from the beginning but unfortunately I've heard a few pastors condemning the pilgrimage tours to the Holy land which makes it clear that they've either not read or maybe not understood what the Scripture has said about loving the Jews and Jerusalem or preaching the gospel from there. These tours encourage the believers in their walk(s) of faith and the name of Jesus works by faith, with the word of God also telling us in [Hebrews 11:6] that – "But without faith it is impossible to please him: for he that cometh to God must believe that he is, and that he is a rewarder of them that diligently seek him." On the pilgrimage tours the Holy Bible makes more sense, particularly in the land of Israel which is where the Holy Bible was birthed. The atmosphere is so peaceful and you are taught the word of God at the various sites where the exact events had occurred. A pilgrim will also enjoy the satisfaction that comes from knowing that you were baptised where Jesus was baptised. The significance of these pilgrimage trips also ensure that they are very great opportunities to experience the walks of Jesus and his apostles. To be able to be a well-grounded witness of Jesus it may be necessary to visit some of these places to get a real feel of what these geniuses went through in serving God and in spreading the gospel. There's a special aura that comes with these individual pilgrimage tours and sites. Experience is always imperative to any divine assignment because a lot of ministers preach about the land of Israel yet they are void of what it feels like to be there. Saying is one thing and knowing is another thing entirely. For instance a preacher can talk about Jesus all day long, but if they haven't experienced Jesus for themselves, how can they know that what they preach or teach about him is right? I'm an ardent supporter of Israel and I wouldn't even let any preacher talk me out of my love for Israel and the Jews. Pilgrimage tours attract God because they show how much we cherish historical Godly sites, even as we appreciate them and the testimonies cannot be underestimated because I came back from my first holy pilgrimage tour of Jerusalem and my wife conceived our lovely daughter, I came back from the holy pilgrimage tour to Rome and shortly afterwards my permanent residence status in the United Kingdom was approved, which then eventually took me to my naturalisation stage as a British citizen and then I went to Canterbury UK on Christmas day 2014 during my very recent and very severe health challenge, four weeks later the Lord called me into the ministry in very clear language. The point is we receive from God when we partake in these holy tours with an open mind.

For instance I had a funny experience in the past because I'd applied for this job and there was a requirement of the fluent knowledge of the French (as well as English) languages and I had told a *lie of faith* to the employer that I was very fluent in French having been on pilgrimage tours in Paris, FRANCE multiple times. In faith I thought my pocket French booklet will be enough to teach me a few words to get over the French language requirement for the role. Well the Holy Bible said in [Joel 3:10b] – "let the weak say I am strong". Somehow I'd managed to go through the first stage of the recruitment process without my French language proficiency being tested, which I was quite pleased with. However during that interview, the interviewer had warned me that after the second telephone interview which was coming up the following week that I'd be required to attend a third stage interview which was the language centre to test my French language prowess and proficiency. Well I'd already started with a *lie of faith* and had to keep up with the tempo of my *lie of faith*, so I maintained my boldness and resolve that I was very ready and competent for it. During the second telephone interview a few days later, it was really going well when suddenly the lady reminded me again that the next stage will require me to attend the French language centre because French language was pertinent to the role I'd applied for. I reassured her that I was aware and ready for it. Unexpectedly out of the blues she asked – "could we switch to French now for a moment please? This is just to make sure you're ready for the next stage of your interview." I just thought 'wow'!!! Well reluctantly I had to say 'yes' to this request because I couldn't have said '*no, I'm not ready for the French interview today*'. Then the lady just burst into that level of incomprehensible French language and I remember thinking for a second that 'this lady must be wicked'. She didn't even start with baby words or sentences that I could understand like "Bonjour Monsieur, comment allez-vous?" She chose to go straight deeper than my understanding or knowledge of the French language. So I chose to respect myself by nicely hanging up the telephone immediately and I felt so depressed after that experience because I wasn't even given the opportunity to get to the language centre stage that they'd constantly '*threatened*' me about and it was indeed giving me nightmares. I felt so ashamed and embarrassed with the abrupt turn of events because I really thought I needed that job back then. A few moments later (but almost immediately) I'd decided to check my email and saw the organisation's lovely worded email in my inbox advising me that I had not made it to the next stage of the selection process. They barely waited for me to hang up the telephone before the email arrived in my inbox. My wife found this very funny and just couldn't stop laughing about the entire encounter. I told her that I'd only applied for the role 'in faith' believing that God could do anything. However I started having different thoughts coming into my mind of what I could or maybe couldn't have said or done: '*maybe the refusal email was even ready for me before the interview began? Maybe I hung up the telephone too quickly? Maybe if I had burst into speaking in tongues over the telephone the Holy Spirit may have interpreted my words to the interviewer in French? Maybe I should have suggested for us to leave the French aspect until the next phase? Maybe her first sentence just needed a simple "Oui" or "Merci" response?*' I started feeling like I'd disappointed myself by not staying calm enough to continue that telephone interview…who knows? '*Could it be that the Lord Jesus was watching me smiling and waiting for me to take the next step of faith for his Holy Spirit to step in and intervene?!'* Above all, it was a lesson for me on how important experience is to whatever message you want to convey or deliver and that the words we learn during our short pilgrimage tours are solely for our edification and awareness. They do not guarantee mastery over any particular type of experience(s) or event(s) that occurred in such areas, but when we talk or preach about places like Israel, we can have a real picture of those experience(s) in our minds that we can in turn be able to transmit to our audiences/listeners through our message(s) for more clarity and it will naturally make more sense as we speak the words that accompany our delivery of the message(s). In all I just look back thinking about these things and remembering the quite embarrassing interview and I'm filled with awe and laughter; but then the pilgrimage tours give me so much joy, satisfaction, peace and great understanding which is surely better than studying the Holy Bible a thousand times without such pilgrimage experience(s).

The place of New-Testament Foundation:

From this instance above I may have failed to exercise the authority given to us in the name of Jesus during the interview as discussed above because I was nervous through this although I believed that it was possible. Maybe I only needed to stir up the spirit within as this has been the failure(s) many people may have experienced while exercising our understanding of the Scripture. The Holy Bible details in [2 Corinthians 3:2-3] – "Ye are our epistle written in our hearts, known and read of all men: {Verse 3} [Forasmuch as ye are] manifestly declared to be the epistle of Christ ministered by us, written not with ink, but with the Spirit of the living God; not in tables of stone, but in fleshy tables of the heart." We are therefore the word of God, the New Testament (epistle of Christ) written with the Spirit of God rather than with ink just like our Lord Jesus Christ. This means we are the *Holy Bible* that some people may ever read and [Colossians 3:4] accounts that – "When Christ, [who is] our life, shall appear, then shall ye also appear with him in glory." There again we are reminded that Christ (the Lord Jesus) is our life. This means that as he lives so we live. This also means it is actually a sin for us who believe in Jesus to die abruptly or prematurely. Why? Because Jesus is the life in us and the life we live. Please do always remember that I am only a student of the word of God and this conclusion is from my personal understanding, belief and therefore interpretation of the Holy Bible that I study. These Scriptures clearly address us as the New Testament and Jesus is the New Testament. We are also made aware of the reality that we have been made able ministers of life and the New Testament is life as recorded in [2 Corinthians 3:6] – "Who also hath made us able ministers of the new testament; not of the letter, but of the spirit: for the letter killeth, but the spirit giveth life. The Holy Bible is life because it is kept alive in our spirits through the Spirit of God resident in us. Scripture tells us that – "…for, behold, the kingdom of God is within you" [Luke 17:21b]. We carry the Holy Ghost in us through Godliness and [1 Corinthians 3:9] reminds us that – "For we are labourers together with God: ye are God's husbandry, [ye are] God's building." Then in [1 Corinthians 3:11] it continues – "For other foundation can no man lay than that is laid, which is Jesus Christ." Unbelievably true we are called God's building with Jesus Christ being our firm foundation and the chief corner stone. We therefore are God's building standing tall and founded on Christ in the name of Jesus. The Scripture also speaks in [Colossians 3:17] – "And whatsoever ye do in word or deed, [do] all in the name of the Lord Jesus, giving thanks to God and the Father by him." Hence we live and move and have our being in the name of Jesus for we are his offspring - [Acts 17:28]. When my sons were younger, Kingdom David (my senior son) used to call Freedom Justice (his younger brother) "baby Jesus". I never knew and still do not know where Kingdom David got that idea from, however I believe it was the Lord speaking through this young son. Therefore numerous events encouraged me to step up to fulfil this revelation that I'd received back in 2009 but refused to write on it as a result of fear and torment from the enemy. I believe many teachers of the Bible could have equally received this knowledge but may not have wanted to write it because of what people may tag it or interpret it as. I struggled for years to come to terms with this understanding and on numerous occasions I was so scared that it may be sin just thinking about it or actually meditating on it, so I tried to forget it yet I could not get it out from my spirit. I put it this way, the name of

Jesus is a gift from God birthed in the New Testament. I gave something to somebody one day and my son Kingdom David asked me this question – "Daddy, did he say thank you?" I said to him – "Son, I'd teach you one thing now that you must remember forever – when you give something to somebody they must not say 'thank you', so do not expect a thank you because you did not give to get a thank you. However whenever someone gives you anything, you must say 'thank you'." Regarding the name of Jesus we must appreciate it, accept it, believe it and honour it by always being thankful even if we have to get into a subconscious habit of reciting it multiple times every day. As often as we identify with that name 'Jesus', it saves (even sometimes when we may falter), thereby we lay claims to our authority as the New Testament foundation which is Jesus.

The place of Salvation:

The Bible says in [2 Peter 3:9] – "The Lord is not slack concerning his promise, as some men count slackness; but is long suffering to us-ward, not willing that any should perish, but that all should come to repentance." In 2005 I travelled to Nigeria and went to a night club one night in the city of Owerri, got so drunk with a few friends and was confident that I would not be able to drive back home to where my family lived at the Shell Camp in the city of Owerri very early the next morning yet I wanted to drive home. We were all too drunk of alcohol and totally knackered. I had opened the car doors with the car keys, got on the steering wheel as drunk as I was while my friends jumped into the car too from the other doors. Some of them dozed off immediately they got into the car not even realising that we could have been on our way to alcohol-induced self-destruction. It could easily have been two crimes committed on the night – *suicide-murder* because I could have killed others and maybe killed myself as well since I believe that every suicide is equally a murder, but thank God it didn't happen. I was ready to start the car when I started looking for the car keys that I had used to unlock the car doors. I could not find the keys and this was within moments of unlocking those doors and hopping into the car. I searched my pockets, the car door from the driver's seat where I'd got in from, I searched inside the car, a couple of my friends who managed to stay awake (even though not very alert) helped; and yet the car keys were nowhere to be found. Then we all slept off in the car. A few hours later we woke up quite sober but surely more alert this time. I just put my hand in my pocket and the car keys were there. The same pockets I had also searched before we all gave in and slept off. I just knew instantly that the Spirit of the Lord took those keys away from me and kept them until I (as the driver) had sobered up. I was just smiling and shaking my head in thanksgiving to God but my friends remained startled at the detail. The strong hand of the Lord had saved us from perishing and on numerous accounts I have always witnessed the hand of God in this magnitude. We were all chronically in what may be tagged as 'sin' at the time and if someone was asking why God saved or protected us, I'd remind them what Jesus said in [Mark 2:17] and again in [Luke 5:32] – "I came not to call the righteous, but sinners to repentance." If God was not a faithful God (even to sinners), you'd surely not be reading my story today. I had always asked God to anoint my going out and my coming in with his Holy Ghost *crude* anointed oil; and God always did. The Bible repeatedly tells us how good God thinks about us and I could not have had that accident on that night because God knew that a year after I'd meet my future wife and we'd have our three children (Kingdom, Freedom and Wisdom) to the glory of his holy name; who we have dedicated to him for his use and glory. God also knew that I was going to serve him and his Church in the ministry. He knew I will be very useful to him by sharing these testimonies in published books and also in many other ways and God prevented me from the danger. I had a very strong relationship with God yet I was deep in sinful activities, activities that defile a man. I was addicted to God and at the same time I was addicted to alcohol *laced* with women. I would go from night club straight to the night vigil in Church and sometimes vice versa. However my problems with alcohol and other sins would not stop there because back in Great Britain I got to that stage of throwing up in public transport after bouts of binge drinking. Twice I forgot my shirt, once at a party and next at a friend's place and then I had to walk home on my inner wear. Multiple times I threw up at the entrance to the block where I lived at the time. Many times I missed my bus or train stop because I was too drunk to be conscious. Few times friends had to drag me home after very drunk outings.

In 2007 I lost a job back then because I was too drunk to go to work and even forgot to call in *'sick'*. The funny thing was that on other occasions, if I had to go to work the very next morning I'd normally be okay for it after a binged night out. During my Master's degree between September 2007 and October 2008, in between lectures I'd have to drink some alcohol… especially my cider then. I got so addicted to it as much as I was addicted and very dedicated in spiritual activities. My University professors caught me drinking alcohol so many times just before, in-between and after lectures, and one once said to me that - *"cycling is better than alcohol"*, while another really tried to mess up my exam scores in his course but I wouldn't let him after I complained to the University and got my exam script in that particular course reviewed by another lecturer. Eventually I passed the course and graduated with my class, glory to God. *I must bless God for 'August 2010' when I 'intentionally and consciously' gave up that drinking-ghost.* No regrets at all. My wife was crying virtually every day. It was that terrible. Once at a night club in Bristol UK I was so drunk and I met this white English girl, pulled her breasts out and was fondling and sucking on them right in the night club which was very inept behaviour particularly in a public area. My friend who had travelled to Bristol with me for this *nightmare* could not believe it because it was so bizarre. My mum used to call me a *night-crawler* years ago but now I think that this stage of my folly was the climax of my *night-crawling* antics. Once I got so drunk in an open park and was staggering to the toilet to ease myself before I stumbled and fell over. It was another English lady that rushed to my rescue, helped pull me up and then dragged me to the male toilets. She then took out my phone from my pocket and used it to call my friend that I'd been to the park with so he could run and pick me up from the dirt I was experiencing. Today it's all a testimony to glorify God, and this was how addicted I was to *killer-drinks and riotous living*. For years it was like the Holy Spirit battled with the spirit of distilled spirits and alcoholism that I had in my blood and veins. The evil spirit behind alcoholism tried to distil out the living spirit in me but it wasn't possible, today I distil alcohol in written words of published books to glorify the same Spirit of the Father that saved me. Through it all, God still preserved my destiny for his glory because I was dedicated in my service to God in his vineyard. I served as an

'*Intercessor*' and in another department called '*Zerubbabel*' in the Church where I used to worship at the time. God was still at work regardless my weakness. Even the great future and destiny ahead of us was orchestrated by God, how could he then slumber?

The [Psalm 121:3-4] tells us that – "He will not suffer thy foot to be moved: he that keepeth thee will not slumber. {Verse 4} Behold, he that keepeth Israel shall neither slumber nor sleep", and we know that we are Israel and Israel (just like David) paints a picture of our Lord and Saviour Jesus Christ having a lot in common. In my first book (Kingdom, Freedom and Wisdom) I argued that '*David was the Jesus of the Old Testament*'. David as a name means 'beloved' or 'the beloved of the Lord' and the voice of God confirmed this likeness observed between David and Jesus as seen in [Matthew 3:17] – "And lo a voice from heaven, saying, This is my beloved Son, in whom I am well pleased." The meaning of David's name therefore equally identified him as the 'beloved' of God, and in the Scripture above Jesus was addressed as the 'beloved' Son of God as well. This for me goes to prove also that Jesus had two real (human) personalities that lived on the earth. The one is 'the Lion' and the other is 'the Lamb'. In the Old Testament which is a testament that taught the '*eye for an eye doctrine*', David was arguably the character that fulfilled that personality in every way as the Lion with a strong, aggressive and very radical character, although he always showed his humility towards God in worship at the times of his failure(s). In the New Testament however which is a testament of the '*peace and love doctrine*', Jesus was the character that fulfilled that deep personality as the Lamb with a humble, firm, calm and exceptionally wise character or demeanour, however also sometimes he needed to address certain issues aggressively as the Lion like casting out devils and rebuking traders and merchants in [Matthew 21:12-13] thus – "And Jesus went into the temple of God, and cast out all them that sold and bought in the temple, and overthrew the tables of the moneychangers, and the seats of them that sold doves, {Verse 13} And said unto them, It is written, My house shall be called the house of prayer; but ye have made it a den of thieves." So sometimes Jesus had to exhibit that rugged demeanour in order to get his message across intuitively. We'd substantiate this argument as explained above regarding the similarities between David, Jesus and the land of Israel and undoubtedly the believer from these Scriptures below:

- [Exodus 4:22] – "And thou shalt say unto Pharaoh, Thus saith the LORD, *Israel is my son, even my firstborn…*"
- [Psalm 89:27] – "*Also I will make him (David) my firstborn*, higher than the kings of the earth."
- [Colossians 1:15] – "Who (Jesus) is the image of the invisible God, *the firstborn of every creature…*"
- [Romans 8:29] – "For whom he did foreknow, he also did predestinate *to be conformed to the image of his Son (Jesus), that he might be the firstborn among many brethren.*"

God called Israel his firstborn and equally called David the same but then Jesus was manifested as the Son of God, the firstborn of every creature and the only way to salvation. These Scriptures tell us that the way God sees the land of Israel, David and our Lord Jesus is without doubt the same way God sees us today because we (the believers) are God's firstborn among many brethren as joint-heirs with Christ. But what? Does getting saved automatically make us a Christian or acceptable to God? That perspective could easily be construed from a religious mind-set and we've always been taught that Christianity is not a religion and even the religionists see their religion as the be-all and end-all. But the word of God tells us in [Luke 3:6] – "And all flesh shall see the salvation of God." If so then, *salvation should be for all* but that 'salvation must come from no other but Jesus' as seen in - [Acts 4:12]. But it was written in [Psalm 24:1] – "The earth is the LORD's, and the fullness thereof; the world, and they that dwell therein." So then all flesh belongs to God, however we need salvation as a means to access God through Christ in the name of Jesus. Salvation being therefore a means to an end (eternity), rather than just an end in itself because some may still backslide after getting saved, although a lot of teachers have argued against this. Salvation hence serves as a guide into the way, but Jesus is the way. Jesus taught us how to follow in [Luke 4:43] – "And he said unto them, I must preach the kingdom of God to other cities also: for therefore am I sent." Jesus wrought might miracles and signs and sent us out to do greater works as already seen in - [John 14:12]. As our

Lord and father, we're meant to be greater than Jesus was and this is why he categorically commissioned us for *'greater works'*. Making my mind up to obey God and write this book did not come so easy because I was scared as explained already but one Scripture encouraged me to go ahead believing God. That Scripture is [Luke 9:62] - "And Jesus said unto him, No man, having put his hand to the plough, and looking back, is fit for the kingdom of God." This was the word that Jesus spoke to tell men to remain focussed on his work rather than on fleshly desires or other sources of discouragement. The later part of [John 10:25] details this desire, focus and commitment even further and I quote – "Jesus answered them, I told you, and ye believed not: *the works that I do in my Father's name,* **they bear witness of me.**" Imperatively my hunger to spread my understanding and knowledge of the gospel of Jesus the Christ hems from an undying urge to stay conscious of the truth that there are probably billions of unsaved people in the world who are waiting for me to step into the full calling of God on my life for their deliverance to come and until I fulfil this call, they may never receive salvation because we are uniquely different just as our stories and realities are. I'm talking about people who can relate very well with my significant experiences, core challenges and notable shortcomings; having had similar (sometimes chaotic) frictions in their individual lives because nobody is perfect, regardless in the moments of your lowest ebb you remain an inspiration to somebody. Although your utmost enthusiasm and motivation in life will equally inevitably scare some people who may even go on to criticise you. The unified results of these encounters are complemented by the outcome that we're all in the same school of life and discipleship in our peculiar endeavours, talents, gifts and callings. It is the Prayer of Salvation that offers sinners into a new life and according to [Romans 10:9] – "That if thou shalt confess with thy mouth the Lord Jesus, and shalt believe in thine heart that God hath raised him from the dead, thou shalt be saved." For every sinner and unbeliever, this is your first or number one **port of entry** into the kingdom of God:

"Dear Lord Jesus, I am a sinner and today I repent of my sins. Please forgive me of my sins, my pride and my iniquities; and accept me into your kingdom. I believe that Jesus you died on the Cross of Calvary and rose again from the dead for my freedom and justification. Jesus I ask for your wisdom as I make you Lord and saviour of my life, and help me to walk in a new experience and revelation of your spirit through righteousness and holiness every new day. I receive the gift of eternal life and I declare that I am born again. I ask for your grace to be steadfast in my new life, to be a faithful steward in your vineyard and I invite your Holy Spirit to lead me forever until eternity, in Jesus name Amen."

The place of Stewardship and Discipleship:

In [Luke 6:13] Jesus called his disciples and from them chose twelve whom he called apostles. This surely says that Jesus had numerous disciples and through his ministry Jesus never stopped making men disciples and he sent all out in his name. We also discover from [Luke 10:1] that Jesus 'appointed another seventy disciples who he sent out two by two'. However the Holy Bible records in [Luke 10:17] that the seventy he sent out returned with joy saying *'Lord, even the devils are subject unto us in your name'* yet these were not the apostles who spent more time with Jesus. Let's examine what Jesus told these seventy in the following verses [Luke 10:20-21] – "Notwithstanding in this rejoice not, that the spirits are subject unto you; but rather rejoice, because your names are written in heaven. {Verse 21} In that hour Jesus rejoiced in spirit, and said, I thank thee, O Father, Lord of heaven and earth, that thou hast hid these things from the wise and prudent, and hast revealed them unto babes: even so, Father; for so it seemed good in thy sight." The steward or disciple is a servant of the Church and if a servant they must be shepherds over the flock (members) and if you must be a shepherd, you must smell like the sheep but many of our Church leaders and teachers today glory more in miracles or testimonies (geared towards marketing their 'business') than in pleasing and doing the will of the miracle worker (God). In the Scriptures above I believe Jesus was comparing his twelve apostles (wise and prudent) to the rest of his disciples (*babes*), yet the Father gave the revelations to the *babes* and I'd explain why. Remember in [Luke 9:40] they could not cast out a demon (which was their original commission) from a young boy because they (it was the apostles although they were still called the disciples from this account) were so complacent and used to Jesus doing it for them. In [Luke 9:41] Jesus called them '*faithless and perverse generation*' and enquired of them how much longer he will be with them?! As long as Jesus walked the earth, his apostles remained unproductive and in [Luke 9:54] they (James and John) were asking the Lord for permission to destroy the city of the Samaritans (which was not their commission) because the city did not receive Jesus; but Jesus rebuked them. These were the same apostles who could not cast out a demon. Jesus saw that their priorities were misplaced and this was as a result of over-familiarity with Jesus. But the same spirits that the apostles could not cast out were subject to the newly appointed disciples who I believe spent a lesser amount of time with Jesus just because they believed in his name and there was no chance or opportunity of over-familiarity with Jesus. It was over-familiarity because in – [Luke 9:1-3] Jesus had already given the apostles power and authority over all devils. Then in [Luke 10:17-20] Jesus applauded the seventy new disciples and renewed their strength to go out and do more, even more than the apostles were not able to do. Also speaking from - [Luke 10:23-24] "And he turned him unto [his] disciples, and said privately, Blessed [are] the eyes which see the things that ye see: {Verse 24} For I tell you, that many prophets and kings have desired to see those things which ye see, and have not seen [them]; and to hear those things which ye hear, and have not heard [them]." This is why prophecy is not a title or a tag, it's an office. Once you adopt it as a title, it fails to produce. Imagine that Jesus said to the seventy that not many prophets see and hear what they see and hear?!

I had another dream on the 30th of November 2014 where my shoes got stolen. In that dream I had tried to catch up with the culprits but could not, I just smiled and let them run with the shoes but I kept moving on barefooted. Immediately I woke up the Lord showed me what this meant – 'the enemy wanted to stop me, they tried to stop my movement and my progress but ended up stealing away my challenges and obstacles. Immediately I understood this, I just thought 'good riddance'. I did not need any prophet to explain this dream to me and I don't disrespect this office in any way, however I revere it so much *as an office of God* but do not revere it *as a title of men*. The commitment and dedication I put towards studying the word of God and writing these books encourages a zealous meditation on these words and the dreams that I have. During these meditation processes, the Spirit of the Lord is then able to explain the mysteries behind my dreams. I have never met any *'prophet'* to interpret my dreams for me, thereby making stewardship and discipleship profitable because they are one and the same, yet we cannot function as a body in the Church without the office of the prophets because they are about the most important in the five-fold ministry even though all the other offices are equally important as well. To confirm the dream I had on my shoes (problems) being stolen away, I had a subsequent dream during my afternoon nap on 02 December 2014 where a man came in my dream and healed me of asthma that I had suffered for about thirty (30) years. In that dream the man took the inhalers I had in my pocket and threw them away saying – "You don't need them. Don't use them again." Nonetheless in that dream I was still too scared to stop carrying inhalers around. I had asthma from birth until I turned twenty-five (25) years in 2004 which is when I relocated to the United Kingdom from Nigeria and then from that time until the age of thirty (30) years in 2009 I never had any further attacks again. However later on in 2009 our flat got damp from wet weather and the damp turned to mould. I tried to clean up the mould-infested flat and it went on to trigger a fresh asthma attack. I've had episodes that could only be controlled with asthma steroid inhalers and I found myself back to carrying and using inhalers again (if/when required) for precaution until that dream. Frighteningly this is where I need to grow my faith even further because I have still avoided not carrying inhalers on me even as I write. But the truth remains that shortly after my shoes got stolen in my dream, I had another dream where this asthma healing took place and the rest of what the devil tries today are all lying vanities because I know I got healed of asthma in my dream regardless the symptoms that may seem stubborn or persistent.

Apostle Paul did not allow his affliction to stop him from fulfilling his ministry. He led by example and said this in [Galatians 4:12-14] – "Brethren, I beseech you, be as I *am*; for I *am* as ye *are*: ye have not injured me at all. {Verse 13} Ye know how through infirmity of the flesh I preached the gospel unto you at first. And my temptation which was in my flesh ye despised not, nor rejected; but received me as an angel of God, *even* as Christ Jesus." Not just that he ministered to the Galatians with afflictions in his body, the climax is that he was still given reception as an angel of God, even as Jesus. That means what was supposed to discourage him eventually stirred him in the Spirit thereby bringing honour rather than shame or reproach. It's unbelievable the rewards of stewardship and discipleship because through them God is honoured. Stewardship and discipleship both require a steadfast and dedicated attitude, and this is why I must continue in the word of God in order to grow the faith I need in order to get rid of carrying any inhalers because God has already healed me. Scriptures tell us in [John 8:31-32] – "Then said Jesus to those Jews which believed on him, If ye continue in my word, then are ye my disciples indeed: {Verse 32} And ye shall know the truth, and the truth shall make you free." Having then received my healing from that plague, my business becomes persistent searching and meditating on the truth of God's word where my healing was born and by so doing the fear of any further asthma attacks will dissipate supernaturally without my awareness or knowledge. For the truth then to make me free, my act of faith is still relevant and [Romans 10:17] tells us this – "So then faith cometh by hearing, and hearing by the word of God." From this argument then we sense a strong correlation between stewardship, discipleship, faith and healing coming through constant meditation of the word of God and particularly of the healing gospels of Jesus. Above this is the intuition that stewardship and discipleship always come through a conscious, dedicated and intentional effort to follow the things of God thereby being persuaded or convinced beyond doubt of its proven reality and ingenuity by the authority of God in the name of Jesus. Assuredly God through his word constantly promises divine health for his stewards and his disciples as already seen from the above Scriptures and [Psalm 89:34] reinstates or rather re-establishes God's covenant promises in this familiar and deity-characteristic tone – "My covenant will I not break, nor alter the thing that is gone out of my lips." When we serve God with all we have, his promises stand sure forever in our lives as the witness and as the testimony to encourage others in the same.

The place of Prophecy:

For some reason I discovered that I am particularly attracted to and admire preachers who address themselves just as pastors (particularly those that function in a particular office within the five-fold ministry yet they refuse to be obsessed with titles) and I further discovered that there are two unique or peculiar phases of pastors (kind of pastor and type of pastor) but all lay claims to preaching the word of God and/or the gospel of Jesus Christ. **Kind of pastors** preach the hardships and pains they went through and endured in life backed up by the gospel of Christ. These are the preachers that greatly command the anointing, power and majesty of God; and people seek to hear and encounter God through them. They use the power of God to wrought deliverances among God's people who may equally be going through similar experiences that they went through in the past or that some of them may currently still be going through. **Type of pastors** on the contrary preach messages from the Holy Bible very well too, although they may not necessarily experienced any strong challenges in life. I strongly believe however that prophecy is for all because prophets are born before very few are *possibly* made and [Jeremiah 1:5] confirms this thought - "Before I formed thee in the belly I knew thee; and before thou camest forth out of the womb I sanctified thee, [and] I ordained thee a prophet unto the nations." Therefore we inherited the gift of prophecy before we were even formed in the womb although few are uniquely called and anointed into that office of authority by God to speak to the Church. This means from the day God conceived us in his mind we already became prophets in his eyes as already verified from the Scripture above. Even unbelievers prophesy (good or evil) in their own lives, their children's lives or into the lives of the people around them and it manifests regardless of their religious belief or unbelief because the Holy Bible says in [Proverbs 18:20-21] – "A man's belly shall be satisfied with the fruit of his mouth; and with the increase of his lips shall he be filled. {Verse 21} Death and life are in the power of the tongue: and they that love it shall eat the fruit thereof." The human mouth is the only vessel required for prophecy in the natural sense and every human being has a mouth but spiritually the Spirit of the Lord gifts it to a select few. The mouth serves the same purposes as a microphone to either echo the mind of God through the voice of men or to reveal the hidden strategies of the enemy over destinies. This tells me that surely prophecy is not a title but rather a spoken word whether from a physical mind or a spiritual mind. For further studies see [James 3:5-11].

Equally in [Matthew 12:36-37] Jesus said – "But I say unto you, That every idle word that men shall speak, they shall give account thereof in the day of judgement. {Verse 37} For by thy words thou shalt be justified, and by thy words thou shalt be condemned." This Scripture was talking to all men, not just to a particular sect of people bearing the title of *'prophets'*. We are like our Lord Jesus and he referred to John the Baptist by this phrase *'much more than a prophet'* [Luke 7:26] and Jesus who we operate in his name is greater than John the Baptist; however Jesus confirmed this in [Luke 7:28] – "For I say unto you, Among those that are born of women there is not a greater prophet than John the Baptist: but he that is least in the kingdom of God is greater than he." Our Lord Jesus was a fulfilled prophecy and surely more than a prophet regardless that Jesus was repeatedly referred to as a prophet; although in [Hebrews 3:1] he was called an apostle. Prophecies are often greater than prophets because prophecies outlast prophets, they are often the words of God and God cannot lie having *'exalted his Word even above his own name'* – [Psalm 138:2]. Most prophecies outlive the prophets that speak them because they are words and those words become (and may remain) life even after prophets are gone. Do not forget that God spoke the world into being. This is a picture of the strength of prophecies and today we live by those prophecies declared many thousands of years ago and the only difference is that God is not a prophet because he is God, but he has declared them for us to live them out. It is God that anoints and appoints to the office of a prophet yet he has given every man the authority to prophesy over his own life and that of others as well. As already quoted above in [Psalm 138:2b] the psalmist says that "God hast magnified his word above all his name". God's words were his prophecies because prophecies speak into the future. For instance if I called myself the most anointed man on earth, that does not automatically make me the most anointed man because the anointing of the Holy Ghost cannot be measured by man. However though, the prophecy is bigger than me because that's not who anybody is, yet God may choose to honour himself in my life with a unique and spectacular anointing. Jesus was the spoken word of God made flesh. He was also a teaching-evangelist because the Holy Bible tells us that *'God anointed him with the Holy Ghost and power and he went about doing good, preaching the kingdom of God and healing all that were oppressed of the devil for God was with him*' - [Acts 10:38]. That is the work of a teaching minister or an evangelist much more than it is the work of a prophet. Jesus was not telling the sick people to be healed tomorrow, he was healing them actively and instantly. Therefore that Jesus idiomatically referred to himself as a prophet in [Matthew 13:57, Mark 6:4 and in Luke 4:24] or that people identified him as a prophet does not make him a prophet because he was prophecy personified and fulfilled. Jesus made twelve apostles which helps me to believe that Jesus had intended for apostles to actually be the 'servants in charge' in the Church and that is why [1 Corinthians 12:28] and [Ephesians 4:11] tells us that he gave the Churches first apostles. He could easily have had twelve bishops or twelve prophets or even twelve pastors, but he called them apostles. His appointment of the twelve disciples to the office of apostleship in [Matthew 10:1-4] also confirms his peculiar attachment to the office of apostleship. However men prophesy, apostles prophesy, bishops prophesy and obviously prophets called, ordained or anointed into that office prophesy even more because they own the office. But our mouths were planted as vessels in our bodies to sow good seeds to ourselves and to others, hence the saying that '*you are the prophet of your own destiny*'. So every man is a prophet over his own family and affairs just as the pastors, apostles, bishops, prophets and other preachers or teachers in ministry-authority are naturally appointed prophets over the church.

In the books of [1 Corinthians 12:28] and [Ephesians 4:11] as already quoted above it was written by the Apostle Paul that 'Jesus made some prophets'. I however do not believe that this confers the title *prophet* on any particular individual or people. For instance when we say 'Apostle Paul' or 'the Apostle Paul', we're only identifying the office that Paul the disciple of Jesus worked in, not his title. I'm sure you reading this book may not be working in any office in the Church at the moment, however you surely have made some declarations over yourself and possibly over your family or even over friends that God chose to honour. Those declarations were prophecies but they do not automatically give you or confer any title on you. While Jesus lived, his apostles remained with him (not under him) although he led and taught them, but after Jesus ascended into heaven as Lord and Christ, the apostles became the main teachers of the Church. Even the rest of the disciples never really made any more impacts that were recorded in the Holy Bible. The vast majority of the New Testament was primarily written by the disciples who later became the apostles, particularly the Apostle Paul. Scripture in [1 Corinthians 14:31] specifically tells us – "For ye may **all** prophesy one by one, that all may learn, and all may be comforted." This was made clearer in [1 Corinthians 14:3-5] that 'prophecies are for edification of the Church and for the greatness of he that prophesieth'. It does not confer a title as a result of the declaration of such prophecies. A prophecy has either of two motives: to bless (exaltation) or to curse (damnation). I am not a teacher, preacher or an expert in this field as we've already established, I am just a lay student being taught by the word and Spirit of God with some insight by the grace of God. I believe that ignorance (without any judgement or condemnation) of this office may be the reason why anybody will call or address themselves by the title of *prophet*, because even the individuals that you speak to are prophets in their own God-given right and this is regardless if they were appointed into such offices or not. Having said this I've fortunately met real God-ordained and called prophets who have chosen not to bear *prophet* as a title and some few others who have chosen to bear it as a title, however I do not condemn these by detailing these ideas from God. Prophecies become more effective and apparent after we accept our Lord Jesus as the saviour of our lives; it becomes a spiritual covenant-relationship once spoken hence binding to the parties involved. If there is any prophet anywhere (as a title), I believe that it should be the word of God (Holy Bible), however it may be noted that the word of God as a book of prophecies is magnified far above the word prophet. It's a book full of prophecies and most of those prophecies are from God. I call the word of God or the Holy Bible - '*the prophecy*', but because the word is God [John 1:1], we therefore know that the Bible is more than just any book of prophecies. Therefore title is irrelevant when offices and callings are involved. Some prophets are called, anointed and appointed by God, not titled by God. What people call prophet are mostly appointed officers in the service post of the office of a prophet. It's an appointment into a spiritual office. It's understandable the things that happen with the teachers of our time who often get fascinated by the '*big idea*' of a physical title rather than the spiritual role and sometimes this is justified by our human nature which often seeks the glorification attained and the satisfaction derived from individual accomplishments.

The difference is grand since these officers are called and ordained by God, therefore no personal gratifications or fascinations should be attached to a God-given destiny.

Even the apostles of Jesus began to fight for his position [Luke 9:44-48] and [Luke 22:24] after Jesus told them that he will be betrayed. They felt no remorse or pity for whatever it was that Jesus was meant to go through, rather they were all interested on which of them will become the 'greatest' and our Lord Jesus rebuked them and debunked their thoughts and arguments by reminding them that greatness could only be attained through humility in [Luke 9:48]. This is the syndrome at work among most spiritual leaders today unfortunately. Moses was used by God as a prophet, Elijah the same, Samuel and many others. What we never read from the words of God in the Holy Bible was Moses being addressed with this title as Prophet Moses. Prophets declare and multiply visions and ideas from God [Hosea 12:11]. The big idea from God concerning the children of Israel was that they were delivered from the hands of their Egyptian oppressors and tormentors. Hence the Scripture says - "And by a prophet the LORD brought Israel out of Egypt, and by a prophet was he preserved" [Hosea 12:14]. That prophet was Moses yet he did not bear a title. Even Jesus never took a title for himself. The religionists have prophets too and [Luke 13:34] quoted Jesus as saying – "O Jerusalem, Jerusalem, which killest the prophets, and stonest them that are sent unto thee; how often would I have gathered thy children together, as a hen [doth gather] her brood under [her] wings, and ye would not!" The epic difference from this Scripture is that although prophecy is for everyone, not all are sent (in that office) by God. It is a sacred office and a call rather than a mere inscription on paper. The certification of prophets sent by God is supernatural, again it is not written on paper. Physical inscription undermines that office or legendary authority. Jesus had no certificate to show that he became the Lord, Christ and King of kings but we know he is who he said he was. Jesus was never issued a certificate after God anointed him with the Holy Ghost and with power but people believed that God was with him indeed through the miracles, signs and wonders that Jesus performed. That was his certification. His titles were probably the 'Messiah' or 'Son of God' or 'Son of man' or 'King of the Jews', I don't know but what I have read from my Holy Bible was that he was never issued a certificate of entitlement. Jesus and the prophets had spiritual entitlements rather than physical titles. Jesus as much as his disciples were unlearned [Luke 2:47] and [Acts 4:13] yet Jesus became the greatest. This also tells me that for a maximum manifestation of the power of God, spiritual offices cannot and should not be certified on paper because it subconsciously attracts pride. For man seeing is believing but for God believing is seeing. "God is a spirit: and they that worship him must worship him in spirit and in truth – [John 4:24]. This is exactly how and what it is for any believer. We believe God in spirit and worship him in spirit. We therefore have nothing to prove to anybody about what office we're called into, God does.

For instance no man of God comes to say to people - '*God has called me*' holding or clutching a certificate in his hand from God. We only believe, see the signs and follow them as our Church leaders. It is a spiritual exercise of faith and trust. This is indeed what faith is about!!! It is so because when they (anointed men of God) are sent, they take nothing therefore there is no evidence other than the miracles manifested; but we have to have a spirit of discernment to know who is from God and who is not. As has already been mentioned in the '*Taking-Nothing*' section of this Chapter, when Jesus sent the twelve apostles, he commanded them in [Luke 9:3] - "And he said unto them, *Take nothing* for [your] journey, neither staves, nor scrip, neither bread, neither money; neither have two coats apiece." The disciples obeyed and the Scriptures record that '*they lacked nothing*' [Luke 22:35]. Here we have a reconfirmation that when God sends you out, you will not need any titles or certificates to prove to anybody that either you're a servant of God or that you've been sent or ordained by God because the anointing of the Holy Spirit will make the difference. We already have evidence that in spite of being with Jesus all the time, the apostles could hardly perform any works because their over-familiarity with the King of kings bred contempt. The apostles got so used to the anointing that it became common-place to them and therefore would not work, hence they still had to rely on Jesus to cast out devils for them. They thus failed in their own responsibilities to the point they needed Jesus to increase their faith because they saw that they could even hardly believe him despite seeing the signs which Jesus performed. Explained further in

[Luke 17:5] – "And the apostles said unto the Lord, Increase our faith." I'd liken the infestation of titles amongst Church leaders today to the apostles of Jesus that probably took the anointing of God as a title while Jesus was still with them, hence nothing was working because of their evident attachments to fleshly satisfactions. No wonder Jesus had to go to heaven before his apostles could become what they needed to become because they had to step up (ascend spiritually and mentally) seeing that Jesus had risen from the dead and ascended into heaven. This can be seen in [John 16:7] – "Nevertheless I tell you the truth; It is expedient for you that I go away: for if I go not away, the Comforter will not come unto you; but if I depart, I will send him unto you." Jesus also said that the comforter shall reprove the world thus in [John 16:10] – "Of righteousness, because I go to my Father, and ye see me no more…" If Jesus said that we'd see him no more, this therefore tells me that today's miracles are not done by Jesus (the Christ) but by the comforter who is equally the Holy Ghost. Having said this we must spiritually ascend to access this power as Jesus in the name of Jesus, not through Jesus because the Christ is now with the Father in heaven although his Spirit remains in us. He has empowered a name for us and gone for us to assume, function and/or operate in that name to be empowered with the same ability to wrought more miracles than he wrought on earth. Jesus taught us how to live in the name of Jesus. Don't forget he was a teacher and therefore came to teach that we are Jesus the sons of the Lord Jesus because we believe *in his name*. He ascended the heavens as Lord and Christ, not just as the same Jesus that walked the earth because the authority in that name was now passed to us his children. It's the same like when a father goes to rest at the bosom of the Lord, he leaves (not wealth, not belongings, not sicknesses and surely not diseases), but a name for his children. As our father, what name did the Lord leave for us? It is Jesus. What children carry along in life is their father's name and that name becomes an immediate identity to you as the offspring of that great man. This is exactly what Jesus did for the believer. The comprehension of this principle re-engineers a new and unique spirit within us. This is why we must open our hearts and minds to record the word of God, open our spirits to receive the word of God and open our souls to retain the word of God for our refreshment and divine profiting through constant meditation therein.

As a Bible student I believe that positions and certificates must remain irrelevant in the house and affairs of God to all in ministry because Jesus admonished us to remain unprofitable servants in [Luke 17:10] – "So likewise ye, when ye shall have done all those things which are commanded you, say, We are unprofitable servants: we have done that which was our duty to do." Unprofitable servants because we serve not to gain or profit from our service because our first fruit is always to bear witness and glorify God. Therefore in speaking also, it is our duty to speak and then whatever we speak is the result we will get as promised in [Numbers 14:28] – "Say unto them, [As truly as] I live, saith the LORD, as ye have spoken in mine ears, so will I do to you…" Prophecy is therefore like the Holy Bible, being that we call it the word (prophecies) and power of God because words are prophecies and prophecies are words that produce power and manifestations. Although it is not every word written in the Holy Bible that is the word of God. The Holy Bible is a book of prophecies from God, men, women, even donkeys [Numbers 22:28-30 and 2 Peter 2:16] and unfortunately the devil in [Matthew 4:1-11] also spoke in the Holy Bible. So we must be clear when we claim "every prophecy" in the Holy Bible, because we may unawares be claiming the curses and reproaches of the enemy or those meant for our enemies. So let's be very careful and more detailed to avoid mishaps. The Holy Bible is a clear guide for daily living, the manual and the book of law and grace. It's a book that is loaded with both prophecies of blessings and prophecies of curses. For instance, that God allowed the enemy to curse and afflict Job does not mean that God cursed or afflicted Job. Job was perfect and upright and offered burnt offerings for his children according to the number of his children [Job 1:1-5] but it could be that Job may have either dug a pit or broken an hedge (through his verbal professions) for the attack because the Scripture says in [Ecclesiastes 10:8] – "He that diggeth a pit shall fall into it; and whoso breaketh an hedge, a serpent shall bite him", and then we also see in [Job 15:5-6] however, Eliphaz the Temanite saying to Job – "For thy mouth uttereth thine iniquity, and thou choosest the tongue of the crafty. {Verse 6} Thine own mouth condemneth thee, and not I: yea, thine own lips testify against thee." From this Scripture I want to believe that although Job remained perfect and upright in God's sight, his words were lame before God and Satan wandered into his life through his own prophecies. Job was ignorantly betrayed by his own words, most probably. There is therefore an imperative that we must profess sound words and [Job 22:28] tells of the power of our speech – "Thou shalt also decree a thing, and it shall be established unto thee: and the light shall shine upon thy ways." Being positive with our words brighten the paths we walk. The strong Biblical argument remains that no matter the chaos that may seem to be appearing before us, our words and confessions determine the outcome of them all.

I had always wished and believed God for my children to serve God in ministry, however on 24 January 2015 a London based Ghanaian pastor (Pastor E Isaiah) got praying for my sons and while laying his right hand on them one after the other he said – "I see light and I hear *Emmanuel* which means *God is with them.* I see one of them a footballer and the other a specialist in the area of sciences, maybe a top medical doctor or so. I see them very great professionals." Of course I was very pleased to hear this but my countenance had to fall for a second because I have always believed God that my children will be in full-time ministry which I am eagerly anticipating following direct revelations from God and confirmatory prophesies from different men of God, and I think the reaction or my countenance clearly showed on my face and the pastor continued – "Please it does not mean that they will not be educated. They will be graduates, very educated but do not stop the one that will play football when he starts playing." I just muttered – "Lord your will be done in their lives." The reason is this, I'm keener on my children maintaining a real relationship with God than them being professionals and bagging all the money on earth. So I could not hide my feelings unfortunately. However everyday I'd meditated on this and then few weeks later the Lord began to speak to me concerning this saying that - '*he (God) was going to use them through every endeavour in life but that they still needed to have some professional career while they served God*' and also that '*their professional careers would not last forever but that they serving God and being used by God is until eternity.*' I felt reassured hearing these words of encouragement and I didn't need any prophet to interpret this to me. Understanding the prophetic therefore requires some deep insight and genuine, heartfelt relationship with God. I recently learnt four prophetic tricks:

- In the first instance the prophet was led to instruct members of his ministry to sow prophetic seeds at the beginning of the year that will represent the exact age(s) they, their wives or husbands and their children will turn within the New Year. That means you calculate the sum of the '*new*' ages of your household for that year and sow exactly the same figure in monetary terms as a seed to God. This is something I consider very wise and will continue to do on the first day of every year, I'd sow the total sum of I, my wife and our children's ages that we will turn in that New Year as seeds to God.
- In the second instance the prophet was led to pour water from a small bottle of water on the heads of everybody that sows prophetic seeds into his ministry. There's so much wisdom in this because every seed needs water to grow or germinate and giving makes you a seed spiritually, therefore you would need to be watered to grow and prosper in the place of that particular seed that you've given out to God.
- In the third instance the prophet was led to remove his shoes and allowed members who would sow prophetic seeds to wear his shoes. This is grand wisdom because prophetically you ascend the level where the prophet currently is and could soar even to greater heights in faith because shoes signify movement.
- In the fourth instance during child dedications, the prophet drops honey in the mouth of every baby before he anoints and prays for the baby. The honey makes prophetic-sense because it would serve to represent the symbol of sweetness. The child is by this act expected to enjoy a sweet journey through life.

The place of God's Word:

The word of God is different from the voice of God which will be talked about in more detail in the second chapter of this book. When we speak about the word of God, often times we make reference to the Holy Bible. The word of God cannot be altered because it's already been spoken and recorded in this book called the Holy Bible while the voice of God is heard every day by men through his Holy Spirit. This is why the voice of God exceeds the Holy Bible or is more than just the Holy Bible. Having said this it may be imperative to confirm that the word of God is the product of the voice of God that became flesh. As Jesus was the word and power of God made manifest in the flesh, so are we as believers. In [John 1:1] Scripture says – "In the beginning was the Word, and the Word was with God, and the Word was God." If the word was there from the beginning with God and became God, that means Jesus became God and we were made gods by this same covenant. Then in [John 1:14] the Bible says that – "And the Word was made flesh, and dwelt among us, (and we beheld his glory, the glory as of the only begotten of the Father,) full of grace and truth." The same word which was God became flesh and that flesh was Jesus who dwelt among us and now lives in us and we live in him. Our lives as believers was written before we came to live it because the only difference we are supposed to have with the Lord Jesus is that factor that makes him Lord, which is the Cross of Calvary. Otherwise every other characteristic or detail that was written about Jesus as a promise of blessedness and glorification was written for man in his form as flesh. This is why the title of this book sounds very controversial, however in depth comprehension tells any believer that it's not. This knowledge does not excuse us from the realities of our challenges because we're meant to experience challenges as men (flesh) living in a spiritual world. It also ensures that our mind(s) are equipped and built to think and act like the sons and children of God, and the Jesus of this day. The Bible says in [James 1:18] – "Of his own will begat he us with the word of truth, that we should be a kind of firstfruits of his creatures." We were made and built of the truth of the word of God, and Jesus became our first fruit to God after which he rose from the dead as Lord and Christ to become the first fruits of them that fell asleep as it is written in [1 Corinthians 15:20] – "But now is Christ risen from the dead, [and] become the firstfruits of them that slept."

The words of life we speak to encourage people and build faith in them is the word of God because life is birthed through it. The book of [John

3:34] tells us that – "For the one whom God has sent speaks the words of God, for God gives the Spirit without limit." The word of God is our picture or our image but it is the words of God that we know and believe that we go on to become, live and manifest. The Apostle Paul wrote in [2 Corinthians 3:2-3] – Ye are our epistle written in our hearts, known and read of all men: {Verse 3} [Forasmuch as ye are] manifestly declared to be the epistle of Christ ministered by us, written not with ink, but with the Spirit of the living God; not in tables of stone, but in fleshy tables of the heart." This was the Apostle Paul confirming to the Church at Corinth that they were the gospel the apostles preached. That means the apostles preached them to them, or simply preached men to men. This is why this book is of great need to the believer because the believer will then understand that the word that men preach is the gospel of Jesus and we are that gospel of Jesus. Many believers assume our Lord Jesus to be our role model in our faith, however we still may have some of our pastors or Church leaders that we assume to be our role models in the physical. We only accept them as role models because we see Jesus in them, just the same way that the younger generation sees us as their role model because they see Jesus in us. However the believers do not understand that what makes us accept a man as a role model is the Jesus we have seen in and through them. This is why the believer is different from the unbeliever, because we are the good news and we spread us in the name of Jesus, whereas most of the unbeliever doctrines are centred on an idol or image that has no life in it. However we do not worship us, rather we deliver the picture of who we are being transformed into. As the word of God, believers are the instruments that God is using to deliver his justice in the earth and [Ephesians 6:17] says – "And take the helmet of salvation, and the sword of the Spirit, which is the word of God." We are therefore swords in the mighty hand of God being used to quench all the fiery darts of the enemy. No wonder the Lord told me in my dream on 21 November 2014 that 'I am natural resources in the hand of God'. That means as believers we're the Lord's arsenal of weapons for warfare in the earth. The Lord is not going to use real guns, axes, machetes or arrows to fight and defeat the devil, we're to be used as both the Lord's physical and spiritual guns, axes, machetes and arrows of warfare because we are the word of God made in flesh but equipped with the Spirit of God.

The Holy Bible speaks in [1 Peter 1:23] – "Being born again, not of corruptible seed, but of incorruptible, by the word of God, which liveth and abideth for ever." This means that we're made of a special kind of seed that cannot be defiled or contaminated and this is the breed of Jesus. We are seeds that came about living by the word of God and we are God's instruments, not just of warfare but of psychology since we're equipped to read and understand the signs and times. The book of [Hebrews 4:12] confirms this – "For the word of God [is] quick, and powerful, and sharper than any twoedged sword, piercing even to the dividing asunder of soul and spirit, and of the joints and marrow, and [is] a discerner of the thoughts and intents of the heart." This Scripture is surely not only talking about words written on paper, it's also talking about the word spoken into life or being through the form of a man (flesh). It's talking about the believer because we have that spirit in us that can read minds, which can discern thoughts, which see and hear what the Spirit of God is revealing and then which go on to act in prayer and warfare to place barriers for the enemy. We are the word of God that cannot be broken because we will not return to God void but must fulfil our purposes on earth as it is written in the prophesies of [Isaiah 55:10-11] – "For as the rain cometh down, and the snow from heaven, and returneth not thither, but watereth the earth, and maketh it bring forth and bud, that it may give seed to the sower, and bread to the eater: {Verse 11} So shall my word be that goeth forth out of my mouth: it shall not return unto me void, but it shall accomplish that which I please, and it shall prosper [in the thing] whereto I send it." This Scripture says that as the rain and snow cometh down from heaven and does not return back but waters the earth for fruitfulness and prosperity, in the same way we're been spoken forth into the earth from heaven and cannot return to heaven until we bring forth good fruit and flourish here in the earth because the real reason why God spoke us into the earth was to bring his presence in the earth by bearing witness of his power. This is why Jesus cursed the fig tree in [Matthew 21:19] – "And when he saw a fig tree in the way, he came to it, and found nothing thereon, but leaves only, and said unto it, Let no fruit grow on thee henceforward for ever. And presently the fig tree withered away." The fig tree had life but it bore no fruit and for some reason I want to believe that Jesus cursed this particular tree because it had never borne any fruit before, not just because it did not bear any fruit at that moment that he became hungry.

Therefore the word of God is who we are as opposed to the voice of God which is what we hear. The word of God is what God has already said that became recorded and has either given birth to life or is yet to give birth to life while the voice of God is active because God is constantly speaking it every day to bring his word to pass. In summary the voice of God confirms the word of God and brings it to pass. For instance God has called everybody according to the Holy Bible, but for it to come alive the voice of God spoken through his Holy Spirit quickens that word that has already been written down and given to believers. This is why God speaks to the believer when he wants to bring his word to pass in that believer's life. The act of speaking at the time of the hearing is done by the voice of God and it is not enough for God to just confirm his word of calling by speaking to a believer's pastor to tell the believer. If God cannot speak to 'the called' with his own voice, then who called the called? Pastors cannot call men into the ministry because the pastors themselves were called into the ministry by God. They heard the voice of God and then acted on the voice they heard which normally would have been confirmed through different men or servants of God. Any and every believer can rely on the word of God for evangelism but we need to hear the voice of God if we must get into the full-time ministry for the gospel of Jesus. This is why we've been made to function as Jesus in the earth because we have been named by his name and [Ephesians 3:14-15] confirms this – "For this cause I bow my knees unto the Father of our Lord Jesus Christ, {Verse 15} Of whom the whole family in heaven and earth is named." How can we be named in his name and not equally called in the same body as Jesus? But [Colossians 3:15] tells us – "And let the peace of God rule in your hearts, to the which also ye are called in one body; and be ye thankful." This easily means that even our bodies are the bodies of Jesus because as he currently is, so are we in this world. Therefore if Jesus is the word of God, then I must be the word of God because I am the physical Jesus here on earth but not the Christ. This logic is delivered in the book of [Acts 13:33] – "God hath fulfilled the same unto us their children, in that he hath raised up Jesus again; as it is also written in the second psalm, Thou art my Son, this day have I begotten thee." If the Scripture said that **God has raised up Jesus *'again'*,** then we (the believers) must be the next Jesus who God has raised up this time for a testimony to our generation. It cannot be an error because Jesus had already been raised up from the dead and if he had to go to heaven, that means he made way for his Spirit to flow through us in full measure and without restrictions. So it is not a mirage that the believer as the spoken word of God represent Jesus, not the Christ. But for the purposes of further clarity, the 'Voice of God' will be dealt with in detail in the second chapter of this book.

The place of Work:

In [John 4:34] the Holy Bible records – "Jesus saith unto them, My meat is to do the will of him that sent me, and to finish his work." Jesus identified that the work of a man must conform to the will of God for their lives, otherwise time and energy is being wasted and this is why he said that he must do the will (work) of him (God) that sent him (Jesus) and to finish his work. Then in [John 9:4] Jesus continued – "I must work the works of him that sent me, while it is day: the night cometh, when no man can work." Every work that God gifts to man to perform elevates man. The results of God's work in man is continually incremental and our Lord Jesus is a great example of this picture being that God elevated Jesus unto Christhood. The Bible declares that "When a man's ways please the LORD, he maketh even his enemies to be at peace with him." – [Proverbs 16:7]. Jesus pleased God with his lifestyle and became Christ only because he accomplished his works. Abram fulfilled his call as the father of faith and was called Abraham. They did their works to fruition and it earned them enlargement and change of status even as their names prospered further. Creation was the work of God and God actually spoke man into being even before he made the flesh of man. The book of [Genesis 1:3] says – "And God said, Let there be light: and there was light." This is when God made man as I've already explained in an earlier part of this book, because we'd later understand that *'man is the light of the world'* as recorded in [Matthew 5:14]. Following this God created the flesh in his image to carry that light that he had made as seen in [Genesis 1:27] an [Genesis 2:7]. The harvest of God's work being that as he planted men in the earth at the beginning, at the end he shall come back to reap the harvest of righteousness from a recreated man right here from the earth. Every work has a reward, more so an assignment from God and [Revelation 1:8] tells us – "I am Alpha and Omega, the beginning and the ending, saith the Lord, which is, and which was, and which is to come, the Almighty." Going through the diary of Jesus while he walked the earth I discovered that Jesus healed all, therefore we as the Jesus of this day are expected to heal all but this is not currently so in our Churches today as multitudes still carry unresolved burdens in their bodies. Then what could be the challenge of the Church that may be hindering the effective execution of this work or commitment? Jesus manifested in his name as Jesus and we use the same name today as a supernatural authority over demons. Jesus was of Jewish heritage and so are we in the Church because we believe in Jesus. Jesus preached in the Synagogues but he built and established the Church for the believer to preach in. So where has this void originated from if we have a better advantage than Jesus had because he made it possible for us, the advantage of the Holy Spirit?! In [Isaiah 56:5] we see this – "Even unto them will I give in mine house and within my walls a place and a name better than of sons and of daughters: I will give them an everlasting name, that shall not be cut off." This is the name of Jesus required to accomplish the works at hand, the same works required of the Church this day yet most of our Churches struggle to reproduce the same results that Jesus reproduced. As a Church the main point or question then becomes *are we working hard* to fulfil God's purposes in the earth or *are we hardly working*?!

Jesus had numerous works that he did within a short ministry life-span amongst which includes being an author. The Bible records this in [Hebrews 5:9] – "And being made perfect, he became the author of eternal salvation unto all them that obey him." Even nature teaches us how to work naturally because I discovered that nature breeds creativity. Whether you're in the woods or at the bay area by the bank of an ocean, these are some of the best places where ideas never run dry. Therefore nature ensures that we could become self-employed by just stirring and employing our gifts, talents and creative revelations from God to work for us. When I started my writing career full-time on 19th February 2013, I equally had a full-time job in retail management at the time and I continued writing even after I resigned this role to encroach in other personal endeavours, try out some business opportunities and although none of these seemed to be working out really well at the outset, yet I remained steadfast and focussed until the Lord spoke to me in a clear vision to get into the ministry and the Lord confirmed his word within hours same day through his prophet. So as much as I had a job when I started to write, I got myself employed in my own way as led by God through exercising my gifts of writing and exploring my potentials by composing songs and poems too. We also read from [2 Thessalonians 3:10-13] – "For even when we were with you, this we commanded you, that if any would not work, neither should he eat. {Verse 11} For we hear that there are some which walk among you disorderly, working not at all, but are busybodies. {Verse 12} Now them that are such we command and exhort by our Lord Jesus Christ, that with quietness they work, and eat their own bread. {Verse 13} But ye, brethren, be not weary in well doing." This Scripture commands us that if we're not willing to be creative with our time and energy, then we should not eat and also that when we are gainfully creative we must not neglect helping the needy. The authority of Jesus became his source of income in the midst of possible lack. When he needed to pay his tax, he ordered the coin out from the mouth of a fish, although prior to this he argued that he should be exempted from paying taxes at his own hometown. The New Living Translation shows a vivid understanding of this story in [Matthew 17:24-27] – "On their arrival in Capernaum, the tax collectors for the Temple tax came to Peter and asked him, 'Doesn't your teacher pay the Temple tax?' {Verse 25} 'Of course he does,' Peter replied. Then he went into the house to talk to Jesus about it. But before he had a chance to speak, Jesus asked him, 'What do you think, Peter? Do kings tax their own people or the foreigners they have conquered?' {Verse 26} 'They tax the foreigners,' Peter replied. 'Well, then,' Jesus said, 'the citizens are free! {Verse 27} However, we don't want to offend them, so go down to the lake and throw in a line. Open the mouth of the first fish you catch, and you will find a coin. Take the coin and pay the tax for both of us.'" As much as Jesus considered himself free from taxes at home, he still needed to avoid the wrath of the tax collectors by paying taxes for himself and for Peter. As a teacher and a leader Jesus also was required to set an example for all men (particularly his followers) to emulate as we practice this in our different societies today.

In [Ephesians 4:28] emphasis is still laid on working to earn to give – "Let him that stole steal no more: but rather let him labour, working with [his] hands the thing which is good, that he may have to give to him that needeth." This then should mean that our only need for working should be focused on giving the needy, although this somewhat restricted idea is challenged by the words written in [1 Timothy 5:8] – "But if any provide not for his own, and specially for those of his own house, he hath denied the faith, and is worse than an infidel." So the need for our work goes beyond just giving to the needy as we must also adhere to Scriptural values by providing for our own family otherwise we're considered as infidels (unbelievers). But why should this statement hold if Jesus fell short of responding to his own mother's requests? On one occasion in [John 2:1-11] during the wedding at Canaan in Galilee, Jesus referred to his mother as "woman" and then later reluctantly he performed the miracle of turning water into wine. However I believe that his response was delayed by his query which could be considered as rebellious and disobedient. Then again Jesus denied his mother and siblings in [Matthew 12:46-50] by these words recorded in the New Living Translation of the Holy Bible – "As Jesus was speaking to the crowd, his mother and brothers were outside, wanting to talk with him. {Verse 47} Someone told Jesus, 'Your mother and your brothers are outside, and they want to speak to you.' {Verse 48} Jesus asked, 'Who is my mother? Who are my brothers?' {Verse 49} Then he pointed to his disciples and said, 'These are my mother and brothers. {Verse 50} Anyone who does the will of my Father in heaven is my brother and sister and mother!'" Does the response of Jesus mean that his mother and siblings were not in the will of the Father in heaven? It could easily have been that they had an urgent need for provision, although the Bible has not made this clear but why did Jesus neglect this call? Yet responding to a call from our own family should constitute a form of provision, maybe of comfort in words because provision is not limited to or defined only by our daily needs. Does this make Jesus an unbeliever? How could he be if he was the author of our salvation?! In conclusion of this sub-title, I'd consider these words in [1 Thessalonians 4:11-12] - "And that ye study to be quiet, and to do your own business, and to work with your own hands, as we commanded you; {Verse 12} That ye may walk honestly toward them that are without, and [that] ye may have lack of nothing." Ultimately the main focus of our working life is to be able to have enough and also possess the courage to give it all away whether in provision for our own family members or for charitable endeavours because when we go we take nothing with us. Therefore our focus must drive our giving spirits away from self towards others as the same was established for the Church.

The place of Children:

A child is a symbol of humility, loyalty and followership. In as much as children are gifts from God, these qualities do not come to any man as special gifts, however men consciously and intentionally strive to build and grow these as skills. The Bible repeatedly likened the believer that will make heaven, as the one that has broken himself down to the level of a child (humility). Is it then a shock that when people get old, they start behaving like children? The Bible has made it clear that this is the state they have to be in to ascend God's throne. Jesus said in [Matthew 18:5] that – "And whoso shall receive one such little child in my name receiveth me." This has two literal meanings. One is that we must *receive* children in the name of Jesus and in so doing we receive Christ but in the culture where I come from, although children are very important, regardless, a son is accorded more honour and respect than a daughter. The argument is that *a son is who you are while a daughter is who they are.* The reason is because your sons are born to stay as your immediate family members while your daughter(s) are born to go (to her husband's family) as your extended family. The sons are therefore treated as a heritage and inheritance is given to sons as *their* birth-rights while they '*may*' be given to the daughters as *a* privilege. But what the Bible is saying from the Scripture above shows that when we come in contact with children, we must see them as though we saw Jesus. Why? It is because they represent Jesus and therefore are Jesus, not the Christ. Jesus was not particular about males (being male) or females, he emphasized the acceptance or the reception of children. Another strange reason why they may marginalise daughters where I come from could be because of this Scripture in [Isaiah 9:6a] – "For unto us a child is born, unto us a son is given." It then upholds their possible argument that *children are born but sons are given*. If then sons be a gift, we must cherish the gift of sons above the gift of children. The second meaning would signify brokenness because it is only the broken that come to Christ. Every sinner is broken and that is the most common or only state a man has to be in in order to accept Jesus (the Christ) as his Lord and Saviour. The Holy Bible tells us in [Mark 2:17] – "When Jesus heard it, he saith unto them, They that are whole have no need of the physician, but they that are sick: I came not to call the righteous, but sinners to repentance." This he said knowing the stubborn nature of man which makes submission almost difficult because of pride, arrogance and man's selfish desires. The Bible (as quoted below) also says that the Lord teaches children, this means that when we humble ourselves like children, we attract the wisdom of the Lord as we automatically tend to be more like Christ. In our quest for charismatic followership then, the place of children can never be neglected or undermined. Hence we see this in [Isaiah 54:13] – "And all thy children [shall be] taught of the LORD; and great [shall be] the peace of thy children." Therefore not only is wisdom attracted by such humility, peace is also granted access into our lives because when we submit to the Church (as a body, not as a building), we submit to Christ (the head of the Church) and our challenges under us submit to us because peace is automatically granted from above down the lineage. The place of children could otherwise be associated to as understanding hierarchy and honouring it. The [Psalm 127:3a] shows us that the place of children is the place of heritage and this is largely because *God resists the proud and gives grace to the humble* - [James 4:6]. Instead of raising people with child-like characters, the Church is now busy raising arrogance, building pride, bragging in self-acclaimed achievements and yet we cry wolf even for our own failures. This is why I'm an advocate for character education which I believe is as important to the Church as gospel or kingdom evangelism and as such should be ingrained in every part of the Church as well as its curriculum, starting from the leadership. The work cannot make any real further progress until the Church raises leaders who'd serve like children and then the rest of the body can follow suit because from experience I know that children do what their leaders do rather than what their leaders say.

The Holy Bible says in [Matthew 19:13-14] – "Then were there brought unto him little children, that he should put [his] hands on them, and pray: and the disciples rebuked them. {Verse 14} But Jesus said, Suffer little children, and forbid them not, to come unto me: for of such is the kingdom of heaven." The disciples of Jesus who were also the Church leaders (under Jesus) at the time rebuked children because pride resists humility, but they ended up getting rebuked by Jesus himself. The children came in their humble spirit to their master and father Jesus but it was an opportunity for Jesus to teach these leaders that the children possessed the character that attracts heaven. We have gambled humility away from our Church leaderships and it has had an extreme effect on our congregations as well. This is the reason why we cannot blame believers *lurking* around everywhere seeking the right place of worship (if there is any such one today) and God is watching the attitude of our Churches (his body). I use the word '*lurking*' because we hope that we don't find the members of the numerous other Churches we've already attended in the next one that we're about to attend lest the relationship we've built with the other pastors be broken through gossip. What works for the doctor seems to be working for the patient too because if our leaders are not consistent in their character, how could the led be consistent with theirs? Believers now indulge in an intentional game of hide and seek as they make their choices of where to go for Church service or not. As I journeyed through a number of Churches seeking help from an affliction I had in the past, I came across Church members that I had already met in some other Churches which I had already visited. I further discovered that believers now had specific Churches for specific issues or needs they have as members of the Church now see the Church in the place of a hospital and its pastors or leaders as doctors that specialise in different ailments. In the process I've heard believers saying – "this pastor is very good in immigration", while another says – "my friend got cured of cancer in this other Church", and then the next says – "when I needed to pay my rent, I went to this Church and the pastor interceded on my behalf, go there he will help you. Just beg him." In the believer's eyes men now take the glory that is due to

God because they have restricted their gifts as they restrict those of the believers *among* (not *under*) them and in the process of pastor and Church searching, believers have even lost faith in their God who performs the spiritual surgeries that sorts out their financial or health woes and bring the healings through his anointed vessels. A number of Churches have opened orphanages for children that they were not faithful to and then had to close them down again. The reason is seen in [Psalm 72:4] – "He shall judge the poor of the people, he shall save the children of the needy, and shall break in pieces the oppressor", because we have refused to remain faithful to [Psalm 90:16] – "Let thy work appear unto thy servants, and thy glory unto their children." Therefore as much as we must encourage children, we must also understand that every believer is a child and must remain so before God. This goes to say that we must observe children if they are our epic role models of who Jesus really was as much as we are the same to them. By Jesus saying that *'whoever receives these little ones receives me'* he meant that we must receive children both physically and spiritually. Physically we receive every child that approaches us with a concern by resolving that concern, thereby we become servants of the child as well as automatically serving Jesus. Spiritually we receive the child by appreciating and/or emulating their character and/or personality. This is because as believers we (adults) and particularly children (regardless of faith) are Jesus, not the Christ, yet without the Holy Ghost we are nothing. The child cannot be associated or attributed to any religious organisation. For instance that a child goes to a Church with his parents/guardians or to a Mosque with his parents/guardians does not automatically make them a Christian or a Muslim (respectively) because they are not mature enough to make their own choices regarding these matters, hence what the Holy Bible is saying here is that Jesus *'received the children'* meaning that he received every single child that came to him, not children that were believers or unbelievers because children are sinless. The disciples may have also rebuked those children probably because they were children of unbelievers. Although the Scriptures have not said this but I'd presume that that was what happened, prompting Jesus to *debunk* his disciples.

The place of Charity or Love:

Charity could be viewed as a life-changing statement because of this rendering in [1 Peter 4:8] – "And above all things have fervent charity among yourselves: for charity shall cover the multitude of sins." Surely these could include verbal sins which we may have spoken against our lives and that of others but because we are uncertain about what kind of sins were being referred to here, our quest for answers just even got stronger. This Scripture reminds me of my late Dad and how dedicated he was in charity. I still believe that I'm yet to witness a man that his life was completely hinged on and dedicated to charitable endeavours like my late Dad was. Some pastors and other individuals are particularly exceptional as well but my late Dad gave all that he had and I associate his character in charity to the testimony of the widow's mite as seen in [Mark 12:41-44] and [Luke 21:1-4]. He gave school-admissions to tens of thousands of people into different levels of education, gave out cars, gave land, saw through political positions and other governmental appointments for people, gave his money, gave love and support thereby engineering the production of a multitude of graduates and professionals who cannot be referenced even in an encyclopaedic catalogue; and this does not include numerous other charitable acts he rendered to a lot more people in Nigeria and possibly around the world, having lived and studied abroad. I'm talking about people that he may have affected in one way or another, including people known and unknown to him and us (his children). He never bothered where you're from, as long as you needed a help that he could assist with, he was committed to it where he could. He was charity personified! Above everything charity can only be charity when it is being done in humility and without being broadcasted just to get a round of applause or some undignified praise. Didn't Jesus warn us in the Holy Scriptures in [Matthew 6:1-4] – "Take heed that ye do not your alms before men, to be seen of them: otherwise ye have no reward of your Father which is in heaven. {Verse 2} Therefore when thou doest thine alms, do not sound a trumpet before thee, as the hypocrites do in the synagogues and in the streets, that they may have glory of men. Verily I say unto you, They have their reward. {Verse 3} But when thou doest alms, let not thy left hand know what thy right hand doeth: {Verse 4}

That thine alms may be in secret: and thy Father which seeth in secret himself shall reward thee openly." I recently realised that I am equally guilty of this ludicrous failure and that is why writing these words myself is very pertinent because it reminds me of certain areas I'd have to improve as a student in order to hopefully become a good or better leader in the future by the grace of God. The Apostle Paul wrote concerning this in [2 Corinthians 10:17-18] – "But he that glorieth, let him glory in the Lord. {Verse 18} For not he that commendeth himself is approved, but whom the Lord commendeth."

It is the Holy Ghost that keeps us chastised for character correction in order for the name of Jesus to stay and remain alive in us because without these chastisements, we easily miss the mark. This was the unique and outstanding quality about my late Dad, he would never help anybody just to have another topic of discussion in the public. He was immensely blessed with such character and grace. My memories of my late Dad remind me of a man that would not eat so that the stranger could be fed. Being a professor of education, it was his passion to train, help and see-through thousands in their academic pursuits and he thrived absolutely fantastically in it. He raised innumerable *children* and writing a tribute for him when he died I could not resist stating the obvious that – '*he was not a preacher but he was a lovely man of God and my friends envied me because of him.*' I always use his charity-lifestyle as a point of contact in my supplication to God saying: '*Abba Father the charity my late Dad did to people, the investments he made in the thousands of lives that he positively affected and blessed will manifest and multiply repeatedly in my own life and that of the generation after me*'. However I must learn from his good acts of charity and goodwill and strive to emulate that great aspect of his life. It was my late Dad that taught me that when you do well to people, you don't count the cost and also that you never expect anything back. I learnt that from my late Dad and will continue to teach my children the same. In [Proverbs 10:12] it was recorded in a very beautiful way that – "Hatred stirreth up strifes: but love covereth all sins." In this rendering the *book of proverbs* identified that love (which is charity) covers ***all*** sins. It takes my mind back to the historical stories we heard about the colonial era and all the atrocities that were committed by the colonialists. These may have been written off by the hands of time and civilisation or modernisation *some may think*, but I personally question the strength of these developments towards abolishing this historical tragedy. My motive is not to deviate from the subject matter, however there may be interesting debates that may arise from this argument wherein we may agree to agree or agree to disagree. I strongly hold the view that great nations like the United Kingdom, France or the United States and a handful of other western and civilised territories may have wisely escaped the wrath of God by aggressively and dedicatedly embracing the Biblical endeavour known as charity. Could charity then constitute a form or sort of redemption or salvation? This view may be idolised by some in their minds as a medium for encouraging the committing of sins, and then volunteering their funds and/or other resources to realising, achieving or fulfilling this sacred act of charity. I'd subjectively refute this stance comparatively. I have a seasoned conviction reserved somewhere within me that charity and grace dwell together. Therefore if grace is without sin, charity is surely independent of sin. Grace is a gift that purifies sins, while charity is a conscious endeavour that covers sins. Explaining that both grace and charity possess the capability to turn the darkness in sins to the light in righteousness.

Scripture in [1 Peter 4:9-10] implores us to – "Use hospitality one to another without grudging. {Verse 10} As every man hath received the gift, even so minister the same one to another, as good stewards of the manifold grace of God." Certainly then we are cognizant with the accuracy of this detail that there is a visible link between grace and charity indeed. Also when you show love (hospitality or charity) to a supposed enemy, it gets them to reconsider how or what they feel or think about you. This is one way charity may cover a multitude of sins. Apostle Paul compared charity to prophecy saying that prophecy is nothing without charity in [1 Corinthians 13:2] – "And though I have [the gift of] prophecy, and understand all mysteries, and all knowledge; and though I have all faith, so that I could remove mountains, and have not charity, I am nothing"; and in [1 Corinthians 13:13] he said – "And now abideth faith, hope and charity, these three; but the greatest of these [is] charity." Therefore as faith without works is dead [James 2:17], so also prophecies without charity is dead in my opinion. Charity (love) is an intentional act of goodwill expressed towards the work of God and towards men and [Ecclesiastes 11:6] encourages us that – "In the morning sow thy seed, and in the evening withhold not thine hand: for thou knowest not whether shall prosper, either this or that, or whether they both [shall be] alike good." This is the gain of charity that we know not which will prosper, thereby encouraging us to be faithful and unfailingly steadfast in this command. Kingdom-giving involves a great understanding and knowledge, and if knowledge is power, then surely financial knowledge must entail financial empowerment which should be geared towards more fervent kingdom-giving, as much as kingdom-knowledge gives birth to kingdom-empowerment.

Finally to summarise this chapter, it would make a world of difference if we could grasp or understand the wealth of this revelation that Jesus was born the son of God but Christ was not born and was never the son of God, although Jesus the son of God would later become Christ the King. Whether in faith or concerning grace or yet regarding prophecies or in performing charity let us do all in the name of Jesus. In [John 5:43] Jesus said this – "I am come in my Father's name, and ye received me not: if another shall come in his own name, him ye will receive." Assuredly we can see from this Scripture that beyond reasonable doubt Jesus came in the name of his Father. Even so today we live and move and have our being in the name of our father Jesus. Sometime ago, precisely very early in the morning (in my sleep) on 21 November 2014 I had a dream and in that dream I and my family were in Church and God was speaking to us, telling us that we are '**Natural Resources in the hand of God**'. I could only recognise my face and that of my family in that congregation but God was speaking from his altar. I woke up from that sleep with those words '*Natural Resources*' echoing in my head and initially I could not understand the express meaning of this word, although I know what natural resources are. Moreover later on during the course of the day the Lord explained it to me that it meant that we are vessels, tools, materials, finished projects that God will use to fulfil his kingdom purpose right here in the earth. If then vessels and finished projects in the hand of God, this therefore means that we are complete and ready to be manifested in the world by the power of the Holy Ghost; just like Jesus was. I knew that God was speaking directly to me (and my family) in that dream, that is why he gave it to me in my dream and is also the reason why I was only able to recognise my family during the course of that dream. We are the Jesus that God will use in this end time and it will all be to his glory, honour and majesty. However, not all our teachers understand this truth. That's why the Psalmist says in [Psalm 119:99] – "I have more understanding than all my teachers: for thy testimonies [are] my meditation." I do not imply the same (*possibly*) arrogant meaning by quoting this Scripture but I believe that no matter one's level in life, you can always learn from people around you and this is regardless your level of leadership in the Church because we're all students and stewards supposedly serving the Church.

Our association and relationship with the Jews could also be identified as a form of charity or love before God. Preaching the gospel to the lost could also be attributed to charity. The Holy Bible records in [Acts 10:34-35] – "Then Peter opened his mouth, and said, Of a truth I perceive that God is no respecter of persons: {Verse 35} But in every nation he that feareth him, and worketh righteousness, is accepted with him." This was reiterated by Apostle Paul in his epistle in [Romans 2:10-11] – "But glory, honour, and peace, to every man that worketh good, to the Jew first, and also to the Gentile: {Verse 11} For there is no respect of persons with God." Why then to the Jew first? Jesus in [John 4:22] – "Ye worship ye know not what: we know what we worship: for salvation is of the Jews." Sometimes as believers, we often forget that Jesus was a Jew and had a particular or keen interest on their salvation. Jesus being a Jew emphasizes that salvation has a Jewish origin and Jesus (Yeshua) gave birth to the Church or what we refer to as the Christian faith, which we believers assume that we practice. This does not mean that we reject or disdain the Jews the way some disgustingly do because if there were no Jews, there will equally be no Churches since Jesus would not have been born. Jesus also commanded that salvation be preached beginning at Jerusalem [Luke 24:47] and [Acts 1:8]. Our Lord is therefore desperate for the salvation of the Jews hence our charity of salvation which entails spreading the gospel must begin from the Jews at Jerusalem. Apostle Paul says [1 Corinthians 9:20] – "And unto the Jews I became as a Jew, that I might gain the Jews; to them that are under the law, as under the law, that I might gain them that are under the law…" He tried to '*become all things to all men*' in order to win them to Jesus. This is the commission therefore, for all to win souls in the name of Jesus beginning from the Jews at Jerusalem as much as we get devoted to other charitable works. In the New International Version of [Matthew 15:24] Jesus revealed – "…I was sent only to the lost sheep of Israel." Our charity must start from soul winning because it is a symbol of love and charity is love, however it must also be backed up by good causes where we see the need for it. Conveying our message of the gospel of peace does not imply that we turn a blind eye to causes where monetary actions may be expedient. Incidentally I had a dream in the early hours of 30 January 2015 where my late Dad was giving a large amount of cash which he had placed in an envelope to somebody that seemed like his driver, for his driver to take the money to a particular charity organisation like one of the '*motherless babies homes*' at the city of Owerri in Nigeria. I believe God was showing me what an exemplary charity-driven life that my late Dad had lived for an encouragement to me and for emulation. Then how important charity (love) is, if the dead still try to give and show love even in our dreams!! Many ministers of God have taught us that giving, love or charity is a means of exchange. For instance in a situation where somebody is sick with say a flu, assuming they had a thousand pounds offering to sow as an exchange for their healing and because it makes sense (I'd assume) that you can only give what you have. If it be so then that you have your thousand pound seed and the flu, whilst sowing that seed for healing you also give away that flu with it to the anointed servant of God who would have been empowered to neutralise the effects of the sickness in your life by accepting that seed-offering from you in the name '*Jesus*'. They therefore take away this sickness not to keep it for themselves but for God to destroy its works and effects in your life and health in its entirety. If then you (the seed sower) have faith, you automatically become made whole completely, not just healed of that flu that had plagued your health but of every form of affliction that hitherto ravaged your life. If charity (love) therefore encourages giving, this means you could truly give out every hindrances in your life through your generous donations of goodwill and gestures of kindness. It has been my utmost desire in life to give food to the hungry, shelter to the homeless, clothing to the naked, build schools and hospitals, train the less privileged, oversee the construction of water-wells and the provision of other essential amenities in the rural parts of the world, plant Churches as well as preach the gospel around the globe; and all these are great acts of kindness or goodwill which could also be referred to as charity or love.

Chapter 2: Jesus – God The Son

(God Of Man)

The place of Character:

CHRIST denotes

C – Character (in Service)
H – Holiness (sees God)
R – Righteousness (exalts Nations)
I – Inspiration (encourages Mankind)
S – Salvation (for Israel)
T - Triumph (through Testimonies)

Christ signifies ownership. Christ was Jesus – God the Son and the 'God of man'. In the New Testament Jesus had twelve Apostles who represented the Old Testament twelve sons/tribes of Israel (Jacob). This typifies the similarities between the divine government of the ancient kingdom of Israel and the divine government of the ancient Church. Spiritually Christ remains the head of both because Israel is a spiritual symbol of the Church. In [Matthew 1:16] the Bible says – "And Jacob begat Joseph the husband of Mary, of whom was born Jesus, who is called Christ." In the New Testament Joseph acted as Jesus's surrogate father because Jesus was conceived of the Holy Spirit and born of Joseph's virgin wife Mary. In the Old Testament Joseph was one of the sons of a man called Jacob. This unique picture shares the profound similarity and testimony of a continuous lineage that began from the Old Testament and ran down to the New Testament. In the Old Testament, Joseph (who was a kind of

Jesus) later became the Prime Minister of the greatest kingdom on earth at the time (Egypt); and in the New Testament, Jesus (who later became the Christ) and was the spiritual Prime Minister of the greatest kingdom ever (kingdom of God). The distinguishing factor is incidentally yet similar being that Jesus also shared similarities with Jacob the father of Joseph. Jesus (who later became the Christ) was the child of the Holy Ghost [Matthew 1:18] and a prince of the kings of the earth [Revelation 1:5]; however Jacob (who later became Israel) was the servant of God [Genesis 27:28-29, Genesis 30:27 and Genesis 31:24, v.29] and a prince of God and men [Genesis 32:28 and Genesis 35:10]. Seems a bit of a mix-up and repetition here I suppose but it's intended for us to solidify our platform for this 'mental' chapter ahead.

Catastrophically a lot of times we confuse and mix up Christ with Jesus in the same manner. Well yes, *Christ is Jesus only because Jesus became the Christ. Jesus as a man had to be transfigured by the Spirit to become the Christ, whereas Christ's personality never had to be altered for Christ to become Jesus. Jesus was a physical being hence limited in his reach, but Christ was a spiritual being hence unlimited in his reach. Jesus had a denomination, he was a Jew but Christ never had a denomination. As we assumed his name Jesus, he in turn became the Lord and thereby assumed the name and authority as Christ.* This is he that was there from the beginning and was with God the Father creating the inhabitants of the world. Now the same Christ walked the earth as Jesus and how possible is this to the natural mind?! Admittedly this mystery becomes even more complex today with the comprehension and understanding that this Jesus is '*seated at the right hand of God the Father as Christ interceding for us*' - [Romans 8:34]. Christ dwells in us now through his Holy Spirit because Christ is a Spirit who never died whereas Jesus died, although his flesh (as Jesus) died and was risen (as Lord and as Christ). Jesus as Christ went through a pre-ordained metamorphosis to become who he is today in us and for the Scriptures to be fulfilled. It is essential that we get a grasp or a very strong hold of his spiritual personality and his divine effectiveness in us lest we frustrate his abilities in us. Christ is the one who initiates the ideas in us and quickens the gifts within us. The book of [Proverbs 18:16] declares to us that – "A man's gift maketh room for him, and bringeth him before great men." That gift in us is Christ who glorifies himself in us through our unique gifts by using them to bring us before the great thereby glorifying himself. Didn't the Scriptures actually say *'Christ in us the hope of glory'* - [Colossians 1:27b]?! Therefore it is the power of Christ in us that transforms our abilities and capabilities for a supernatural manifestation displayed in the physical. This is also because with Christ in us we are exposed to an unbelievable wealth and array of opportunities, gifts and talents. The same Christ through the immeasurable power of his Holy Spirit gives us spiritual signals whenever those opportunities arise or even when threats are about to creep in or cross our divine paths thereby catapulting us beyond any spheres of threats and challenges through dreams, visions, intuition and the inspiration he holds within us. It's an often misconstrued message to the natural mind yet commands such clarity and precision because Jesus is with the Father in heaven and the works of miracles and manifestations we see today in the Church are being done by the Holy Ghost and not by Jesus as many believe, although they are done in the name of Jesus. I'd further narrate that who Jesus was to his apostles and other disciples is who the Holy Ghost is to man today.

Prior to this understanding, selling this kind of message to the Church in the exact words of the Bible has often seemed either quite unclear or the meanings conveyed have been devoid of revelation. My humble understanding and such wisdom ensure that I come short of calling myself a Bible teacher being that we talk about the acts and the demonstration of the power of the Holy Ghost which is revealed to men and there's no avenue to measure or weigh what constitutes a teaching character or qualification in men in the absence of revelation knowledge from God. I'd categorically conclude that the link between Jesus and Christ is the Spirit of God, and without the Holy Spirit Jesus had no chance at being the Christ. The Holy Spirit made the difference, that's why when you're possessed by the Spirit of the Lord, then you are Jesus not the Christ. This is an argument of zealous chasm and possibly privy contentions thus hindering a philosophy of further explanations since the Holy Bible is a sacred book and therefore should not be open for a public spectacle of strengths or flaws and/or criticisms. Meanwhile as deep as I was in writing this book, I still had reservations about it and almost deleted this book several times (as already testified earlier) after I faced repeated and severe health attacks and challenges whilst writing this book. I started thinking that maybe God wants me to delete this idea or that maybe I had offended God through this writing. In the process God brought hope to encourage me through it and I had absolutely no other explanations to it the fulfilled delivery of this dream. It's an idea that has lived through over six years of conception in my mind after I saw this whilst studying the Holy Bible for myself in January 2009. Prior to this time I had never heard any preacher ever say anything similar to this and God is my witness regarding this. Maybe they had (I don't know) but the Lord showed it to me by himself in his holy word. Regardless, the depth of comprehension contained herein may still not yet be understood by many teachers of the Holy Bible today. Christ is therefore an experience more than he is a personality.

Let this book be an encouragement to every student of the Holy Bible that regardless the error messages or discouragement from the enemy, you must fulfil your destiny and write the books you need to write because you have peculiar experiences and as such many people to encourage and lecture through the words of your testimonies. I discovered that on every particular Bible topic or life experience, the Lord may give the same topic or allow similar experience to different individuals but all get totally unique revelation, interpretation and learn different lessons from it and this encourages me never to discourage myself because I will through my testimonies save someone passing through similar challenges that I had to endure in my past. Scripture in [Ecclesiastes 12:12] encourages us to write – "And further, by these, my son, be admonished: of making many books [there is] no end; and much study [is] weariness of the flesh." Therefore as much as we must study, we must also write more. The book of [Acts 10] teaches us a lot about character and Peter an Apostle of Jesus Christ served as the example in this passage. The angel of God had spoken to a devout and God-fearing man named Cornelius in Caesarea through a vision to send men to Joppa to fetch Peter who was supposed to tell Cornelius what he must do. It was surely an unbelievable task for Cornelius to send for a servant of God; and then it would have been daunting for Peter as well, being a servant of God how could he condescend so low to go to an *'ordinary'* or *'common'* man's house?! But the apostles of the early

Church were more of servants of God rather than being men of God like what we have today in many Churches. Meanwhile about the same time (I believe), God was equally showing Peter a vision not to call what God has cleansed 'common'. In [Acts 10:28] Peter spoke saying – "And he said unto them, Ye know how that it is an unlawful thing for a man that is a Jew to keep company, or come unto one of another nation; but God hath shewed me that I should not call any man common or unclean." I'd identify that it was Christ in Peter that encouraged him to remain humble unto the obedience of this possibly questionable (in this age) instruction. Otherwise imagine a man of God today of the magnitude of Peter, an apostle that walked and dined with Jesus being summoned to the house of a man he did not even know existed. I doubt if this could be possible today but it would depend on the personality involved. Then Peter speaking through the mind of Christ said these words in [Acts 10:34-35] – "Then Peter opened [his] mouth, and said, Of a truth I perceive that God is no respecter of persons: {Verse 35} But in every nation he that feareth him, and worketh righteousness, is accepted with him." I was then able to realise that character is the most reverend part of the believer's walk of faith and life. Character is the lifestyle a person leads more than anything else. I further discovered that not going to school does not make one an illiterate. It is not *'uneducatedness'* that constitutes illiteracy. What makes anybody qualify to be called an illiterate has to do with their wrong character or negative attitude. Emulating the character of Christ comes with the knowledge that Christ is more than a Christmas tree with lights on it. Christ is the believer's light and that light shines from within us, thereby glowing through to radiant manifestation on the outside by the power of the Christ (Holy Spirit) in us. Wherefore we are thereby taught how to live in the spirit rather than in the flesh. This explains why ***the flesh (Jesus) had to leave for the Spirit (Christ) to come*** because Christ (in us) came to teach us the spirit-led life. This life transfigures us through a new experience thereby transcending us into the spirit by crippling the flesh in us.

The book of [Acts 10:46-47] shows us more to ponder about character – "For they heard them speak with tongues, and magnify God. Then answered Peter, {Verse 47} Can any man forbid water, that these should not be baptized, which have received the Holy Ghost as well as we?" At Caesarea they received the Holy Ghost before baptism which was contrary to the original doctrine that people had to be baptised first before the Holy Ghost came upon them like was the case with the apostles and the disciples of Jesus. ***This is why character is about being like Christ more than it is about being like Jesus and the only difference is personality***. Like Christ means that believers flow as led by the Holy Ghost in an unlimited space and sphere whereas like Jesus means that we operate in our natural form which obviously has its limits. So then we know that sometimes protocol may need to be broken over the physical as permitted by the Holy Spirit of God. From this detailed account in [Acts 10], protocol was broken at least twice:

- First a servant of God and an apostle of Jesus Christ (Peter) was *summoned* to pay an '*ordinary but cleansed man*' a visit and he did without hesitation. This is the express character of Christ who comes through his Holy Spirit to dwell in cleansed men and women known as his *vessels* thereby operating and manifesting through them.
- Secondly protocol was broken when the men in Caesarea received the Holy Ghost before being baptised.

Character therefore exhibits very important virtues: humility, honesty, gratitude, courage, faith, kindness, service, self-control, fairness, resilience, creativity among others. Jesus exhibited most of these virtues but because he was still flesh, he did not want to die but Christ in Jesus '*forced*' the will of God through because Jesus came to die and had to die. Using the word '*forced*' here may be duly criticised and I welcome all criticisms because if Jesus asked the Father to take the cup from him, that tells anyone that he did not want to die and it was because of his nature as flesh. *This is why character is more of Jesus yet most of Christ because character most times would involve a lot of courage*. The Scripture in [John 8:58-59] records another instance where Jesus actually ran away from death – "Jesus said unto them, Verily, verily, I say unto you, Before Abraham was, I am. {Verse 59} Then took they up stones to cast at him: but Jesus hid himself, and went out of the temple, going through the midst of them, and so passed by." This reaction from Jesus I believe was spontaneous (as flesh) and could also be attributed as wisdom because it has to be wise to prevent or rather protect yourself from danger or death. The difference is that the character of Christ scares danger. The personality of Christ cannot be frightened. Character most often than not is caught, although it can equally be taught to a profitable extent. Jesus was teachable and a number of instances were recorded in Scripture where he learnt and asked wise questions in the temple [Luke 2:46] as a child, Christ on the other hand is the teacher because Christ is an embodiment of the Spirit of God. Character education is therefore of grave importance amongst schools and must be added/included as part of the curriculum thereby teaching young children how to conduct and behave themselves wisely through life and in relationships with people, particularly in the 'believing' or what we call 'Christian' countries and communities. A good example of the dangers of teaching character education wrongly is the term called 'radicalisation'. It's "something like something." This is my senior son's language when he does not understand the need for a particular thing, he'd say 'it's something like something'. Radicalisation remains unacceptably incomprehensible and therefore is something like something. Character is the direct opposite of the murder-word '*radicalisation*'.

Character is a lot more than the knowledge or understanding and believing that you're either British, Polish, European or American and so on. It's an idea that was sown into your mind from birth and as such there's no evidence for such details. You only resolved to believe whatever you were told at birth and then you were trained and raised in a particular pattern or culture to concur with the idea that had been planted in your mind from birth. You were given a certain mind-set but no part of your body looks different from what you were told that you're not. For instance being British does not mean that you're made up of body parts peculiar to the British because there's no such unique body features. This tells me that character is more than your belief system. You may have been educated that your family or ancestral lineage is French, not knowing that if you searched into your history, you may suddenly discover that you are inherently Irish, Australian or Jamaican or maybe from any other part of the world. The people that raised you up may not even be your parents and you cannot know this detail because such secret information often remain secret even to the larger family members. Your siblings may after all not be your real siblings but you will still not know until your truth and reality is revealed to you. I personally grew up with a brother who my Dad would later tell me many years later (as a full-grown adult) that he is my half-brother and this was irrelevant information to me because it came at the most unwelcome time. I grew up knowing and loving him because he was supposed to be and is still (I believe) the only brother I had and still have from same parents. If what my Dad later revealed to me in 2012 is the truth, then it'd mean that all male siblings I have are half-brothers. That means I am the only son my Dad and my mum had together, plus it would also justify the special love both parents had for me being that both of them knew we were living a lie in our family (if that information is true). It may also have been the secret of their constant logger-heads that we never knew what the cause was. Having said this if you would then believe human beings without evidence and started to act like them just because you were trained to be like them, how dare you not to believe that Christ is Lord and start to learn how to behave Christ-like because the Holy Bible says in [1 John 5:9] – "If we believed the witness of men, the witness of God is greater: for this is the witness of God which he hath testified of his Son." This argument is very logical and thought evoking. It requires common sense but not everybody applies it. For instance, I remember my late Mum always say to me that whenever I get married and have children, I should get a DNA to ensure that my children were mine because there are many cases where fatherhood of a child had been called into question. I thought it was wise and to this effect I did a double DNA test from two different testing centres on my three children. I did it twice just in case the first place had made an error. My wife accused me that *'I did not trust her'* but I knew what I had in mind and it cost me some good amount of money, yet I had to satisfy my innate appetite. My wife called it a 'waste of money' but I told her that I had been advised and raised with a mind-set which I had to justify. I could bet anybody with anything that my children 'are my children' but I needed a valid proof to that effect. I thought that it was not just enough to believe that because I am African (not black) and my wife is European (not white), therefore that this should prove that our multi-racial (not mixed) children automatically are mine. That is what I considered 'dumb' because we're talking about flesh and character is more than flesh or your belief system. The result is that when I talk about my children, I talk with such pride, justice and dignity because I know that truly they are mine.

But in real Christ-like mindedness, I may think that this was the human mind being unduly manipulated by some external spiritual force otherwise should it really matter if I produced the babies or not? If I truly believe that God is the giver of babies, my selfish research was unnecessary and the findings biased. For this logic to be credible, does it then mean that the need to marriage to one wife is undermined? If the DNA was irrelevant, then I may also argue that marriage is equally irrelevant because marriage to one wife does not ensure that the parties in the marriage have one sexual partner. If then marriage is relevant and needful, therefore the DNA equally makes sense in verifying and reassuring the husband that his wife is trustworthy and not an adulterer. This is because there is then that reassurance that the children belong to the man. This may well not remain the case overtime, but as events unfold the truth and realities of the future unveils. Also if DNA was an unnecessary idea, there would not be the need for this Scripture [Matthew 5:32] – "But I say to you, That whosoever shall put away his wife, saving for the cause of fornication, causeth her to commit adultery: and whosoever shall marry her that is divorced committeth adultery." This Scripture proves the unquestionable relevance of DNA. So character here is justified because it involves a knowing and because you know, it becomes your evidence rather than merely believing. However in our relationship with God, believeing takes prominence. Also if I had another ten children with a ten different women (which I know will never happen), my utmost enthusiasm will certainly be to do a DNA test on every single child before I may accept paternal responsibilities in this manner. I can raise another man's child very happily and willingly, but I need to be aware and conscious (not biased) when I do it. It has to be an intentional and voluntary endeavour because a lot of people may do a DNA test and be shocked to know that their children are not theirs which will inevitably be very disappointing and I don't intend to break anybody's marriage by saying this. However the knowing of character has to be positive because the fruits of character are good fruits. This may sound weird and very rare a thought but it gives a deeper insight that the aim of character is to ensure that people behave very well or act responsibly through all challenges and situations. Also there is a saying that it is only the woman that knows the real father of her baby and this thought *frightens and surely threatens* character in relationships, however the DNA fulfils and nullifies this possible threat that may affect relationships. Resemblance to any man or child does not guarantee or confirm fatherhood or parenthood. The DNA will never give you a one hundred percent (100%) result or assurance, however you feel reassured when you see the results at (99.99%). It wells up some sort of immeasurable peace within you and this may equally sound stupid but when my children grow up and get married, I may advice my sons to ensure that they do a DNA on every child registered in their name(s). I'd equally warn my daughter that I may advise her husband to do the same. This is intended to maintain character in my children, thereby ensuring alertness and as close to 'responsible' as possible. Also this knowing will help mould and control their minds and reasonability, thereby steering them towards doing right naturally.

The place of Headship:

The place of Christ is the place of headship and the Holy Bible tells us in [1 Corinthians 11:3] – "But I would have you know, that the head of every man is Christ; and the head of the woman *is* the man; and the head of Christ *is* God." In the same way there is always a hierarchy to be respected in a place where the Holy Spirit of God dwells as much as there must be order in the house of God. This is where the Church struggles a lot because a lot of leaders act like they are the head of the Church. Yes physically they have spiritual authority, however that they started the ministry does not make them head and as such Christ remains the head. This is why I argue extensively that leaders must be leading-servants for their role(s) to be respected and relevant. Churches where the leaders are disorganised in this aspect, we often find that they end up losing the respect and authority they were instituted to command. This is the reason why many members of various ministries while leaving such ministries go on to write upsetting letters, emails or text messages of a not so honourable tone to the Church leadership in a desperate and frustrated attempt to hopefully right wrongs. So Church leaders must strive to recognise and honour Christ, else they lose theirs. It is the same in a home where the wives do not respect or honour the husbands, their children equally lose their grasp on the need for the exchange of honour. My mum used to say that *'respect is reciprocal'* and that **'an elder who expects greeting from a young child must also be willing to greet the child first as much as they'd be willing to respond if the child greets first'**. By so doing you teach the child what is right by *doing what is right*, not just by *saying what is right* because children more often than not do what they see adults do rather than what adults say they should do. There has also been a lot of debates and arguments on who is equal with who in the Church. Regarding this and controversially so Apostle Paul said in [Galatians 3:28] – "There is neither Jew nor Greek, there is neither bond nor free, **there is neither male nor female: for ye are all one in Christ Jesus.**" If this is narrated from a mental perspective, we could then argue that there is no need to honour headship or authority regarding Church leaderships where men are identified as the leaders. However in [1 Corinthians 14:33-35] Apostle Paul *subjected* the Corinthian Church to observe this doctrine – "For God is not *the author* of confusion, but of peace, as in all Churches of the saints. {Verse 34} Let your women keep silence in the churches: for it is not permitted unto them to speak; but *they are commanded* to be under obedience, as also saith the law. {Verse 35} And if they will learn any thing, let them ask their husbands at home: for it is a shame for women to speak in the church." So is it then one rule for one Church and another rule for another Church being that the Galatians were admonished that males and females are all one in Christ whereas the Corinthian Church were advised that their women keep silence in the Churches? Is there confusion with God? Well the same Scripture says that God is not the author of confusion. This identifies that hierarchical orderliness must then be observed and honoured. This later Scripture also raises a few questions as detailed below:

- Lady Pastors and ministers: a trend or a Call?
- What happens to already female ordained pastors and ministers in the Churches?

- Was their ordination right or was it in line with Scripture and how or why?
- What about women who don't have a husband at home to speak to at home, will they remain silent and in ignorance of the answers that they seek?
- Does this entail segregation in the Churches and why?
- Was this instruction strictly for the particular Churches at Corinth or was it for all Churches?
- Was Apostle Paul *conscious or sober enough* when he made these comments and if he was, why was the Apostle Paul very controversial then?

I have battled with these questions for years and having asked a few pastors, they have not really been able to answer these questions convincingly. I also discovered that many teachers and scholars of the Holy Bible avoid explaining or discussing some of these issues and I still cannot comprehend why or how this is so. Do we then choose where and where-not to preach about in the Holy Bible? But [Hebrews 13:17] emphasizes that we – "Obey them that have the rule over you, and submit yourselves: for they watch for your souls, as they that must give account, that they may do it with joy, and not with grief: for that *is* unprofitable for you." If so then what about the Churches that have women as their leaders with tangible evidence that the Lord is also using them to command testimonies. If they should then not speak in the Churches, why are they at the helm if the Apostle Paul declared to the Corinthian Church that this was a shame, thereby rendering it an unacceptable practice? I don't question these words, however I seek sincere explanations regarding these. I hope to provoke some thoughts by asking these detailed and comprehensive questions with the intention that some thoughtful suggestions or constructive criticisms or debates may arise from these with the intention to exert knowledge or understanding and not to ridicule. The first epistle of Paul the Apostle to Timothy in [1 Timothy 2:11-14] further complicates this mental picture that we're already meditating through – "Let the woman learn in silence with all subjection. {Verse 12} But I suffer not a woman to teach, nor to usurp authority over the man, but to be in silence. {Verse 13} For Adam was first formed, then Eve. {Verse 14} And Adam was not deceived, but the woman being deceived was in the transgression." If this being the case, how then could we argue this case of *sexual equality or inequality* strongly without being considered discriminatory or without it being derogatory by so doing? Whatever happens, I believe that Christ (as the head of the Church) must be honoured as much as the man (as the head of the woman), although not every Scripture teacher agrees to this notion. I discovered that most of the men appointed to Church leaderships argue this case in favour of the men while the women in similar positions insist that both men and women are equal in Christ, although both cases have Scriptural basis or foundations as already seen from above. The word of God (Holy Bible) also takes us through this further narrative in – [Ephesians 5:21-25] – "Submitting yourselves one to another in the fear of God. {Verse 22} Wives, submit yourselves unto your own husbands, as unto the Lord. {Verse 23} **For the husband is the head of the wife, even as Christ is the head of the church**: and he is the saviour of the body. {Verse 24} **Therefore as the church is subject unto Christ, so *let* the wives *be* to their own husbands in every thing**. Husbands, love your wives, even as Christ also loved the church, and gave himself for it." Having said all this I think our female ministers should be encouraged and applauded in every way because we've had a flood-few of them that God is still currently using, amazingly too. We could then also summarise by testifying this reality that the vast majority of these Scriptures insist that women submit to men whether at home or in the Churches as much as *all men* submit to the leadership of Christ. Christ when he walked the earth as Jesus showed that leadership can only be defined by one word – '*SERVICE*' and this is one explanation that you may never hear from our Christian leaders today. Leadership or headship exerts but does not abuse its authority.

The place of Causes:

The personality of Christ in the Old Testament (even though 'Christ' was never mentioned in the Old Testament) portrays *radical judgement* as opposed to the personality of the Christ in the New Testament which portrays *faithful justification*. When I named my second son *Freedom Justice*, a much senior family-friend of mine (Martin by name) rang me asking – "are you fighting for a cause?" I just laughed over the telephone and answered his question with this question – "Is there not a cause?" A cause is simply a justified need. Scripture in [John 18:37b] identifies this cause in the words of Christ (as Jesus) – "To this end was I born, and for this cause came I into the world, that I should bear witness unto the truth. Every one that is of the truth heareth my voice." Christ still bears witness of this truth today through the gift of his Holy Spirit in men with signs following them that believe. For instance in our lives and endeavours there is always a cause and whatever cause it is justifies the need for it. David observed this in [1 Samuel 17:29] – "And David said, What have I now done? [Is there] not a cause?" This story was a particularly intriguing one because in [1 Samuel 17:26-30] Eliab who was David's eldest brother tried to rebuke and discourage him from fulfilling his cause and thereby hinder his destiny, but David refused to be deterred because he understood that there was a genuine cause. The fight for the kingdom of God and the gospel of Jesus Christ (which is what this book is about) is arguably the most important cause in life and let nobody discourage you that we cannot do this together. I'm naturally a psychologist which means that I study and observe people quite a lot; and I discovered that a lot of African preachers will hardly encourage people to go out and preach the gospel if they perceive the call and gift of God in such people. It's bizarre and somewhat awful because they forget that they were encouraged by someone when the call came on their own lives. Its widespread today particularly in the African pastored Churches and I don't mean to generalise it or be judgemental in any way but it's really detestable doctrine and very contrary to what Jesus preached and practiced because Jesus took disciples from everywhere and encouraged believers to *'make disciples of all nations'* - [Matthew 28:19]. It is rather a destructive doctrine that has crept into the current Church today thereby depriving and frustrating the cause of Christ to bear witness to the world. Again I believe in the call of God before an actual encroachment into the ministry is started or established, but believers have to be encouraged to start from somewhere first. After I was told by a number of pastors that I had a calling, I never rushed into the ministry because I made a vow that until I heard God sending me, I'd never jump in. Eventually he did call me through numerous dreams and visions, and would eventually confirm the call to ministry over my life through a prophet who had never met me before until that very day the Lord had spoken to me to go and start, the Lord spoke to me as well. So if I had any reservations or doubts as to whether I was sure or not that I'd been called, God strategically positioned me on the same day to later have an encounter with him through his servant the prophet. I didn't need any further proof of my calling because it was so real. This is why I do not take permission from any man before I write to publish and I don't intend to sound arrogant here please. It is God's work and every man has a Biblically justified right to do it and this does not make 'ordinary' or 'common' men (with extraordinary abilities) preachers or teachers in any way. I must therefore insist that I'm just a student that has been called into the ministry and I am only trying to express my understanding of Scripture in words.

There is a real cause not just to spread the gospel of Christ but pertinently beginning from the Jews at Jerusalem. This was the gospel of Christ emphasized by Jesus to help the believer understand the heart of God towards the Jews. Although I've hardly heard major African preacher say something *'really positive and encouraging'* about the Jews unfortunately. There often seems to be a void in the wealth of understanding they have regarding the Jews being that most African preachers criticise the Jews for killing the Lord Jesus without the open-mindedness that this was intentionally orchestrated and initiated by God for the birth of salvation. Some have often claimed that the Jews of today were not the real Jews without the knowledge that every believer is a spiritual Jew according to [John 4:22b] – "...for salvation is of the Jews". Personally I have always had a very strong passion for the Jews and forever will. I personally believe that the voice of Israel is the voice of God. Matter of truth if I had a choice I'd probably save a Jew first before a believer (Christian) because Scriptures repeatedly encouraged believers to reach out for the Jews first. I am that radical and at the same time very outspoken with the love I have for the Jews, even though I'm a believer in Christ. If God loved them that much as seen through the Scriptures, then who am I not to? I even love the Jews the way I love myself and sometimes I wish that physically I was of Jewish heritage as a believer. That's how much I really adore the Jews. Jesus that we believers teach and preach about was a Jew and many of us actually forget but Christ has no denomination or what some may call religion. Jesus was never a Christian even though Jesus gave birth to the Church. Jesus was also never called a Christian, his disciples were called Christians (first) at Antioch. Even during his death Jesus was addressed as "KING OF THE JEWS". That was his crime, not "KING OF THE CHRISTIANS". Many believers seem not to even understand this including the vast majority of our Church leaders in ministry today and I say this truth with all due respect and humility to all. The unfortunate thing in the Church today is that our leaders are too big, too proud and too wise to be corrected by or to learn from a 'novice' or an 'apprentice' (if you may call some of us that). It is indeed acceptable. The word of God is not a story book, it's a revelation I believe and that is why the Holy Bible admonished us in (2 Timothy 2:15) to "STUDY" (not READ). I probably said it in my last book that – *"If I was not considered a Christian, I would surely have been a Jewish-Christian or preferably a Jewish-believer in Christ."* I got attracted to the Jews so much after studying through the Scriptures. Sometime last year in 2014 I told my wife that by the grace of God one of my sons will marry a *Jewish-believer in Christ* and I'd prefer it to be my first son. Above all, every instruction that Jesus commanded his disciples on spreading the gospel, he often emphasized them starting from the Jews at Jerusalem (first). God's word can never be broken because he repeatedly said in the Scriptures how he loves Israel and that he has chosen Israel as *"his first born son"* - [Exodus 4:22]. This tells me that Israel (as much as David) were the Jesus of the Old Testament and Israel, David and Jesus were all Jews. We believers claim to be the new Israel forgetting that some people were placed as "the Israelites" by God himself right from the beginning of creation and [Psalm 122:6] instructs – "Pray for the peace of Jerusalem: they shall prosper that love thee." Jerusalem is the city of the Jews (first) before any believer or other foreign claimants of that great city. Why would God focus his creation on Jews if they were irrelevant? It's a question and you don't have to answer me, just ask yourself and then meditate on your answer.

From the foregoing we can see that defending the Jews is a cause set for us to fight dedicatedly by God. Equally the Lord Jesus (our role model) never preached in a Church. Jesus was taught and then he also taught in the Synagogues of the Jews. This does not go to undermine the strength of the believer's faith in any way, however my motive as a writer on the principles established by the word of God is to give the reader a clear picture of the urgent cause to win the Jews for Christ. A cause established and led by our Lord Jesus for us to emulate and continue. This cause is a strong *responsibility* imposed on the believer. I call it a 'responsibility' regardless of my argument in my last book that '*Nobody is responsible' because everybody has a disability and your disability is your irresponsibility, since it is the responsibility of God (which is Christ through his Holy Spirit in us) to sort out our disabilities.* The same Spirit of the Christ triggers the genuine motivation to pursue our destined causes in him. I decided and determined that by the grace of God nothing will stop me from spreading the gospel of Christ from this year 2015 after I was repeatedly called by God through dreams and visions, and repeatedly anointed and commissioned in my dreams. The problem is that sometimes 'Church centres' or what we may refer to as 'Christian centres' try or rather tend to restrict us instead of encouraging us. Some pastors often see their members as '*potential competitors*' instead of '*potential propagators of the kingdom of God and the gospel of Christ*'. They think or maybe assume that their member(s) may open a ministry to enable them to share the gospel and stall the growth or expansion of theirs. By so doing, they try to restrict not only the spread of the gospel of Christ but then also the growth of the ministry they preside over because whenever you (as a pastor) raises a spiritual son in ministry, spiritually your own ministry just got expanded without your knowledge. *The message of the gospel is not about a man's ministry, it's about God's ministry* really. This is why I told God that I am open to anywhere he will send me to this year, any ministry that will help me grow without counting the cost and shortly after this I heard God speak to me in a very clear and audible vision on 23rd January 2015 to go and start the ministry that he had repeatedly shown me in numerous dreams and visions, and make disciples of all nations; and he confirmed the same word same day through his servant the prophet in a Church I attended for the first time on that self-same day. Many people will live and die worshipping Church buildings and pastors without fulfilling their own calling. What a shame and I refuse and reject to be like that from this year of the living God and forward. A stranger once addressed this challenge quite beautifully – 'You do need to get planted in a good local Church where people can love and be like-minded with you and where you can learn and you can grow.

You know Churches are not perfect, sometimes you get hurt by people in Churches, sometimes they don't quite know exactly what to do with you. *But let me tell you this – if you try a couple of Churches and you don't find the right one, don't give up. You keep trying until you find the place where you feel like your home.'* This I consider as possibly the most intelligent and most reasonable advice that could be given to any child of God or even to a new convert who is *actively seeking a home called 'the Church' rather than a building called 'a church'* because the home encourages the positive movement of the cause(s) rather than the building which hinders or stalls the growth and progress of such.

The place of Force:

The force of God works by the spirit of the grace of God in the name of Jesus but the role of effort cannot be undermined. The Bible reads in [Matthew 11:12] – "And from the days of John the Baptist until now the kingdom of heaven suffereth violence, and the violent take it by force." This is the order of events in the physical just as it is the order of events in the spiritual. A lot of strategies that work in the physical also operate in the spiritual realm. When you are violent in the physical, violent in prayer, violent in character, violent in exercising your authority, you do not only effect changes in the physical, you equally effect spiritual changes as well. This is why the enemy needs to experience force from the believer before he may release every of the believer's hitherto stolen potential. Jesus went on the Cross of Calvary by force. He only went because he had to go otherwise the menace that Adam instituted would still have remained. Jesus came to clean and clear things up. It's the same in the physical world, when Benjamin Netanyahu was re-elected as the Israeli Prime Minister for the fourth time on 18 March 2015, I was principally excited about this. I used the word 'principally' to emphasize my peculiar joy at this achievement not just for the Prime Minister but for the great nation of Israel. I was reassured within me and very confident that he should remain Israel's leader because I determined that it was crucial that Israel needed a real force at the helm, not a dummy that will maybe be subjected or rather subdued by the governments of the other parts of the world in Iran,

Russia or other relevant areas. I believed and still believe that Israel needs someone with the brain of President Barack Obama and the heart of maybe President Vadimir Putin. A person who can be very constructive and still be very calculated at the same time if they must remain strong, firm and particularly 'recognised' in this present world. I'm not a fan of Mr Putin but the real truth is that he has the heart for the sort of language that the world understands at the moment. The only language that puts any nation at the very top of the map of this world is *force*. If you (as a nation) cannot exercise force in a way that is arguably justified and possibly gets the world to notice you, you will remain down under. This is why African nations have remained somewhat '*irrelevant*' and severely neglected in deciding or determining the affairs of the current world because they are '*too peaceful*' to make a relevant mark of recognition required for a place in the elite nations of the world today.

The Roman empire only worked 'by force', the greatest empire that ever existed (the British empire) was attained because Great Britain was determined to conquer the world when they did and they achieved it 'by force' and the result is that until this day Great Britain is still enjoying the rewards of their sacrifices centuries ago, Germany tried the same and almost succeeded 'by force', Russia attempted the same and almost succeeded but today Russia leads what one may refer to as *the radical world* 'by force' and I don't believe that this is because they just want to but rather so that they will always be talked about and recognised, the United States of America leads the financial and economic world today 'by force' and they also lead the world in the fight against terror 'by force' because we're all in the battle against criminal terrorist groups who unfortunately will not relent in their exertion of force, and China leads the development world today 'by force'. Therefore Israel can only apply *force* as their strategy, otherwise risk being dumped under like Africa or even some other nations of the world we live in that have remain too calm and therefore lost their honour in the world. Force could be applied for good or for bad. When applied for good, there is a peaceful transition to attainment or achievement, but when applied badly a war may ensue. That is why this is not a gospel of violence, no, this is a gospel of knowing and using your strategy well enough to be recognised and thereby considered relevant in your world. It's a very simple and very clear strategy. Any nation can either choose to remain too peaceful, playing pity-parties, remain humbled forever because they may often require financial bail-outs like Greece, Spain or even Ireland and get celebrated only on St Patrick's day and then forgotten again until the next St Patrick's day, or, they can determine to apply force (where required) like their next door neighbour – the United Kingdom, put themselves on the elite map of the world and get celebrated everyday forever, even when you (as a nation) may not even deserve to be celebrated every day. This is what runs this world – power, and that power must be exerted through some kind of calculated force fortunately or unfortunately. It's the same principle in the kingdom of God and we can see this from [Exodus 6:1] – "Then the LORD said unto Moses, Now shalt thou see what I will do to Pharaoh: for **with a strong hand** shall he drive them out of his land." This explains that even God could only achieve his purpose for the children of Israel by force. He is God and could have done it in an alternative manner, however he needed to show us how to deal with *Pharaohic* spirits in the Church and in our communities. Force can easily be exercised by persistence or in several other ways, it must not involve some sort of violence because it could take a professional tone in order to push it through. However an effective Christian life can only be achieved through the force of fasting and prayer or other spiritual exercises because we're warring against spiritual terrorists who fight day and night to take our lives through incessant spiritual attacks. I've personally had a fair share of these experiences in my own life, attacks that came through the spirit (maybe in dreams) but their effects began to manifest in the physical as I'd suffered in my health in times past. The Scripture in [Matthew 11:12] speaks thus – "And from the days of John the Baptist until now the kingdom of heaven suffereth violence, and the violent take it by force." The reason and need for the application of force by any believer is found in [Ephesians 6:12] – "For we wrestle not against flesh and blood, but against principalities, against powers, against the rulers of the darkness of this world, against spiritual wickedness in high *places*."

For instance when I was still battling with the United Kingdom Border Agency (UKBA) for my permanent residence in the United Kingdom, I had to apply persistently before I eventually got it. The UKBA repeatedly insisted that I had not yet qualified for permanent residence, but I refused to give in to this argument. I had a five-year residency at the time that was meant to expire on 26 October 2014, but in the year 2011 I applied for permanent residency which got refused although I was given a right of appeal which I refused to exercise for some reason and then I sent my application for review to the agency for a second time and it got rejected again. I made up my mind to request a review for the third time insisting on my argument that in my own mind and from my own calculation, I had already qualified for the permanent residence status. This time I did not just receive a normal reply from the agency, but on June 2011 I received some sort of professional threat dated 31 May 2011 and written in this tone – "Consequently, your documentation is being returned to you, including your children's British passports and your Nigerian passport. If you submit a further letter maintaining your demand to be issued with an EEA permanent residence card all passports will be returned to the issuing authority. In the case of the British passports this will be the Identity and Passport Service and the Nigerian embassy with regards to your Nigerian passport. I would be grateful if you would take note of the contents of this letter." I'd note here that the Identity and Passport Service would later become 'Her Majesty's Passport Service'. In all, it was an intelligent and very professional threat that got me because I became scared to make any further requests for permanent residence. Although it was not violent in any way, but the tone of the letter exerted the force that it was meant to exert, intended to deter me from further applications until whenever the agency believed that I become qualified for it. Within a year in the year 2012, I was stirred to apply for British citizenship which was subsequently refused and my psychological immigration trauma had to continue until 17 January 2014 when I was eventually issued with an EEA permanent residence card after I dared to reapply on 07 November 2013. My persistence eventually paid off. It was equally non-violent in any way, but the intended results were achieved. So force can be applied without a threat to life because is justified by persistence. Force for a believer is declaring and exercising the authority of the word of God over the works of the enemy. There is physical force which inevitably may incur some violence but the Bible says in [Zechariah 4:6-7] that – "Then he answered and spake unto me, saying, This *is* the word of the LORD unto Zerubbabel, saying, Not by might, nor by power, but by my spirit, saith the LORD of hosts. {Verse 7} Who *art* thou, O great mountain? Before Zerubbabel *thou shalt* become a plain: and he shall bring forth the headstone *thereof with* shoutings, *crying*, Grace, grace unto it." This reemphasizes and re-establishes our opening words that *'the force of God works by the spirit of the grace of God in the name of Jesus but the role of effort cannot be undermined'*. There is then the spiritual force which every believer exercises even when we speak and pray in the spiritual language of tongues because the Bible says in [1 Corinthians 14:2] that – "For he that speaketh in an *unknown* tongue speaketh not unto men, but unto God: for no man understandeth *him*; howbeit in the spirit he speaketh mysteries." Enforcing or establishing the force of God from the spiritual realm into the physical can only be achieved by the Spirit of God.

The place of Anointing and Anointed:

As a believer who has also been a dedicated Church member at different Churches, I came to the understanding and realisation that the anointing is the Spirit of God and therefore represents God. Therefore in Church, whenever I heard the pastor say "receive the anointing", I understood that it either meant "receive God" or "receive the Spirit of God" and I also was able to understand that under such unction the pastor was not the person speaking but God, so I always responded to every declaration or prophecy made from the altar of God in Church with these words "Yes Lord, Amen". This imagination or thought and understanding is backed by the following Scriptures written in [1 John 2:20 and 1 John 2:27] – "But ye have an unction from the Holy One, and ye know all things. {Verse 27} But the anointing which ye have received of him abideth in you, and ye need not that any man teach you: but as the same anointing teacheth you of all things, and is truth, and is no lie, and even as it hath taught you, ye shall abide in him." We have been called by God through his word as believers and that anointing resides in us until we activate it through the Spirit of God that has put it in us. The Bible says that we are 'partakers of the heavenly calling' in [Hebrews 3:1] – "Wherefore, holy brethren, partakers of the heavenly calling, consider the Apostle and High

Priest of our confession, Jesus Christ." Then the book of [1 Corinthians 7:17] goes further thus – "But as God hath distributed to every man, as the Lord hath called every one, so let him walk. And so ordain I in all churches." The Apostle Paul identified the specific call of the members of the early Churches and ordained them in the same specific offices. The place of the anointing and the anointed are therefore one and the same, because the Spirit of God anoints men to behave or act like God and the God that men witnessed as our model was Jesus. The anointing empowers or 'shoots' the anointed to captaincy and leadership. The Bible says in [1 Samuel 10:1 and 1 Samuel 10:6-7] – "Then Samuel took a vial of oil, and poured [it] upon his head and kissed him, and said, [Is it] not because the LORD hath anointed thee [to be] captain over his inheritance? {Verse 6} And the Spirit of the LORD will come upon thee, and thou shalt prophesy with them, and shalt be turned into another man. {Verse 7} And let it be, when these signs are come unto thee, *that* thou do as occasion serve thee; for God *is* with thee." This story chronicles the moment Samuel the prophet of God anointed Saul as the king of Israel and the anointing on Saul attracted the Spirit of the Lord to come upon Saul and he was saluted and blessed by men. It will also be wise to take note in this Scripture [1 Samuel 10:1-12] that not only did Saul get transformed, he also contacted the spirit of prophecy which was released through his immediate contact with a company of the prophets of God who were returning from the high place and the Bible adds that the moment Saul turned his back to go from Samuel the prophet, God gave him *'another heart'* and all the signs prophesied to him by Samuel came to pass that day. This is emphatic because it shows how the anointing dispels delays from the path of the anointed. The anointed Saul's reaction to the anointing was questioned by the people that knew him before and they asked questions that eventually became proverbial as to whether Saul was also among the prophets?! Saul prophesied because *like begets like* just as humans and animals give birth to their kinds. Seeds also produce fruits according to the kind of the tree that they've been plucked down from and as a result Saul received a double anointing of kingship and prophecy.

The anointing activates automatic deliverance spiritually in the anointed and we read this from the book of [James 5:14-15] – "Is any sick among you? let him call for the elders of the church; and let them pray over him, anointing him with oil in the name of the Lord: And the prayer of faith shall save the sick, and the Lord shall raise him up; and if he have committed sins, they shall be forgiven him." In many Churches today (particularly the Pentecostal Churches), this Scripture has been made dormant thereby leaving many sick and afflicted in the Church. Although the pastor of a Church may also be considered as an elder of the Church, however this Scripture implores us to *call the elders of the Church to pray over the sick and they will be healed*. Many pastors today have been obsessed with power to the point that it begins to work against them and the ministries they lead. They become power-enthusiasts hence hindering the power of the Holy Spirit to work and express healings in people. If we will have elders in our Churches and not use them, then the motive for having them is defeated. If we will have elders in our Churches who cannot advice our pastor(s) because of the fear of possible bullying or aggression, then we have no need for those elders. The elders are there primarily to assist the pastors in the work of the ministry, otherwise we would have no need to have elders in our Churches. Pastors have become so dominant that they begin to dominantly stagnate the growth of the same Churches they preside over. There have been numerous situations where pastors have repeatedly prayed for the afflicted in their Churches yet the healings are not manifesting, still they refuse to apply the wisdom of gathering their elders or even other believers to assist them to pray for the sick in the Churches. We get this image from the New International Version of the Holy Bible in [Mark 5:40] – "But they laughed at him. After he put them all out, he took the child's father and mother and the disciples who were with him, and went in where the child was." When Jairus lost his daughter at his home, Jesus got there and told the people that she was not dead but sleeping and they laughed at him. Jesus did not need the crowd that gathered there to weep, he only needed some like-minded people to help stir the power in him up. So he took the parents of the dead girl with him into where she was laid to serve as witnesses but then he took his disciples (Peter, James and John) for their knowledge. He needed them to learn how to trust and depend on each other because shortly after his demise and subsequent ascension into heaven, the disciples would become the Jesus that the Church will run to for physical refuge and solace, and for spiritual growth. They would have to depend on themselves and the power of the Spirit would be released through them. The disciples would receive the anointing but they needed cooperation to stand firm as a team as we have been lectured in [1 Thessalonians 5:11] – "Wherefore comfort yourselves together, and edify one another, even as also ye do." Comforting and edifying one another is supporting one another in the Church ministry. It means coming together in mutual agreement towards an anointed cause in order to teach and build effective discipleship and thereby enhancing followership.

For instance when there is a recurrent health challenge in a patient in the hospital and their doctor has not been able to make any breakthrough in ascertaining the cause of their sickness, he seeks the help of his medical colleagues or other specialists in the field to dig deeper into the root of the issue and immediately the cause is established, then they analyse it and try to resolve it. This is the spiritual role pastors should equally lead in the Churches. We're ashamed to confide in the elders of the Church or in fellow believers regarding the enormous challenges we face or encounter in the ministry and it eventually either ends up in the self-destruction of the ministry or even tarnishing our image as Church leaders in a very embarrassing way. The only reason is because the sickness that you refuse to disclose will inevitably disclose itself in an open and often shameful way. It happened to me on Sunday 21 December 2014 when I suffered so much with my breathing. I would send text messages to the pastor of the Church where I used to attend and he probably really didn't think it was too serious, but then on this day I had gone to him for prayers during the Church service. After the service I had barely walked out from the Church building when I suddenly experienced another chronic respiratory attack and it became so embarrassing that I had to wait for an ambulance for two (2) complete hours because nobody in the Church was willing to rush me in that state to the hospital. I had never been so embarrassed in my life and that was the day I really began to rethink my Church life. I had to review whether I was worshipping the Church building or the living God that we serve. Within those two critical hours that I waited for an ambulance I never saw the pastor walk down from his office to come and intercede any further for me and I still don't want to believe that he never heard of how sick I got but I'd still give him the benefit of the doubt and have since forgiven him and the Church for that and moved on. That was the same day the Lord spoke to me very clearly that 'he wanted me to learn from this experience'. Those words became my reassurance that I was not going to die from that *nightmare* but exactly thirty-three (33) days after my shame, the word of my change came on Friday 23 January 2015. The Bible says in [Matthew 6:13] – "And they cast out many devils, and anointed with oil many that were sick, and healed [them]." If the Bible used the word '*they*' rather than Peter or Paul or any of the other apostles or disciples of Jesus, which means it was not an individual effort. They must therefore have done it together. These were anointed servants of God and had the power to cast out devils, but still not all the demons were subject to them *individually*, making for the need to sometimes gather together as a body to cast every stubborn spirit that hitherto tormented God's people out. This is why the elders are there in our Churches because their dormancy in the Churches orchestrated by our pastors has not only triggered divorces but has also caused other weapons or strategies of the enemy to prosper against the Church, and has also slain many in the Church. The Bible says in [Hosea 4:6] – "My people are destroyed for lack of knowledge: because thou hast rejected knowledge, I will also reject thee, that thou shalt be no priest to me: seeing thou hast forgotten the law of thy God, I will also forget thy children." Forgetting thy children may not necessarily be that the Lord will forget your children, however it could mean that the Lord will leave your family to be prey for the enemy prompting sicknesses in homes and divorce cases among pastors which has been rife and seems to be celebrated in recent years in our Churches.

But I'd desist to blame the health challenges I suffered on the Church because after I fully recovered and got called into the ministry, I was able to comprehend that the challenges I experienced was the Lord calling me to the ministry without my knowledge or comprehension. The Church I once suggested to people and referred them to, suddenly became uncomfortable for me to now stay in. While I was still struggling to accept the Church I had been in and enjoyed for over four years, the Lord allowed the enemy to afflict my health. Even the pastor that I believed in so much prayed for me and the condition seemed to get worse. During this time I had a lot of dreams and saw a lot of visions of myself in ministry but it all did not make sense to me because I never heard any pastor saying exactly what one could face when they're being called into the ministry by God. My affliction would eventually force me out of the Church I really called home, the Church that had saturated my heart. The tipping point was after the pastor prayed for me in Church yet before the end of the service I was already waiting for an ambulance to get me back to the hospital where they could still not ascertain what was wrong with me. I was still discharged home that day even with the suffering that I had to endure within me. I started hopping from Church to Church for a clue and would only get better on Friday 23 January 2015 after the Lord instructed me to go and enter and fulfil my calling in ministry. I stood up from where I sat in my leaving room and said to my wife – "The Lord has been speaking to me very audibly that I must start his ministry now." I went to the room and brought out a notebook that I've had for a few years but never used and wrote down every instructions as I heard them. I heard the Lord speak to me saying – "any Church you decide to attend for an evening service, ensure that you take this notebook with you and lift it up in worship to me so that I will speed up my word to perform it." So a couple of hours later in the same evening I said to my wife – "I am led to attend evening service in a Church that I've never been to before." She asked where I hoped to attend and I said – "There is this Ghanaian prophet that I've often watched on the TV, maybe I'd go to his Church for the first time today and hopefully the Lord will confirm his word." So I set out with my first son for the evening Church service and after the Church service the prophet called me out to confirm that the Lord told him that he had called me to the ministry and that I should start now. I never asked for further proof or evidence of my calling from the Lord because it was so real and unbelievable, yet undoubtable. I actually bought the DVD from the Church I'd attended on that evening of that prophetic meeting to always remind myself that God spoke to me and spoke through his servant the prophet on the very same day. I was not dreaming.

Still I had a lot of doubt on how to start because I've never been taken through the ministry basics by any pastor or shown what to do or how to do it. I had to learn everything afresh by the help of the Holy Ghost and from a lot of searches through the internet. A very encouraging friend of mine also suggested that checked the websites of the charity commission and stewardship to see if I would find any information on how to register the ministry or on how to start, and these websites were quite helpful indeed. Yet I embarked on a procrastination game, proposing to start in February 2015 and eventually did not, then I changed our start date to March 2015 and still would not. But then I prayed over it and the Lord spoke to me telling me to start on 'resurrection Sunday' 05 April 2015, so I put in every effort to make this a date. On 25 March 2015 I got easy hall approvals which got our venues confirmed and I paid for an initial hourly service every Sunday beginning from the Easter Sunday, then two days later on 27 March 2015 I went to press to print the fliers for our Church meetings and was helped in every way. Then on leaving the press office, I heard the Lord repeatedly saying to me – "Because you dared to obey me, you will end well. You will end well. You will end well." I was constantly replying – "Yes Lord, Amen" even as I walked along the way. Eventually on Easter Sunday 05 April 2015, with the help of the Holy Ghost alone we started the COME Global Gospel Ministries with hourly services (every Sunday) from 9am – 10 am, our first worship song (which is the song the ministry is established on) was - "Come Holy Spirit Come", the first message/sermon/topic the Lord gave to me was - "Alive, Arise", while the first Scripture reading was taken from [Acts 1:8] of the King James Version of the Holy Bible as I was instructed by the Lord. So the ministry started with no prior knowledge of what to do or how to go about anything, although our first service was only physically attended by myself, my wife and our three children, however during the service I kept seeing endless multitudes from the four corners of the globe *'coming'* to the kingdom for their freedom and to gain wisdom. Above all the Lord has always been very faithful, still speaking and directing me on what to do. No real pastoral guidance whatsoever but it was good so that only God will be glorified in his ministry because this had always been my prayer – 'that no man would take God's glory over my life, family and ministries. If you've ever been discouraged before, or maybe you've been called into the ministry but have been confused as I was or maybe you have no guidance on what to do or on how to start, this testimony serves as an encouragement to you. When you get despised by the people you believed would guide you, I tell you what,

it is for a testimony that will only glorify God alone and exalt his majesty.
The four Scriptures that encouraged me through this hurdle were these:

- [Romans 11:29] – "For the gifts and calling of God *are* without repentance."
- [Luke 9:62] – "And Jesus said unto him, No man, having put his hand to the plough, and looking back, is fit for the kingdom of God."
- [Zechariah 4:10a] – "For who hath despised the day of small things?"
- [Revelation 3:8a] – "I know thy works: behold, I have set before thee an open door, and no man can shut it."

The first Scripture ensures that you do not doubt your calling into the ministry because God will never change his mind, so it is only you that can discourage yourself. The second Scripture ensures that you don't look back once you've started the ministry that you've been called into. The third Scripture ensures that you are encouraged no matter how insignificant, little or humble your start in the ministry is. The fourth Scripture was an assurance of what I refer to as '*supernatural transfiguration*' in ministry, and spiritually I saw that these four Scriptures are the North, East, South and West open-borders of this global ministry.

The place of Wealth:

Wealth is deeper than having money because wealth encapsulates a level of total economic and all-round financial well-being. It is a level that identifies to us and to others that God is our source. It goes beyond just believers because there is an ability that God has put not just in every believer, but in every man to have the power to create wealth and [Deuteronomy 8:18] summarises this notion thus – "But thou shalt remember the LORD thy God: for *it is* he that giveth thee power to get wealth, that he may establish his covenant which he sware unto thy fathers, as *it is* this day." This is why the Jews as well as the Arab nations remain so blessed. Wealth is from God and the Bible says that "money is a defence" – [Ecclesiastes 7:12]. 'Every good thing comes from God' - [James 1:17] and this means both wealth and money (which is subject to wealth) comes from God, but there is a difference making or having 'as much money as you can' and 'having as much money as you will'. When you make as much money as you can, your source surely has a limit because it depends on your ability and God cannot be limited. This means that there's an amount of money you can't make and reveals that there's a barrier somewhere. This I believe was the level Jesus remained at until he ascended the Cross of Calvary where he became poor for us to become rich. Unfortunately this is where majority of the Church people have remained today, even most of our Church leaders regardless of the exchange that Jesus made. However when you have the access to make as much money as you will, your source is endless and it has to be the supernatural God. This is the will of God for us (believers) in Christ through the Holy Ghost and his will has no limits to what it can and will surely do, yet we have struggled so much because we are too scared to explore the ideas we're given from above. As much money as you will means that the choice is yours to put a stop to the flow at your own wish. That means every provision that identifies with the financial level that catapults you to the realm of wealth or what I call 'financial kingdom' is at your disposal or at your own beck and call. This exceeds the level of work or personal effort. It confronts the power and audacity of the Holy Spirit for supply and full provision. Didn't the Bible say in [Isaiah 45:11] – "Thus saith the LORD, the Holy One of Israel, and his Maker, Ask me of things to come concerning my sons, and concerning the work of my hands command ye me." This is the level where we assume our authority to command God and God is duty bound to respond to every request and demand we place on him. I enjoy washing dishes at home because most often the Lord speaks to me while doing it and very early on 23 September 2014, I was washing dishes at my kitchen sink when I heard the Lord ask me this question and gave me a clue with it – *"How can you be poor in a world with too many people in it? How can you be poor in a world where I've put in billions of people and all of them have some money that they are willing to spare if you will genuinely use your skills and talents to serve them?! The rich people, people made them rich."* I felt terribly embarrassed whilst washing those dishes and it got my mind intensively engaged in thoughts. He did not even say 'some' of them have money to spare, he said 'all' of them have money to spare if you will serve them genuinely with your gifts and talents. I began to think – 'does it mean that adults as much as some babies have my money?' It was a deep revelation that really got me confused in meditation. However it would later start making sense to me after I considered the suggestion that – "*the rich people, people made them rich.*" I also remembered that my birth (names) initials are "C.E.O", before my surname which also starts with an 'O'. It could not therefore add up that I struggled with money even after my parents gave me three birth names whose initials subconsciously called me a Chief Executive Officer (C.E.O), although I would later choose to be identified by just my first name and then surname. It still does not and will never change the truth that I was born to be a CEO. I therefore believe that if it has not happened for the believer, it only has not because the believer has not made the right move that the believer is supposed to make in faith, and the believer has not made the right move that the believer is supposed to make because the believer probably does not know the exact move that the believer is supposed to make or does not have the courage to make that right move. We must therefore be cognizant with the Spirit to lead us aright.

Wealth is manifested in different people through their individual stars of glory. The Bible says in [1 Corinthians 15:41] – "[There is] one glory of the sun, and another glory of the moon, and another glory of the stars: for [one] star differeth from [another] star in glory." Nations are individuals because they were originally built by communities of different people that came together to build together, but just as sources of individual wealth vary, sources of national wealth also vary. Most people of this present age or nations accumulated the wealth they have today through *peace-keeping and reconciliation* endeavours. They went on peacekeeping missions around the world and ended up looting or rather claiming the wealth of some of those nations and their natural resources. This could be referred to as an extreme style of inheritance. It's probably known as inheritance-stealing and Jacob (our father) unfortunately master-minded or made this style of wealth-gain prominent and Russia's gazumping of the Crimean peninsula from Ukraine could be classed as one of the most recent of the sort but I'm not here to condemn any nation or people but to differentiate this sort of wealth-gain from the sort that is really God-ordained and Holy Ghost driven. The Bible says in [Proverbs 13:11] that – "Wealth *gotten* by vanity shall be diminished: but he that gathereth by labour shall increase." Most of the military might in our nations around the world are unfortunately funded with wealth we gained through deceptive means and strategies. With an attitude of *robbing Peter to pay Paul* around us (particularly our Christian nations and peoples), could it be the real reason why our national debts among the nations have eclipsed to astronomical levels and very complex state(s) today?! Think about it – '*wealth gained through deception will diminish*'. This is a clear scenario of what happens when believers avoid paying their tithes because tithing attracts increase which sums up to a state of financial kingdom or wealth. The Lord asks the believer a question regarding this written in [Malachi 3:8] – "Will a man rob God? Yet ye have robbed me. But ye say, Wherein have we robbed thee? In tithes and offerings." I've tasted and witnessed how tithing works for the faithful tither because when I had a little struggle trying to get my driving licence here in the United Kingdom, I made a vow to God after failing to pass my driving test on the first attempt. My instructors told me that I wasn't ready for it and actually a former driving instructor told me categorically that I'd fail my first test and I did. When it was time for the second test he said the same thing, so I decided to change my driving school to a private one since I didn't want any negative assumptions diverting my focus. I booked for a second driving test and the lady who became my driving instructor also insisted that I was not ready for it. So I made a vow to God that if I passed on that second attempt I'd start paying my tithes. On 01 September 2006 I passed my driving test and I attribute this victory solely to the power of vows and this was not an ordinary vow, it was a vow to tithe. God expressly rewarded it because he would always find a way to encourage us to tithe otherwise we rob, not man but God. I also was able to verify that many times I'd struggled financially in the past, it was either because I had not paid my full tithe or I may have paid my bills before searching for money to pay my tithe with. The tithe is easily the most important seed in the Church because the Bible attributes it's non-payment to robbery and I'd dare to believe that the tithe supersedes the first fruit. The first fruits are fulfilled or covenanted anytime we have a new source of funds, however our tithes are paid continuously and consistently whether there's an increase or not as long as we (the believers) have a steady income.

The tithes are therefore more reliable that the first fruits and as such its considered robbery when not fulfilled or paid. It does not become your tithe after Church leaders pray over it, it becomes your tithe automatically the moment the funds enter your account and you set them aside calling it 'tithe' to honour God and preserve yourself. You honour God by paying the tithe to support his gospel vision and you honour/preserve yourself by not robbing God. It's almost as powerful as the name of Jesus because it works like the life insurance for yourself and your children, just the way the blood of Jesus works for the believer and I may be criticised for saying this.

The place of wealth may not just be about money or about financial increase because money (like a lady) may need some persistence to come and would only not come in a situation where the zeal or interest to access it diminishes. A great health condition adds up as wealth hence the saying that '*health is wealth*'. I left a previous role in retail management on 24 January 2014 and had asked the Lord to show me a sign that it'd be the start of a fresh adventure in my finances. At the time I left this role, I hoped to start in another role and whilst it wasn't coming through immediately I had to make desperate efforts to get out of some other challenges I had and getting out of them required money but I didn't have the funds. So I encouraged myself to step out in faith. Favourably on my very last day in that role in retail management, I was at work when my office phone rang and I picked up the phone and it was my wife and she said – "I think you have a parcel, I believe your application for permanent residence has come back from the United Kingdom Border Agency (UKBA). Just take a short break at work and run home to check." I said to her – "open it (the parcel)!" She did and it was my permanent residence card which I had struggled to get since 13 May 2004 when I arrived the very first time on a visit to the United Kingdom, although I'd later return home to Nigeria to get my study visa for the United Kingdom which then gave me the status of a legal resident from the day I arrived to the shores of this great nation with it on 01 October 2005. This was the beginning of a lengthy immigration journey and it carried on until that faithful day of 04 November 2013 when I applied for this status after a brief family pilgrimage trip to Rome. By the law, I had still not qualified to gain a permanent residence status when I made that application but I still dared to apply in faith after previous numerous attempts failed. Then on my last day at work as mentioned earlier, I got a surprise in the post and had to rush home after my wife opened the package and confirmed to me (over the phone) that a journey of about ten (10) years suddenly ended in great joy and victory. Although the next phase of my career remained unclear at that moment but it was a sign that God was about to deliver authority into my hands so I remained hopeful and optimistic. My permanent residence had been issued exactly a week earlier on 17 January 2014. It was the week of my second son – (Freedom Justice)'s fourth birthday which was on Sunday 12 January 2014 and I believe gaining this freedom on the week of his fourth birthday meant that God had granted me freedom in the four corners of the earth. It was a remarkable way to celebrate my freedom, being then justified to reside in the United Kingdom without any further restrictions. I couldn't thank God any better than I did, I shed *tears of joy* joyfully. Having received it on 24 January 2014 I was determined to end my immigration battle in the country that I now called home, so I wanted to apply immediately for my British citizenship even though the law insisted that I'd have to hold my permanent residence status for one full year in order to qualify to apply for my naturalisation as a British citizen. But then on my last day at work I got paid my final wages in that role and the funds were cleared up from my account from rent and bill payments. That meant that I didn't even have the funds to either pay my tithe or to fulfil the covenant of the first fruit for the year 2014. I was in a fix, during my time at that job I never missed a tithe or first fruit seed so how could I miss sowing them with my very last wages from this role that really blessed my life, family and some others in tremendous ways. I just couldn't live with the mentality of pondering the possibility that I did not pay my tithe or my first fruit in January 2014, so I decided to take a small amount of loan just to give something to God that would represent both seeds, however I knew I had already failed with this covenant, however I constantly reminded myself that God is and remains a merciful God. Yet I was still making plans to apply for my British citizenship with no funds in my accounts and seemingly no hopes at that moment.

Eventually I went to a loan company where I was approved for a loan of £400. This was just crazy because I didn't have a guaranteed job right then at that point and didn't know how I was going to survive with a wife and three children. Regardless my wife had been very supportive in all things and it was a mutual decision that I resigned the role at the time I did because my wife was due to return to work after her maternity leave and we needed one of us to stay home and take care of the children anyway. We ended up with the decision that I was the right person to stay home for the moment with the children until I was able to get a job that was not going to clash with my wife's working schedule since the law required that my wife remained at work until my permanent residence was granted and we had no clue whatsoever that it was going to be grated this time because I was not yet qualified for it (as has already been mentioned above). So I got to Church and sowed the seed of £400 for my tithes and first fruit even though it would normally have been a tad bigger than the amount sown. I just needed to get my name on God's register for the year 2014 and somehow I pulled that off. I was very pleased with my guts but then again I required money to apply for my citizenship exactly two (2) weeks after I was granted permanent residence status. I refused to let the fact deter me, that by law I still did not qualify for what I was about to apply for until I've held permanent residence status for one full year, coupled with fact that I had no source of income at this time. But I believed God and my spirit was so strong willed towards achieving this citizenship status and acquiring this life-time wealth of a privilege. Committed as I was I found and gave myself reasons to do it rather than reasons not to because all odds were against me and I avoided a cloud of the negative minded people who had questioned my ability to become a British citizen when I had not qualified for it. I only kept reminding them and myself that I did not even yet qualify for the permanent residence and God still favoured me for it, so I knew he could and would do the same. I discovered that the only poison that pollutes the mind is the poison that you allow to pollute your mind. There's absolutely no poison that could hurt or kill a positive mind-set as much as there's no medication that could heal or give life to a negative mind-set. I eventually went on to apply for a further loan from another company within a week of the former loan which I used as my first seeds in Church for 2014, but this second loan was for my citizenship application that I was not certain about the outcome. On 07 February 2014 I took that risk and applied for my naturalisation as a British citizen and by 06 April 2014 (2 months later)

I lost my Dad in Nigeria. Another financial challenge to deal with whilst I was still dealing with the loans I had already taken out in faith. But the very next day on 07 April 2014 after my Dad's death, my application for British citizenship got approved to my shock and utter amazement, the huge financial gamble I made in faith had paid off. Same week I managed to get an appointment for my naturalisation ceremony at my local council (Lambeth) to take place exactly seven (7) days after my application got approved which was also eight (8) days after my Dad's death.

To the glory of God on Monday 14 April 2014 I naturalised as a British citizen. On this same day I applied for my first British passport and on Tuesday 20 May 2014 I had that gruelling interview for first time passport applicants and on Monday 26 May 2014 (a British Bank holiday) my first British passport was issued. Prior to this triumph I always asked God these questions – "Lord when will my face appear on the British passport? When will I see my own name printed on the British passport?" It was a huge test for me, seemingly insurmountable. But now it has become my testimony. This was a strange testimony to me because protocol was suspended for the passport office to work extra shifts on a Bank holiday to issue my first British passport. However I made a vow to God that when I receive my passport, I will not rush to open it, rather I will let his servant to open it. So after I received my passport on Thursday 22 May 2014, I refused to open it even though I was really tempted, but I had to fulfil my vow to God and at the night vigil in Church and in the very early hours of Saturday 24 May 2014 I went out to share my testimony where I handed my sealed passport to Pastor Alex Omokudu and he opened and dedicated it to God for me in Church. I reminisce on these events and I still ponder how else a man can prove to any pastor that he loves them better than sowing financial and material seeds to support them and their ministry, and then when you receive such an honourable document as your first British passport from the post, you don't open it until the next Church service to hand the sealed parcel over to the pastor in the presence of the living God and before God's altar to open and dedicate it to God, on your behalf? However this later testimony is by the way because it's just food for thought for any pastor reading this. I consider this (the journey of my citizenship) as a huge part of what I term as '*my accumulated wealth*' because it offered me the privilege to exercise my faith in order to be able to hold a passport that gives me visa-free travel to the vast majority of the nations that I admire the most and also the grand opportunity to automatically become an automatic citizen of the European Union. It was an unbelievable feeling of achievement but my radical seeds of faith in God paid off. This is why the best definition of faith is simply 'stupidity'. A friend of mine recently shared a testimony of how he went to Church and didn't have no offerings to give, however he felt that urge to give something out to God. He would eventually get his sim card out from the only mobile phone he had at the time and put the mobile phone in the Church offering basket and that would have been stupidity. Sowing your entire wages for a month to a Church/ministry must also be considered stupid by many. Taking a loan to sow a first fruit or tithe when you don't have a job equally constitutes stupidity. Taking a loan to apply for British citizenship at the point of joblessness must also be stupid. Receiving your first British passport through the post and waiting for Church service only to hand it over to a pastor to open it for you must be stupid. Sowing a valuable property you inherited from you Dad as a seed to a Church/ministry you don't attend must surely look stupid. But these are just some acts of faith that I've had to either 'enjoy or endure'. Therefore I'd conclude that as much as faith is stupidity, faith is wealth.

The place of wealth belongs to Christ and you cannot be in want of any good gifts if you are real-radical towards your belief and relationship with Christ. Wealth is therefore not just the possession of financial capability or capacity, it is the possession of every good thing needed to make life enjoyable and comfortable but the process of getting to such heights or position(s) of wealth does not always come so easy and may attracts costs in cash, mentally or otherwise but most importantly '*insane faith*' and the belief that it is possible. Scripture says in [Proverbs 13:22] – "A good *man* leaveth an inheritance to his children's children: and the wealth of the sinner *is* laid up for the just." However wealth is not achieved by the strength of man if the words in [Romans 9:15-16] are anything to go by – "For he said to Moses, I will have mercy on whom I will have mercy, and I will have compassion on whom I will have compassion. {Verse 16} So then [it is] not of him that willeth, nor of him that runneth, but of God that sheweth mercy." This then goes to confirm that it is the mercy of

God that takes men (not only believers) to the stress-free place of wealth and comfort. That also means that our personal efforts or religious belief system have nothing whatsoever to do with the compassionate mercy of God and [Ecclesiastes 9:11] puts it thus – "I returned, and saw under the sun, that the race [is] not to the swift, nor the battle to the strong, neither yet bread to the wise, nor yet riches to men of understanding, nor yet favour to men of skill; but time and chance happeneth to them all." If the Scripture says that 'time and chance' *happen* regarding the affairs of men, it cannot then be the efforts we make, the wisdom we have or the energy we employ that sets the pace of the victoriously wealthy because when it happens, we're void of the knowledge how happenings happen, take place or occur. Yet God can do nothing without our *blind* acts of faith. I use the word *blind* here because faith has to be *blind* enough to ignore the threats that are presented with every breakthrough in life. This is why tithes are really essential because [Psalm 112:1-3] shows us how – "Praise ye the LORD. Blessed *is* the man *that* feareth the LORD, *that* delighteth greatly in his commandments. {Verse 2} His seed shall be mighty upon earth: the generation of the upright shall be blessed. {Verse 3} Wealth and riches *shall* be in his house: and his righteousness endureth for ever." Obedience to the Lord's commandments attract wealth and tithing is a commandment from God [Malachi 3:6-12]. If tithing is a commandment and since obedience to commandments create wealth, that tells anyone that tithing on its own is actually wealth. A tither can only be a tither because the tither fears God. Tithing is an enormous way to reverence God as the divine deity that we must avoid stealing from. If Jesus had to pay taxes on his journey to become the Lord and Christ, then we must also pay our *spiritual taxes* or tithes to become more like Christ. The gospel-goal then is for us to be moulded to behave more like Christ, since we're already like Jesus. Our model as a Church is Christ who is also the head of the same.

The place of Jerusalem:

Jerusalem is a very important part of this book because it is probably the only city in the world currently still being fought for or dragged by three of what we call (major) religions of the world:

*The Jews – They are the original owners of the land or simply put it is the land given to them by God and they hold a sacred place in the heart of God.

*The Christians – I prefer calling these 'the believers of the Christ'. They have a strong argument to laying claims to the land because they were given birth to right in the heart of Jerusalem in a place called the 'upper room' and are very closely related to the Jews.

*The Muslims – They have their third holiest mosque located in this great city and as such have refused to give up laying claims to the land. However being their third holiest mosque, it can then be argued that their claim to this city is not a priority.

During my first pilgrimage tour of the land of Israel in 2012, I saw a signpost in Jerusalem that I believe was intended to upset the Jews and the Christians apparently put up by the Muslims boldly claiming that the land belongs to their *god*. It gave any visitor to Jerusalem a clearer understanding of the battle for this land and the reason for this misunderstanding could be traced to the fact that Jerusalem is the land of the promise or what some may refer to as the land of the covenant. From my close observation I have discovered that any place where God lays claim to, devil is attracted to such places and this is not different in the case with Jerusalem. The book of [Zechariah 14:4] reveals that – "And his feet shall stand in that day upon the mount of Olives, which *is* before Jerusalem on the east, and the mount of Olives shall cleave in the midst thereof toward the east and toward the west, *and there shall be* a very great valley; and half of the mountain shall remove toward the north, and half of it toward the south." If the Holy Bible was not real and specific in its prophecies, the land of Israel will not be going through a storm today and this is why the Scripture encourages us in [Psalm 122:6-7] to – "Pray for the peace of Jerusalem: they shall prosper that love thee. {Verse 7} Peace be within thy walls, *and* prosperity within thy palaces." It's an encouragement that comes with a promise of prosperity. Jerusalem is one of the names I admire most in the world and this Scripture gives life to it because if you bore Jerusalem as a name, whenever people prayed for Jerusalem (intentionally or unintentionally) they pray for you. Again this Scripture explains the reason for the peace felt by pilgrims when they tour the holy land. Jerusalem is a city where so much of real peace is experienced or felt regardless the chaos that sometimes erupts within its walls. It's easily the best place on earth and has so much to do with the believer's faith because Jesus died in Jerusalem, rose in Jerusalem, gave birth to the Church in Jerusalem, ascended into heaven from Jerusalem and returns to the earth for the very elect from Jerusalem. Jerusalem is a reverend city and the Bible calls *'Jerusalem the city of the great King'* – [Matthew 5:35b]. Jerusalem is also in my opinion the holiest city on earth and the proof of this is that three of the world's main religions are *'fighting'* to claim it.

The word of God says in [Galatians 4:26] – "But Jerusalem which is above is free, which is the mother of us all." This is heaven being addressed as Jerusalem and as the mother of us all. This makes it obvious that Jerusalem is a unique name that is in the plan of God for the fulfilment of his purpose both here on earth and above. If it bears a great significance here in the earth and also in heaven, that means we must cherish Jerusalem and give it every support that we could ever afford to give. The psalmist made a declaration of grand honour and covenant to Jerusalem in [Psalm 137:5-6] – "If I forget thee, O Jerusalem, let my right hand forget [her cunning]. {Verse 6} If I do not remember thee, let my tongue cleave to the roof of my mouth; if I prefer not Jerusalem above my chief joy." ***These Scriptures always put me in the mood of Jerusalem, they remind me that there's a city where hope and faith are built without a preacher. They remind me of a great city where peace heals the sick even before they pray. They remind me that life gains automatic renewal and refreshment just at the thought of Jerusalem.*** Christian television channels like GOD TV, Trinity Broadcasting Network (TBN) TV, Inspiration TV and a few other TV channels give us an almost real encounter of what Jerusalem feels like and this is the only city in the world that I advise *every living thing* on earth to endeavour to see and experience before they die. The Psalmist wrote in [Psalm 125:2] that – "As the mountains [are] round about Jerusalem, so the LORD [is] round about his people from henceforth even for ever." This reveals that even in all the terror that could ever lie within Jerusalem, it is a city watched over, protected and preserved by the mighty hand of God.

Jerusalem is a city built within fortified walls and the prophet Isaiah talks about the city in [Isaiah 62:6-7] like this – "I have set watchmen upon thy walls, O Jerusalem, [which] shall never hold their peace day nor night: ye that make mention of the LORD, keep not silence, {Verse 7} And give him no rest, till he establish, and till he make Jerusalem a praise in the earth." This makes Jerusalem not just the most peaceful place but also the safest place on earth because it is supernaturally secure and kept by the God of the universe that shall neither slumber nor sleep.

The Holy Bible says that God will defend the inhabitants of Jerusalem and seek to destroy the enemies of Jerusalem and we see this written in [Zechariah 12:8-9] – "In that day shall the LORD defend the inhabitants of Jerusalem; and he that is feeble among them at that day shall be as David; and the house of David shall be as God, as the angel of the LORD before them. {Verse 9} And it shall come to pass in that day, *that* I will seek to destroy all the nations that come against Jerusalem." Jerusalem is a symbol of every believer and the Holy Bible says that '*the weak in Jerusalem shall be as strong as David*'. This means that there will not be any sick inhabitant in Jerusalem. Then it says again that '**the house of David shall be as God**'. The house of David here also signifies the inhabitants of Jerusalem. This is unbelievable and explains why Jerusalem is royally honourable, hence the battle over Jerusalem can only have one winner and God's victory is undoubtedly assured. Jerusalem is the only city on earth that is worth visiting or seeing multiple times every year because of its welcoming atmosphere, particularly it's amazing and transforming attractions. The Holy Bible says that '*within its walls lie the perfection of beauty for the Lord shines forth*' from Jerusalem – [Psalm 50:2]. It is no surprise therefore the thousands of pilgrims that this spectacular city of the living God attracts and entertains annually because these were prophesies from Zechariah as recorded in [Zechariah 8:21-22] – "And the inhabitants of one *city* shall go to another, saying, Let us go speedily to pray before the LORD, and to seek the LORD of hosts: I will also go. {Verse 22} Yea, many people and strong nations shall come to seek the LORD of hosts in Jerusalem, and to pray before the LORD." Similarly [Zechariah 14: 16-17] portrays the same light – "And it shall come to pass, *that* every one that is left of all the nations which came against Jerusalem shall even go up from year to year to worship the King, the LORD of hosts, and to keep the feast of tabernacles. {Verse 17} And it shall be, *that* whoso will not come up of *all* the families of the earth unto Jerusalem to worship the King, the LORD of hosts, even upon them shall be no rain." I discovered also that anywhere the Holy Bible speaks about Jerusalem, it speaks about *'going up'*, thereby showcasing Jerusalem as a place of transfiguration, a place of ascension, a place of elevation, a place of lifting, a place of rising and a place on a mountain. This is also made vivid in the *Pilgrimage Certificate* issued and signed by the Israeli minister of tourism as well as the mayor of Jerusalem to the innumerable pilgrims that flood their shores everyday with these words written therein – "*By this attestation be it known that* (your name) *by virtue of fulfilling the Biblical calling, has ascended to Jerusalem, the Holy City, Capital of Israel and is henceforth authorized to bear the title of* JERUSALEM PILGRIM." This therefore goes to confirm that Jerusalem is a place where all men go up to meet with the God of Israel and of the Holy Bible and this notion concurs with this rendering seen in [Isaiah 66:13] – "As one whom his mother comforteth, so will I comfort you; and ye shall be comforted in Jerusalem." Jerusalem is therefore an ordained house of refuge for all flesh and the undisputed natural meaning of the term *'heaven on earth'*. A further summary of the detail on the Lord's stance on Jerusalem stands clear in [2 Chronicles 6:6] – "But I have chosen Jerusalem, that my name might be there; and have chosen David to be over my people Israel." Therefore the name of the Lord is resident and in the atmosphere of Jerusalem, explaining that the air we breathe in from the mountain of Jerusalem is the breath of the life of God. But nations have threatened Jerusalem today, nations without the fear of or reverence for God. Jerusalem has become a spot where the nations of the earth surround ready to explore the might of their arsenal of weapons and nuclear warheads. The city of God is now being ridiculed even by some of our so-called Church leaders with pride and undue arrogance claiming that '*they don't need Jerusalem to experience the power of God*', making me question the origin of the gospel they preach. We no longer tremble at the words of the Bible we preach to our congregations. We no longer cringe at the thought that this word is God yet we ask why we have members among us who have proven not to be as loyal as they once were. We even forget that anointing (as much as wealth) does not and cannot buy anyone loyalty, they only delay '*guaranteed*' betrayal. The only thing that guarantees loyalty is humility and the fear of God, and respect for God's Church. If we could treat God anyhow, surely we must expect the same from the men we're supposed to be serving. We neglect the warnings infused in [Zechariah 12:2-3] – "Behold, I will make Jerusalem a cup of trembling unto all the people round about, when they shall be in the siege both against Judah *and* against Jerusalem. {Verse 3} And in that day I will make Jerusalem a burdensome stone for all people: all that burden themselves with it shall be cut in pieces, though all the people of the earth be gathered together against it." Herein (again) is Jerusalem reassured that it is a city fortified and empowered by the great, mighty and *terrible* God we serve. The Lord through the Prophet Isaiah in [Isaiah 65:18-15] makes a detailed chronicle of covenant promises and blessings to Jerusalem and the word of God stands sure forever.

The place of Relationship:

There's nobody that reads the Holy Bible the very first time that understands what they read about, particularly when you start from the King James Version. But through fervency and commitment the Holy Spirit begins to unfold and reveal the mysteries of the word of God to us. This can only be an evidence of a relationship with the Lord. Relationship is certainly and single-handedly our connection with God through Christ in us. This relationship which is often founded on the principles of Godly living engages us through constant communication with the mind of Christ. Again discernment is vital in this relationship because through it we know what we are required to do and when to do it in order to please God and fulfil his call on our lives. Our relationship with Christ (through constant communion with the Spirit of God) must be a genuine father-son relationship. Although Christ is not the Father, he is our master and Lord; but Christ and the Father are one. Therefore in [Matthew 23:8-10] Jesus detailed who the Father is – "But be not ye called Rabbi: for one is your Master, even Christ; and all ye are brethren. {Verse 9} ***And call no man your father upon the earth: for one is your Father, which is in heaven.*** {Verse 10} Neither be ye called masters: for one is your Master, even Christ." This explains that on earth no man has a father because the Father is one and he never dies, however the authority of a father-figure in the life of his children or family is the authority of God. This means that whatever a father-figure says, God has spoken or you could put it this way – *'the voice of a man in authority is the voice of God'* and [Romans 13:1-7] justifies this assertion. However what men should have on earth is a Daddy because our Father is God the Father who is in heaven. Remember [Matthew 6:9a] – "***Our Father who art in heaven…***" Father and Daddy are not quite the same. In the Lord there *'may'* arise this argument that there is nothing like a 'father or spiritual father'. However we may also have either or both of a 'Dad' and a 'spiritual Dad or pastor'. The word Father comes with a strong responsible attachment and/or relationship…a very close, very strong and very personal relationship. The difference is that when you have a Dad or Daddy, you may not be able to reach them in your most desperate moments or they may be extremely busy for you to get through to. This is why we have a Father in God. With a Father you will gain instant access anywhere and at any moment, in any given situation. Not having a contact or not communing (fellowshipping) with the Father means that you have personally chosen not to make that contact or commune (fellowship) with the Father. Therefore the word Dad or Daddy comes with a not-so-strong relationship, although it still commands honour, respect and is very reverend as well, however not as much as the word Father. Also because a Dad is made of flesh, he has a limit to what he can or cannot do for you. The Father will never switch his telephone off because his only contact telephone number is your prayer and supplication to him which is available to anyone that needs that number at any moment. The Father will never fail in his responsibilities. For instance if you ever got sick (God forbid), the reality is that your Dad or spiritual Dad (pastor) may not immediately know that you're sick. In a case where you reside with your biological Dad at home, he may notice these changes before you tell him, however he may be helpless particularly with spiritual attacks. While a spiritual Dad (pastor) who has been anointed to cast out such spirits may not be residing with you under the same room and therefore immediately unavailable, as a result contacting him may not go through in a straight forward manner. So one (Dad) may notice and be ***unintentionally unhelpful***, whereas the other (pastor) may be able to help but **unintentionally unavailable** making both your Dad and spiritual Dad have certain limitations to responding to your immediate challenges, hence the need to directly contact or connect with the Father which is in heaven.

So you may agree with me that your biological Dad or father (if you will) under normal circumstances should 'naturally' be concerned about your welfare. On the other hand your pastor or spiritual father/Dad may 'subconsciously and unintentionally' seem not to bother about your welfare and this is not really because they do not care. This however may also not be because they necessarily don't want to, it may be because they have no idea about it and understandably they may have many spiritual children too, possibly in thousands and quite often more children than your biological Dad or father may ever have. While it is possible for a biological Dad/ father to meet most of the needs of his biological children depending on his wealth prowess and/or the number of children he has, it is not possible that a pastor or spiritual Dad/father will be able to meet most of the demands or challenges of his spiritual children and this is the reality that many Church-goers do not want to come to terms with. Another tangible instance is a situation where for example you (this is just an assumption) have an urgent business need for one million pounds sterling (£1,000,000) loan, I can argue that it is more practical and therefore more realistic that you may be able to get the loan very easily from your biological Dad/father (assuming that they have it) rather than from your spiritual Dad/father and the truth is that no pastor or spiritual Dad will make such investments in your life no matter how much they are worth. They may want to know how your investment will be beneficial to their lives and ministry (not to you) because their focus is them, not you and they still will never '*risk*' it. They wouldn't even see it as a seed, they may conclude that you possibly want to defraud them. This is equally true even when we may tend to deny it, hence we don't tell ourselves the truth about our situational help. Also you may be able to inherit wealth and properties from your natural or biological Dad/father, however a preacher or your pastor and/or spiritual Dad/father has to be in *so much of the Spirit* to be able to believe that God has instructed them to leave an inheritance for an (permit me to use this word please) '*ordinary*' member of their ministry/Church. This for me may justify or clarify the true picture of who or what a father's position and responsibility is rather than just who a father should be. This is why we must only call God our 'Father', and if we must call any man 'father', we must review the real relationship we have with them first. Pertinently it is also very advisable to reverend the relationship you have with your pastor or spiritual Dad otherwise you may become too familiar with him and subconsciously the anointing on his life may become common to you because you know him personally. So it will be almost difficult (although not impossible) for one to have a genuine father-son relationship with his pastor or spiritual Dad without that relationship diminishing the value you've placed on the man of God. This is clearly not the case with your biological Dad/father with all things being equal. The reason is not farfetched because through the help of the Holy Spirit we have the ability to choose or change our pastor(s) at will but we cannot choose or change our biological Dad/father, God chooses them! If God did not trust your biological Dad/father with the care-taking responsibilities over you, you'd not have come through him and God retains the power and ability to make your biological Dad/father your pastor if he ever wished to do that. Also in the situation where they've failed to live up to their responsibilities, it'd probably be for your good and testimony. So your biological Dad/father is actually supposed to be God's original representative in your life for a physical father-figure and until he fumbles or dies, he's intended to remain so. I remember my late Dad always saying that it is very important for a biological Dad to bless his children because of the original authority given to them by God over those children and also because no man can speak over the life of a child more than the biological Dad that begot him. Jesus was a good example of this because his supernatural (not biological) father was the Holy Ghost. My Dad also went on to say that in the event of a curse-pronouncement from a biological Dad, it is likely that the child may have to endure many years if not a lifetime of spiritual and possibly physical bondage that may only be cancelled or reversed by God himself and that is if God does it.

On another conversation my late Dad had advised me in these words – *"**Chimezie Okonkwo I'd give you an advice and make sure you DO NOT (stressed) forget it. No matter what your children do tomorrow,***

make sure that you DO NOT (stressed again) curse them. Never curse your children otherwise they may never find a man that can break whatever curse you may have placed on them." In [Genesis 49:26] Jacob (Israel) was blessing some and cursing some of his twelve sons and concluding on Joseph he (Jacob that is Israel) said – "The blessings of thy father have prevailed above the blessings of my progenitors unto the utmost bound of the everlasting hills: they shall be on the head of Joseph, and on the crown of the head of him that was separate from his brethren." In the New International Version of the same Scripture it reads thus – "Your father's blessings are greater than the blessings of the ancient mountains, than the bounty of the age-old hills. Let all these rest on the head of Joseph, on the brow of the prince among his brothers." There are a number of instances in the Scriptures where biological fathers had placed seemingly irreversible (possibly not unbreakable) curses on their children. Jacob was a good instance regarding this as already noted. When he was about to die, Jacob called his twelve sons together and '*blessed*' them - [Genesis 49:1-28], giving each the blessing appropriate to him. This is why God anoints men to break *some* of such yokes of hard labour. Your biological Dad/father therefore should where possible lay the solid foundation of blessing by constantly speaking words of life into you for your spiritual Dad/father to build on by equally speaking fruitfulness into your life. Every human being is like a cup and the words spoken into your life stay there (in the cup of your body) because that cup is never full, however the predominant words rule, control and manifest in the life. Therefore God uses your biological Dad/father **to lay the foundation of your life**, then God uses your spiritual Dad/father or pastor or other anointed men and women (or servants) of God **to raise the building of your life**. This is because everyone will first have a strong foundation ever before they'd have a reliable future, but all submits and therefore aligns to the divine purpose of God for our individual lives. This does not in any way undermine your pastor's role or his spiritual responsibilities in your life as a spiritual Dad or spiritual father (if you may). With this in mind I'd suggest that if you have not had a wonderful relationship with your biological Dad/father and they're still alive, this may be the right time to make amends but I must also stress that without them God will still bring his divine purpose to manifest in your life if he wishes to. It is also very important for one's biological Dad/father not to be unequally yoked with unbelievers or for him not to be an idol worshipper otherwise laying his hands or *legs* on you may only turn to further curses in your life. A clean and clear righteous history or foundation cannot be purchased with money. It is only the living God that breaks yokes through/using the father-figures in your life or his anointed servants. I'd only lay hands over my children in prayer because I have repented of, condemned and rejected/broken every evil idol worshipping that may have prevailed in my lineage or history by pleading the blood of Jesus who is now my Lord and Christ.

We may be reminded that under certain conditions a Dad or a pastor may be referred to as a father (small letter 'f') and [Ephesians 6:1-4] shows this – "Children, obey your **parents in the Lord**: for this is right. {Verse 2} Honour thy father and mother; (which is the first commandment with promise;) {Verse 3} That it may be well with thee, and thou mayest live long on the earth. {Verse 4} And, ye fathers, provoke not your children to wrath: but bring them up in the nurture and admonition of the Lord." *Parents in the Lord* may not imply the terminology knows as *God-parents* in the Churches today. This Scripture therefore reveals to us that your biological/earthly Dad could equally be referred to as your '*father*' because he has direct and immediately care-taking responsibilities to provide for your cares and needs as long as you remain a child under his custody. However once we become adults, we then become responsible to our own family yet we must be under authority no matter our level in life. The Scripture above may also be referring to your pastor because it says 'parents in the Lord', in which case you submit to them *until you are led to leave their ministry for another*, particularly when they have not fulfilled their role as a spiritual Dad or pastor. I'd advice that you do not call a man 'Daddy' when he does not care about you or fulfil the duties of a Dad in your life, but you must submit to them if they deserve it. This is humility before God towards those placed in higher authority. Seen again in [Ephesians 5:31] – "For this cause shall a man leave his father and mother, and shall be joined unto his wife, and they two shall be one flesh." God '*chooses*' and '*brings*' every man *through* their biological Dad, however also God allows every man to '*choose*' and be '*led*' to their spiritual Dad who they may also call their pastor depending on their particular challenge at any given moment or on the relationship they have with them. I'm sure most of us have had personal issues which the Lord did not reveal to our pastor(s). The reason is simple, when a man of God or a pastor has done what the Lord wanted to use him for in your life, you will be wasting your time remaining under the leadership of their ministry and it is then your will to choose, although to be fair in some situations your issue may just require some patience before God resolves it. This is why it is a sound thing to be led by the Spirit of God because God is a God of upgrade and will not direct you wrongly. This is why Scripture says in [Psalm 37:23] that – "The steps of a *good* man are ordered by the LORD: and he delighteth in his way." I had a personal encounter which gained me this experience. I attended Churches where I said - *'I'd never leave this Church because my seat cannot be empty in the House of God'. However I discovered that my seat in the House of God was not a 'physical' seat, but rather a 'spiritual' seat. Leaving a Church does not amount to leaving the presence of God. This is why we must always allow God to lead us. A pastor may be anointed to deliver you from immigration troubles, but he may not be anointed to deliver you from a spiritual attack. This does not mean that the Holy Ghost has not anointed him to heal, but the Holy Ghost may not have anointed him to heal 'you' of a particular ailment.* If you've ever been attending a particular Church where you got a healing from back pain, yet while in that Church the enemy afflicted you with a chest pain, then you will understand my language; or you've been in a Church where you believe in the man of God (they're preferred when they are servants of God) so much and still God did not use him to heal you, therefore you needed to attend another Church to receive a particular healing. Believers don't love facing the truth. No one man of God has or knows it all. God truly gives all men talents each *'according to their abilities'* - [Matthew 25:15]. That was probably the *'divine or holy error'* being an *innocent error* I made in my last book, heaping praises on a particular man of God and ignoring the rest because Christ (as the head of the Church) anointed all men of God with their peculiar gifts for servitude. We were taught by Jesus (who became the Christ) how to exhibit servitude or servant-hood, not manhood, hence men of God become the servants of God *'only'* when they actually serve but not all men of God are servants of God. Christ is the giver of the gifts and therefore must be referenced in every totality. May I use this opportunity to offer my sincere apologies to men of God around the world who may have found some of the words of my last book, this book or future books insulting because they were not meant/intended to ridicule. Only remember that I'm but a student and will humbly remain so yet I must also think, write and speak for clarity as I am led by God because I was called to do this and thereby reveal secrets to the glory of God. Although I still believe that God allows our errors to happen on purpose, knowing that I may realise my divine error and correct it in this book just as I may make some errors here and correct in future books.

As such the place of a spiritual Dad cannot however be undermined because he is the divine carrier of the power of God wherein he was called and chosen to be who and what he was intended to be. Paul the Apostle said in [1 Corinthians 4:14-16] – "I write not these things to shame you, but as my beloved sons I warn you. {Verse 15} For though ye have ten thousand instructors in Christ, **yet have ye not many fathers**: for in Christ Jesus I have begotten you through the gospel. {Verse 16} Wherefore I beseech you, be ye followers of me." Therefore spiritually Paul the Apostle of Christ begat the Corinthians as his spiritual seeds. In summary *biological father/ Dad is 'from' God, while spiritual father/Dad is 'of' God, hence 'man of God' or 'servant of God'*. The complex idea is that every human being at some point in their life is likely to have three Father/father figures (as seen below) but the only thing that marks the difference being *relationship*:

- Heavenly Father (God the Father)
- Earthly or biological Dad or father (the man that begat you)
- Spiritual Dad/father (your *'current'* pastor or another minister who you believe in and have accepted as such)

I personally also believe that calling a man of God (a pastor) 'Daddy' and then the preacher introducing you as his 'son' attracts some *treasured measure* of spiritual power and authority. No man wants to be greater than his own son because it will mean a curse to the man and to his son. In the same light every son wants and strives to be better than their Dad. So where a man of God has a spiritual son and accepts him as a son and the spiritual son also accepts the man of God as his *'spiritual'* Dad, that 'son' prophetically and automatically ascends the *throne of 'greater-ness'* with a multiplied measure of the power and anointing being transferred from that man of God to that son spiritually. It happened to Elisha after he contacted a double portion of the same spirit that was in Elijah in [2 Kings 2] through dedicated service to the servant of God. The unction was so severe on Elisha that even men began to notice it [2 Kings 2:15]. It also goes that the word 'father' holds a stronger attachment to responsibility than the word 'Dad', just as it is with the words 'son' and 'boy'. Consider calling your child 'my son' and/or 'my boy'. The word 'son' commands an original covenant-relationship and real revelation of attachment. They are not mere words. The word 'father' rather than 'Dad' and 'son' rather than 'boy' attracts an eternal commitment. Using 'Dad' or 'boy' tends to be quite informal and without any connection. For instance Jesus was the 'Son of man' not the 'boy of man'. He was the 'Son of God', not the 'boy of God'. It's quite some revelation here and it is also quite similar to us identifying ourselves like *the children of God rather than the children of men.* **A child of God is a spiritual or supernatural being, a child of man is a physical or natural being.** In the same light I have personally refused to believe that the concept of God-father or God-mother exist as much as there is nothing like step-father or step-mother and the like. It's all English language giving names to the unnamed and they're not necessarily Biblical concepts anyway. We therefore must also learn to be very careful how we address people around us because the way we address *'us'* determines the level of relationship that we'd lead amongst *us* (ourselves) as individuals or as human beings and most importantly as believers because we have been called to lead rather than to follow. Christ in us is a leader because Christ leads us to lead others. We follow Christ to learn how to be able to lead others to Christ. This is why the role of our leaders or shepherds in Christ is very vital and relevant to our spiritual growth as the sheep. But God has promised in his word in [Jeremiah 3:15] – "And I will give you pastors according to mine heart, which shall feed you with knowledge and understanding." Then warning our leaders/pastors in the Acts of the Apostles, Paul said this in [Acts 20:28] – "Take heed therefore unto yourselves, and to all the flock, over the which the Holy Ghost hath made you overseers, to feed the church of God, which he hath purchased with his own blood." The role of the spiritual father thence requires critical and supernatural leadership because **the LORD *calls* men, *chooses* few but *sends* servants**.

Relationship makes us sons of God but the servants of the Church and [Galatians 4:7] speaks in this manner – "Wherefore thou art no more a servant, but a son; and if a son, then an heir of God through Christ." Therefore God has not called us servants but sons but Jesus said that 'whoever will become the greatest in the kingdom of God (which is physically 'the Church') must be a servant first' - [Matthew 23:11] and [Luke 22:26] because ***without service greatness has no value for experience***. Relationship gives direction to the believer and [Acts 16:6-10] gives us a detailed account of how the Holy Spirit restricted the Apostles from preaching the gospel in certain areas. They kept trying until Paul saw in a vision in the night that the Lord had called them to preach the gospel to the Macedonians. Entering the supernatural to discern where we are called to function is a seed of relationship. I never struggle to write these books, songs or the poems that I write particularly as I respond in obedience to write them. I also discovered that I never struggle to preach the gospel since I preach very often at home to my family because every man's ministry actually starts from their own home; and as men and leaders in the home when we speak, heaven responds. It comes easily because I preach from my personal experiences which include moments of suffering and moments of enjoyment. However when you are domiciled in a Church where the pastor has a selfish interest only in building and developing his ministry, himself and his very inner circles or where such pastor(s) try to ridicule every endeavour you involve in for your benefit instead of encouraging you, sometimes you may need to leave such environments in faith, trusting God and he'd take you to where you will be more appreciated and where your invaluable skills, gifts and talents will be employed, encouraged and maximised for the glory and majesty of God. You can decide to roll on the ground every day in honour to God, I can assure you that as long as your environment is self-centred and not ready to help develop or help grow what God has put inside you, your rolling and shouting may just be void or in utter vain in the eyes of God because you have kept your skills dormant within you and have allowed other men's religion to restrict your abilities. ***If they cannot encourage you, they cannot lead you. Therefore***

do not let them lead you if they cannot be your leader. After I published my first book, the pastor of the Church where I always attended never encouraged me and I believe he surely instructed the video department of his Church not to show the testimony of my first book on his television channel because I never saw it on there, however the man I sent the very last copy that I gave out for free (the late Dr Myles Munroe) who was even more honourable around the globe, to my very shock wrote me a letter of encouragement signed by himself. The really unbelievable truth was that I wrote about a topic that the late Dr Myles Munroe was a guru in and I felt quite worried as to how a person of his magnitude may react to my limited knowledge on the subject, but shockingly he wrote. The thing is that where you think your encouragement will come from is most often where your disappointment arises from. This is why when you leave an environment where you do not see a tangible result of your gifts and talents being encouraged, God will not leave your life. Always remember that you had God before you got to that ministry and God had always protected you and will keep protecting you even after you leave them.

All believers should never make any Church building or pastor their God because that is the spirit of religion at work. They may preach to scare or frighten you and thereby keeping you in a mental prison but ignore their strategies when you need to. They could even tell you that you will be afflicted or die when you leave them but how can they know since they are not God. When they don't agree with the style of another pastor or when they see that this pastor's ministry is bigger and more successful than theirs or when they feel that that other pastor does not recognise them, they start spewing swords of lies by claiming that '*God told them that he will put that pastor down and raise them up*'. I've really heard a pastor say this in a Pentecostal Church here in London UK and therefore it's not fiction or an imaginative tale. However shortly after the pastor made this claim before the altar in his Church, God gives the same pastor that he'd claimed that God was putting down soon to raise him up '*a forty-five million pound Church property for only five million pounds*'. God is not a man that he should tell such lies, it's just pastors battling with their competitive mind-set and envy at the success of another!! *Today's Church is plagued with pastors who battle with temperamental issues, however being anointed does not take away your temper, anger or animosity towards others. You control your own temper, not God.* Our pastors have become celebrities who are often fame-minded and recognition thirsty. Some ministers have gotten rid of the truth and embraced foul lies and strategies to entice their congregation. We all seek our own selfish ecclesiastic dynasties and royal empires, forgetting the gospel of the majestic kingdom of glory that we're supposed to evangelise to the world. A Church of God preaches the gospel of Christ and that is our first priority, not gathering members to exploit and bully them mentally. God will not throw you away for leaving a building called *Church*, God will not even throw you away for leaving his presence because he seeks to bring you back, build you and use you, so he'd surely seek to win you back in his own unique way and this is what grace is about. The New Living Translation shows this in [Luke 15:7] – "In the same way, heaven will be happier over one lost sinner who **returns** to God than over ninety-nine others who are **righteous and haven't strayed away**!" If this Scripture uses the word 'returns', that explains it is referring to a believer that once backslid and has been called back to himself by the Lord. It also shows that if you ever left the kingdom and presence of God, God's utmost desire is to always seek you afresh and find you, and then draw you back to himself (God). You are even more valuable than a righteous man that never went away from the presence of God. However leaving a particular Church for another does not even mean that you've left God. **It is not the building that is the Church, the relationship it encourages in Christ makes it the Church.** When I really make up my mind to leave any Church environment (and I'm talking about the building now), I never look back. That is when they may start calling and texting you so that they can draw you back again, but resist and reject them and remain focussed on the Lord's direction for your next level in life. The departments that you wanted to join in such places and they refused, once God shows you that your spiritual uprising lies in your exit from that building, that is when they start trying to contact you to come for a chat regarding joining the department but you're already gone. It happened to me. Don't look back because the devil uses everybody these days, even our so-called Churches. The Holy Bible says in [Job 1:6] that – "Now there was a day when the sons of God came to present themselves before the LORD, and Satan came also among them." That tells me that every place of worship attracts the devil and I'm talking about 'right in the presence of God'. Now if you're a Church leader and the words of this book upsets you in any way, it means that your ministry (which is actually the Lord's Church, not yours) is not doing something right. This book was not written to upset but to challenge and inspire you to change for good and if God allowed me to write it and publish it, then he intentionally allowed you to read it now. The truth is bitter but not when Jesus is told. Jesus is the only truth that is not bitter and the saying that '*the truth hurts*' does not entail that Jesus hurts because 'Jesus is the way, the truth and the life' [John 14:6]. His truth may be bitter when we're told '*his truth*' in our sins, but not him.

A friend of mine recently gave his life to the Lord Jesus and once asked me how do I hear from God and how do I know that it is God? Well I told him my personal experience that I have known that God's voice is 'one voice' very firm, audible and clear. I further explained that when God is speaking all other voices remain silent, so there is no doubt in your mind because only God's voice commands authority like that. I told him that at other times he may hear two voices which may confuse him, explaining to him that the mind will always entertain two voices and at that point you will have a clear inclination that it is not God speaking. One is your mind probably steering you towards good and the other is surely the voice of the deceiver trying to confuse you. But from my own encounter I know that the voice of God is never your mind. This is because God cannot share his speech with any other voice. I reminded him of an encounter I had in early 2011 during a conversation with God that left a memorable impression on my mind. I was trying to get school admission for my first son – Kingdom David, and before I left home I had this conversation with my wife which schools I could try. So I went to the first school (that I wanted) and got application forms from them, headed for the second school and did the same. However by the time I closed in on the third school (which I did not really want), I was at their gate when I heard God speak to me saying – "What if I tell you that this is his school?" I slowed down my walking pace whilst listening and then I audibly responded and said – "But Lord you have not said it!" Then I heard God say – "This is his school!" I was just bewildered because I didn't want that school initially and then I walked through those gates and picked those forms. I got home that day and told my wife my encounter with the voice of God. That same day I filled out and sent off those three applications. Within weeks I received the first reply and to confirm God's word it was the same school I did not want that had offered my son a place because God spoke. I was just smiling having come to terms with the reality that my son will attend this school and it took a few months before I received the other two letters from the first two schools I contacted equally offering my son places. I knew it was just God confirming his word. In [John 10:27] Jesus reminds us that – "My sheep hear my voice, and I know them, and they follow me..." Having said all this, I advised my friend who newly got saved to build that relationship with the Lord and Master Jesus even as I strive to build, improve and establish mine too because I know that it is the bed-rock of an eternal salvation in Christ.

To end this *lecture*, relationship is a choice. This world is a corridor leading to either of two destinations and we're just passing through either of them. We can't blame or criticise anybody for our fortunes or misfortunes regarding our choices. Choice is the only difference between where we are right now (our reality) and where we desire to be at (our dreams, desires and aspirations). Our realities may be obvious, however our desires are enclosed within the mind. Our realities can't tell lies to the people around us, but then our aspirations sometimes will because we wish for one thing and claim we're comfortable in the other. It's only human and it's been in man for ages. This is the disguised reality of man. Relationship is also an experience. We've all probably heard the saying that *'people become products of their environments'*, but I say to you now that *'human beings become products of their individual and personal experiences more than they become products of their environments'* because in every environment you have a mix of different characters and each character's evolvement depend on their peculiar challenges or encounters within the same environment which is *'always'* different among the same inhabitants. So it is your experiences that really mould your relationship-character more than your environment or even more than any other thing does; and to be the best in any endeavour in life, you must be prepared and as such equipped to handle the worst case scenarios that life may naturally throw at your characteristically unaware resolve yet one thing is certain, your personal relationship with Christ determines every outcome because Christ has already fulfilled his part by building a relationship with us in the name of Jesus and through the in-dwelling presence of his Holy Spirit in us. It is therefore our responsibility as individuals to reciprocate the same gesture of love towards Christ our Lord and saviour by building and developing our relationship with him through the love life we lead in him.

The place of Unity:

Growing up was okay until disunity crept into our home and I tried to play alongside it. Whilst I remained committed to my education, I also tried to get busy loafing around as part of my extra-curricular activities and attempted burning up my youth by smoking cigarettes and Indian hemp (weed) albeit without much success after it gave me an initial knock in my brains which God would eventually sort out. Meanwhile some other children who were the same age as I was and from the same neighbourhood as I was invested their own time engaging in Godly matters, serving as choristers in the local Anglican Church and learning new skills as well as improving on old skills daily which they had gained from a united home, also because their parents were together to encourage and inspire them. This is why I believe that my attitude had absolutely nothing to do with the neighbourhood I grew up in, although I used to think that was the case at some point because our neighbourhood equally raised some *insane* youngsters at the time and the plague of inertia eventually didn't achieve much in the neighbourhood since over ninety percent of the once seemingly inept culprits from my neighbourhood turned their lives around to eventually become graduates, medical doctors, engineers, lawyers, ministers of the gospel and other professionals around the world today. I therefore believe that my attitude had all to with my personal experiences and it is the experiences that mould the character, not the environment. After all there have been repeated stories of people who were raised in gang infested environments around the world yet they ended up preaching the gospel of Christ. Children raised in united homes build character regardless of their environment and in most cases a lot of them will certainly go on to become reasonable and responsible adults because a family as much as any environment where children are raised seems like a root and roots are the symbol of unity. Like the branches on a tree they may grow in different directions, but the root normally keeps the branches together by having a strong grip of the stem. In the same manner the children may eventually grow and disperse or live in different societies, but this should normally not take away the united culture that they assimilated while growing up together, although inevitably sometimes it does as a result of greed and some other selfish interests exhibited by some of the family members. In such instances, any disunity becomes unavoidable and therefore justifiable. Unity is like *a marriage with Christ* in character and discipline. This union identifies that there is a head. It's like team-work, in every team there is a team leader and Christ is the team leader for the church. In the real life sense the absence of unity with strong leadership is the reason for chaotic situations in marriages today. Yes there is a union but in that union there must also be a head and like in a family or marriage the man is the head and as critically observed earlier in this book [1 Corinthians 11:3] shows this – "But I would have you know, that the head of every man is Christ; and the head of the woman *is* the man; and the head of Christ *is* God." This shows us that **marriage is like the Church at home**. It is spiritual rather than physical. This means that the ceremonies we perform in Church (called marriage) is not the actual marriage because it is a physical event and marriage is not a physical event. It also means that the parties we throw, photographs we take and the certificates we are issued with as a symbol or evidence of marriage are all irrelevant because they are intended to satisfy the flesh whereas marriage is a union made of the Spirit. If we are truly made 'one flesh' in marriage - [Mark 10:8] and [Ephesians 5:31], that means when the husband is physically sick and the wife is physically healthy, automatically there is already a *spiritual divorce* in place in that marriage without a physical divorce being agreed by both parties who are actually supposed to be 'one flesh'. The truth is that there are many things we don't know in life and we don't know that we don't know them. Understanding this *union principle* even further, we draw from [Ephesians 5:21-25] – "Submitting yourselves one to another in the fear of God. {Verse 22} Wives, submit yourselves unto your own husbands, as unto the Lord. {Verse 23} For the husband is the head of the wife, even as Christ is the head of the church: and he is saviour of the body. {Verse 24}

Therefore as the church is subject unto Christ, so let the wives be to their own husbands in every thing. {Verse 25} Husbands, love your wives, even as Christ also loved the church, and gave himself for it." Unity identifies and honours its head, just like the Church should and then the body is saved, because this is the order of unity.

I'd take instances from my experiences growing up under the watch of my parents because submission to the head albeit with a united front is the reason why marriages are celebrated as achievements or accomplishments. I discovered that most of the children who turn into hoodlums or vagabonds are from broken homes. For a number of years my parents were separated and that single experience gave me a leeway to a certain level of freedom which under normal circumstances, had they been together I wouldn't have enjoyed it. During these years I started smoking and drinking some alcohol in secret. As already mentioned above, sometime in 1995 I had a mental challenge from smoking Indian hemp (cannabis), although God would later heal me but I had to go through and endure this trauma for many months stretching to probably a year. The good news was that I did not go through it alone, as much as God was in it with me, my parents suffered the pain too because as at the time they were already separated for over five (5) years. I'd think and therefore argue that this challenge was vital to bringing my parents back together again after these trying years. Prior to this unification they were in a very long and seemingly inconclusive divorce battle during all those years. At home if my Dad got me upset I'd smash things up and curse out because I had an alternative. I'd run to my mum's place. While at my mum's, if she offended me in any way I'd do the same and run back to my Dads who by then would have calmed down from my erratic misbehaviour. It became my Sodom and Gomorrah experience but I really enjoyed it. The union in the family was broken, the head was '*spiritually*' already divorced and therefore the body could not be saved either. My parents '*totally*' lost control of their actions and reactions as well as those of my siblings and mine because I had to deal with my realities the way they hit me. This is what happens in a broken marriage/home. Marriage is like a baby, if you don't treat that baby well there will be brokenness apparent and you'd have to pay for it somehow and may then choose to live in self-denial of your reality if you wish. This is why we must maintain, reverence and fear our union with Christ. We know that Christ will never fail, so if we fail on our part we must also be ready to endure the consequences of our failures which may be detrimental to the body. Unity with and in Christ is one of the most important virtues of the believer's (Christian) life. I'd give more instances with real life situations.

I was meditating on the word '*united*' some time ago and discovered that most of the nations and organisations that have the word 'united' attached to their names are some of the greatest. For instance we have United Kingdom of Great Britain and Northern Ireland, United States of America and Manchester United amongst many others. We'd easily discover that these nations and organisations are actually some of the greatest we have in the world today. That reminds me of the power and possibility of togetherness. The maxim *united we stand, divided we fall* gives a lot of detail about this. If in doubt consider how many centuries of relevance in world affairs that has been accumulated by a nation in the magnitude and majesty as Great Britain for instance. During my time as a master's degree student studying management, I coined the term **team war** as opposed to *team work*. I coined this term considering the friction, irregularities and failure(s) that sometimes erupted in teams. It was a wake-up call to my team to stick together and together we became strong enough to conquer any adversity or challenge that we encountered. I'd take *Great Britain* as the preliminary case study here for clearer understanding. A friend of mine rang me from Africa very recently and went on a spasticated attempt to crank up accusations and ridicule against the United Kingdom as a nation. He went on to claim that the United Kingdom was governed by a demonic and greedy interest which they use to usurp secret funds from the less powerful and/or the less privileged nations of the world. I was quick to advise him to be very careful in his criticism because 'most times' people accuse or try to degrade someone or something, it's not necessarily because they hate them/it. Most times it is envy. You cannot hate or claim to hate an experience you've never really had. I reminded him that the United Kingdom is surely one of the most admired and easily the best country on earth. How do I know this? Unity breeds a stronger force. Regarding this [Genesis 11:6] gives us an image – "And the LORD said, Behold, the people *is* one, and they have all one language; and this they begin to do: and now nothing will be restrained from them, which they have imagined to do." It's therefore 'unity' that placed the United Kingdom at the centre of the world map and the focal point in Europe. The United Kingdom is a nation that boasts arguably the best healthcare and benefits system in the world today. Just look at the whole world trooping into the United Kingdom to see it and others to live it. Europeans can't wait for their parent nation(s) to become a member of the wider European Union before they all happily purchase their transit tickets to relocate to the United Kingdom. I know because my wife is proudly European and I've had the privilege to live in the United Kingdom these few years. Then consider their generosity too. The home of the English language which is the number one central language of the world today. The United Kingdom understood the power of language and managed to *force* their tongue into the world's system. Such feat could only be achieved in unity or with a united front. The United Kingdom is the only nation on earth with '*GREATNESS*' attached to its name (Great Britain) and it is a land of royalty which I have already addressed from the introduction of this book.

The United Kingdom is considerably a very tiny island nation that gave birth to a multitude of nations and people tend to forget this fact yet they've achieved so much for themselves and for others in such a way and magnitude that history will never be forgotten. They've given and keep giving so much to the world yet we criticise them, sometimes unintelligently with closed and biased minds. My mum used to say this – "*what the great do, the little prattle of*". It's a nation that has the hand of God shining on and through it. The United Kingdom has made an indelible mark in the word and still has so much going on for it because it boasts one of the best travel passports on earth and has held the number one spot for at least three years and running. This is clearly the result of being united in your vision, in your mission and in your endeavour for conquest. The United Kingdom gave the world the King James Version of the Holy Bible and introduced most of our ancestors and the vast majority of the world to what we call Christianity today and the teachings and knowledge of Christ. So how could we then suddenly develop hatred for the one who God has clearly not hated? The critics of this great nation have always cited *acclaimed* atrocities committed by some of these great nations in this past. They were only able to achieve whatever they had or still have today because of their great union. This is the resilience and power we must begin to exercise in Christ as believers. We could also see that God has not destroyed the nation because of his mercy on it. Let us consider some other great nations around us and then we may see how obviously blessed the United Kingdom really is. Look at the Asian countries and the rest of them battling with earthquakes today, hurricanes tomorrow, landslides, tornadoes, cyclones, floods, sink holes and so on. Too many disasters and they start naming them after human beings. All over the world there's always one major natural disaster or the other somewhere and these are the direct result(s) of sudden deviation from the Lord and Christ. The United Kingdom has always narrowly missed this plague, although the nation has unfortunately deviated in recent times by accepting certain destructive norms that are against what was ordained at the institution of this great nation. For instance the plague of gay marriage which the Holy Bible profoundly spoke against, but we must fight to support this great nation to fully get it back on God's lineage and agenda as much as we pray for the likes of the United States, Australia, Ireland, Spain, Greece and Italy amongst others to return to God because their errors directly or indirectly affect or destabilise the unity of the entire world. The weather hazard in Russia today seems to be their *'Mr President'* - Vladimir Putin but I'd actually love to meet Mr Putin someday to really enquire of him what his real motivation through stirring up chaotic situations around the world has been or (hopefully) was and maybe he'd have something really interesting to say. Every one time strong nation that turned their backs on God has had some sort of grievous issue(s) since then. Name them…!

Meanwhile from a critical mind-set the United Kingdom is supposed to have more enemies than any nation on earth because the country have fought a lot more battles than any other nation on earth yet the United Kingdom is still considered safer than most of the western nations, still at that the British Police Officers don't have to carry guns except it is extremely necessary. It tells me that this nation must have had some sort of *'everlasting or enduring covenant'* with God. Sometimes I see the United Kingdom much like the land or kingdom of Israel which is the original *land of the covenant* as recorded in the Holy Bible. I further discovered that everything about the United Kingdom was taken from and founded on the Holy Bible. Think about the monarchy/royalty/majesty - [1 Corinthians 29:25], the British national anthem '*God save the King/ Queen*' - [1 Samuel 10:24] and [2 Kings 11:12], the Prime Ministerial office rather than Presidency - [Genesis 41:41 – 43] and [Genesis 49:26], the name - *the United 'Kingdom'* - [Daniel 2:44] and [Mark 11:10], the Parliament is either the mother of all parliaments in the world or one of the oldest which is a picture of - [Matthew 10:1-4] where it was recorded that Jesus had twelve disciples that he made apostles and they were clearly his *members of parliament*; and we can count the rest of the exploits this great nation has made and keeps making through the wisdom and knowledge it acquired from the written word of God because a larger chunk of the principles and doctrines that govern the land was '*nicked*' from the Holy Bible which is why the United Kingdom remains an acclaimed believing or Christian nation. The United Kingdom is a kingdom-state rather than a mere state and a world renowned royal kingdom at that. It is a symbol of unity at its peak. I think God established this very tiny island nation for it to be admired as a role model and a source of encouragement to people or nations that can see these unique features in it so that the people of other nations may understand that you don't need to be a multitude before you can conquer the world. It is a nation that has purely functioned on the undisputed grace and power of God because many other nations have in one way or the other attempted to achieve this amount of greatness initiated by the United Kingdom and all have undoubtedly failed in their quest to be the best. I believe *the United Kingdom is the King David of the world* today because judging by its size it is unbelievably the "***smallest of the greatest***" and no one nation on earth has a prouder history than the United Kingdom as has already been mentioned in the Introduction (The place of Royalty) part of this book.

The United Kingdom is currently made up of four countries within its borders: England, Scotland, Wales and Northern Ireland and the glory of this great nation was masterminded by a tiny fraction of this unit which also went on to arguably become the mother and surely the heartbeat of the unit. This brief analogue is about one of the countries of the United

Kingdom called England. The four units of this great kingdom sometimes seems divided amongst themselves, particularly in sports related events. However I think their difference also goes to their advantage because when bodies like the Football Association (F.A) recognises four (4) countries within the United Kingdom in footballing competitions for instance, at the end of these competitions when the trophies of the United Kingdom are being counted, all trophies won by all four countries within this country will be counted as one. Meanwhile I've come to understand that as much as numbers have meanings, it may equally be fair to say that any number above one (1) is a symbol of 'UNITY'. Once you have at least two people, you are already a team and qualify for the term *'united'*. Hence the country remained united from its conquest of other territories through the process of granting them independence whilst also maintaining their territorial integrity as a truly united and strong nation. If we also decided to consider another united nation (the United States of America), we'd discover that they've also been birthed from Biblical prophesies hence their status as one of the most powerful (if not the most powerful) nation(s) on earth, although this has been greatly contested by the likes of China and Russia among others. However the strength of the United States as a result of unity has been evident being that they have the grace to currently determine the economic status of the current world with their currency (the United States Dollars) being arguably the most accepted currency of the world. Finally I'd consider a football club in the magnitude as Manchester United which has undoubtedly been the most successful football club in the English premier league and one of the best clubs in Europe and the world with numerous achievements, trophies, records and accolades empowering their name. To this effect millions of people around the world refer to this club simply as 'UNITED'. It's just a simple word that changes the world. This can only be the express power and glory of God in Christ expressed through the manifold works of God on the planet earth. On this light since we believe that Christ is the head of the Church, we can then argue that for the centre of the Church to hold, we must acknowledge that we are more than one as much as we are all one because together we make up the kingdom of God. The Church is the physical kingdom of God and the kingdom of God is the physical Church. Going further with our simple and original case study of the

United Kingdom as a symbol of unity, we may be wise to conclude that above all the triumphs of the United Kingdom and their greatest feat may yet be the humble colonisation of the undisputed land of God (Israel), which I'd rather not discuss any further in this seemingly lengthy chronicle and tribute (if you may) to what we may portray as "the united nations/ organisations" since our beloved Israel harbours the only city in the world that we could consider as the heaven on earth which is Jerusalem. Israel is on a spiritual realm when compared to the other nations of the earth. The problem in the world is as a result of spiritual disunity which has led many to practice religion. If every nation on the planet earth was founded on Biblical principles like the land of Israel, the United Kingdom, the United States, peaceful Canada and a few other nations; we'd all be very safe and it's a privilege to talk about this in detail. What the United Kingdom and a few other nations may have lost though is the wisdom to support Israel and this seems to be the one edge that the United States has gained over these other nations being a great force in their support for the land of God – Israel – and therefore the financial capital as much as being arguably the number one military power in the world today even though they (the United States and the United Kingdom) respectively also currently owe the highest amount of national debt of any nation today probably since records began.

Going further we also may realise that these two nations (the United Kingdom and the United States of America) particularly may have been the focus of [Genesis 48] and as a direct result being effectively the grand-sons of Jacob (Israel) with similar tales that may be likened to that of Ephraim and Manasseh (respectively). Manasseh was the firstborn but Israel made Ephraim his senior [Genesis 48:13-20] which displeased Joseph their father. After Israel crossed his hands to bless the lads by laying his right hand on Ephraim who was the younger and presumably the smaller of the two and his left hand on Manasseh who was the older and presumably the bigger of the two, [Genesis 48:19-20] gives the following account – "And his father refused, and said, I know *it*, my son, I know *it*: he also shall become a people, and he also shall be great: but truly his younger brother shall be greater than he, and his seed shall become a multitude of nations. {Verse 20} And he blessed them that day, saying, In thee shall Israel bless, saying, God make thee as Ephraim and as Manasseh: and he set Ephraim before Manasseh." This could really depict the story of the United Kingdom and the United States of America because England's seed birthed through colonial conquest went on to become a multitude of nations and unsurprisingly the preamble of the United States constitution today is - '*We the People*', while Britain adopted their greatness as a prefix to their name '*Great Britain*' as has already been stated. However I may also point out that physically Ephraim and Manasseh were brothers, however spiritually Ephraim became a spiritual-father to Manasseh. Israel clearly said 'he (Manasseh which is arguably the United States of America) also shall become a people and he also shall be great, but truly his younger brother (Ephraim which is arguably the United Kingdom) shall be greater than he'. I'd also assume that the real reason why Ephraim (United Kingdom) was able to achieve greatness quicker or first before Manasseh (United States) was not just because Israel laid his right hand on Ephraim, but also because he laid the first hand (regardless whether it was the right hand or the left hand) on Ephraim and [Genesis 48:14] confirms this – "And Israel stretched out his right hand, and laid *it* upon Ephraim's head, who *was* the younger, and his left hand upon Manasseh's head, guiding his hands wittingly; for Manasseh *was* the firstborn." Israel was conscious and intentional to accomplish this before his demise and there was no intention of a dichotomy or bias in any way. The New International Version of [Psalm 60:7] reads – "Gilead is mine, and Manasseh is mine; Ephraim is my helmet, Judah my sceptre." The Bible says that Manasseh (United States of America) belongs to Christ and Ephraim (United Kingdom) is Christ's helmet. If Ephraim (United Kingdom) is the royal crown of glory on Christ's head, it is no wonder then that the United Kingdom is the land of royalty we know today. I also went on to conclude that if Ephraim did not hit the limelight, Manasseh would not have become a people because if Ephraim was not blessed first, Manasseh would not have been blessed. This means that Manasseh's greatness and power was hinged on Ephraim becoming great first being that the blessing of their grandfather fell on him first. So it may not just be logic that these (arguably) brothers have even today unitedly conquered the world, regardless that oppositions still arise against them. Yet with all this glory and majesty, these great kingdoms and powerful nations will crash someday at the second coming (of Christ), but

Christ stands forever as head over all. The world cannot be still standing and yet standing still watching the gradual demise of our (supposed to be) united Charismatic values. Unity conquers and exalts but the day of the Lord will surely come like a thief [1 Thessalonians 5:2, 2 Peter 3:10 and Revelation 16:15] and until then the expectations and triumphs of a world unified by '*blood*' in Christ remains tremendous.

The place of Gathering:

There can't be any union or unity without a gathering and the truth also holds that anywhere there is a gathering of the children of God (the Church), the enemy gets attracted to such places as already addressed above. Scripture in [Job 1:6] shows this – "Now there was a day when the sons of God came to present themselves before the LORD, and Satan came also among them." As much as praise and worship attracts the Spirit of God, principalities and power also gather to scatter the flock where they possibly can. However this should not wither our enthusiastic spirit towards our gathering for worship in the Churches. David said in [Psalm 122:1] – "I was glad when they said unto me, Let us go into the house of the LORD." In the entirety of that Psalm, David clearly referred to '*Jerusalem*' as the house of the LORD and a place of gathering [Psalm 122:4]. David was a literary genius and from his rhetoric the house of God was a place where one derived the most joy or satisfaction from - [Psalm 137:6]. But the question is 'do our Churches today possess this emphatic description that connotes peace and acceptance?' The Holy Bible refers to the Church as the body of Christ, laying down principles as to what and what not should keep the body together. The book of [1 Corinthians 12:25-28] accounts for this thus – "That there should be no schism in the body; but that the members should have the same care one for another. {Verse 26} And whether one member suffer with it; or one member be honoured, all the members rejoice with it. {Verse 27} Now ye are the body of Christ, and members in particular. {Verse 28} And God hath set some in the Church, first apostles, secondarily prophets, thirdly teachers, after that miracles, then gifts of healings, helps, governments, diversities of tongues." From this last verse, the different offices do not encourage segregation because all should function as the members of the same body. This is where I really ponder about the motivation behind the thousands of Churches around the globe today. From my understanding it should be one Church, one God and one Lord [Ephesians 4:6] and [1 Corinthians 8:6]; with all these offices working as part of the same Church body. The Holy Bible stipulates the need, how and day of this gathering in [Acts 20:7] – "And upon the first [day] of the week, when the disciples came together to break bread, Paul preached unto them, ready to depart on the morrow; and continued his speech until midnight." The disciples always came together to have the communion on Sundays (actually every Sunday), but in today's Churches the disciples (which are the offices of the five-fold ministry) devise their own strategies quite distant from what the early Churches were about. Members of today's Churches suffer in seclusion and ignominy but the Church most times is careless about the state of the affairs of its members and yet we are the acclaimed body of Christ. The book of [Revelation 1:10] spoke on this wise – "I was in Spirit on the Lord's Day, and heard behind me a great voice, as of a trumpet..." Every day is the day that the Lord has made, but a particular reverend attachment is placed on how we invest our Sundays in the things of God because Sundays are the Lord's Day. Christians world-over have lost their dire, insatiate and once zealous appetite they had for the things of God because of our polite game of *humble-politics* rife in our Churches today. Our preachers could now afford to order some 'unwanted' members out of 'their' Churches without any remorse or fear of the Lord. Also most pastors of Pentecostal Churches (particularly the ones of African origin) tend to withdraw from believers the moment they discover that such believers are unemployed and they will never entrust any financial responsibilities to such people until their financial situation is fully examined and *trustworthy*. However even after such people eventually become gainfully employed, pastors tend to observe them for a while to ensure they've come to a point of financial safety and are persistent seed-sowers in the Churches these pastors lead before they can first test, and trust them only in situations where they've passed the test/trial. But this was not the message of our Lord. Hence instead of encouraging ourselves to attend unbiased services, we deduce schemes and strategies to only welcome members who can afford to pay us and of course they must also be loyal to our Church *cartels* and governments.

But I've read these exciting words from my Holy Bible which says in [Hebrews 10:25] – "Not forsaking the assembling of ourselves together, as the manner of some [is]; but exhorting [one another]: and so much the more, as ye see the day approaching."

Our gathering is of essence to the fulfilment of our faith if Christ is the head (our head). With the state of affairs of our Churches today, I would expect the head of the Church to be experiencing a lot of migraines and/ or headaches because of the tatters and segregations that we have subjected his body (ourselves) to. The Church is the place believers gather to serve and worship God, and God is not a story you tell people; God is the reality people see about you. A Church cannot call itself 'the gathering of the saints', if it's actually 'the gathering of the sins'. I call it thus because we segregate, we divide, we scatter, we destroy, we humiliate, we bully and we discourage. Another Scripture that absolutely draws my attention could be found in [1 Corinthians 16:2-3] – "Upon the first [day] of the week let every one of you lay by him in store, as [God] hath prospered him, that there be no gatherings when I come. {Verse 3} And when I come, whomsoever ye shall approve by your letters, them will I send to bring *your* liberality unto Jerusalem." Apostle Paul was thus advising the Church to save offerings from their wages every week for the Church at Jerusalem. But with the chaos in Churches today, discouragement swells the minds of worshippers and as such the work of God is being hindered by the political affinity exercised in our Churches today. The body of Christ cannot be strangers in a gathering of the saints where Christ is *supposed* to be the head. The summary is here in [Ephesians 2:19-20] – "Now therefore ye are no more strangers and foreigners, but fellowcitizens with the saints, and of the household of God; {Verse 20} And are built upon the foundation of the apostles and prophets, Jesus Christ himself being the chief corner stone…" In summary I'd conclude that no child of God should be a stranger or segregated in the house of their very own Father and God. Preachers who are supposed to be men of the spirit and undoubtedly *servants* have often been over-heard saying "*in my ministry or in my Church*". It is not anybody's ministry because it is not about you the leader (but about Christ), however your role as a leader should be the role of a team-leader to your '*fellows*' (not followers) and above all a servant of

God and that is if you decide not to write your own Holy Bible (as usual) for your own comfort and we'd always device a strategy to shove our mind-Bibles down the throats of our congregations otherwise *off they leave 'my Church'*. In all this we show no remorse whatsoever towards Christ yet we all claim to love God and [Proverbs 16:2] tells us that – "All the ways of a man *are* clean in his own eyes; but the LORD weigheth the spirits." A similar picture is displayed in [Proverbs 21:2] – "Every way of a man *is* right in his own eyes: but the LORD pondereth the hearts." Our desires now outweigh the gospel we share for a God we are supposed to tremble at his presence and in the process of our malicious acts we discourage *'the gathering of the saints'* and instead encourage *'the scattering of the saints'*. Instead of gathering as saints together in order to scatter all the stratagems of the wicked as a team, we end up scattering the Church in our bid to gather wealth and for our self-glory; and this goes on as long as we dictate the shots. Instead of lions, we seem like cubs on the pulpit. Scripture says in [Jeremiah 3:15] – "And I will give you pastors according to mine heart, which shall feed you with knowledge and understanding." This word did not promise to give the Church pastors that are widely egocentric or who will divide and scatter the Church, rather pastors that will nurture the Church. However being the current trend in our practice of *Christendom* today and as human beings, we tend to find it easier to copy others that do wrong and proudly make reference to them on the altar of God rather than being normal ourselves and helping to correct their wrongs because we possess the faith and the focus to force through our divine assignments and purpose according to the will of God which is rather significantly our utmost accomplishment and satisfaction in life and destiny. If our pastors and leaders in the Churches today now see other pastors as their role models (instead of Christ) in order to justify their wrongs, then who is leading who and why should we gather if it be in vain?!

The place of Generational Wars and Generational Warrior:

The devil is totally homeless and his homelessness has kept him merely struggling to survive via his antics geared towards frustrating believers but he just can't succeed. I know this because [1 Peter 5:8] – "Be sober, be vigilant; because your adversary the devil, as a roaring lion, **walketh about**, seeking whom he may devour." This Scripture tells me that the devil is homeless and his homelessness is unquestionable, so I'd advice people (particularly believers) to keep him homeless and clueless. We must not give the enemy hope, space, comfort or a resting place. ***The devil is the only homeless person that must remain homeless.*** His homelessness does not however exonerate us from his wiles, therefore every day is a day of war and every war consists of several battles that must either be won or lost because the devil is constantly on reinforcement. But through Christ we received a name and an identity to function in because [Proverbs 18:10] tells us that – "The name of the LORD [is] a strong tower: the righteous runneth into it, and is safe." We are '*in*' the name of the Jesus who became the Christ therefore we are safe. His name '*as a man*' became our covering as believers because we ran into it at salvation. If there are generational wars and battles, then at some point God will surely raise himself some generational warriors to clear-up the backlog of calamities left by the enemy. This is the vessel who God uses to put or bring a stop to every generational and recurrent calamities, reproaches, sicknesses, diseases, plagues, poverty, afflictions, infection, anger, envy, hatred in a family line or in the Church to an utter end. The stage of the switch from a generational curse to a generational blessing is a very critical stage in the life of any family but the great news is that through every battle, Christ in us remains the hope of that glory and I write from some experience. Abraham and David shared a lot in common, particularly because they were *vessels of recovery* and therefore the generational warriors of their time. In [Genesis 14:16] an account was rendered of how Abraham recovered all that was stolen from him thus – "And he brought back all the goods, and also brought again his brother Lot, and his goods, and the women also, and the people." Similarly in [1 Samuel 30:18-20] David was praised as having recovered all thus – "And David recovered all that the Amalekites had carried away: and David rescued his two wives. {Verse 19} And there was nothing lacking to them, neither small nor great, neither sons nor daughters, neither spoil, nor any *thing* that they had taken to them: David recovered all. {Verse 20} And David took all the flocks and the herds, *which* they drave before those other cattle, and said, This *is* David's spoil." In Abraham's lineage there was an initial trend of generational war made up of several individual battles which included barrenness, lying and doubt. This was apparent because Abraham was arguably either *faithlessly* hoping to protect himself from getting killed or just unbelieving, yet he went on to become the *father of faith*. Abraham first fought and apparently transferred some of these negative generational trends down his lineage:

Barrenness

Sarah (Abraham's wife) was barren - [Genesis 11:30]. Abraham's son Isaac, his wife Rebekah was barren too - [Genesis 25:21]. Isaac's son Jacob, his wife Rachel continued the generational *cursed-culture* of barrenness as seen in - [Genesis 29:31]. But these initial curses of barrenness in the Abrahamic lineage were eventually broken.

Lies

Then was the plague of telling lies which clearly dominated Abraham's blood line. Abraham lied *'as Abram'* to Pharaoh in Egypt - [Genesis 12:13-19] and then Abraham lied *'as Abraham' (father of faith)* to Abimelech in Gerar - [Genesis 20:2] and again in [Genesis 20:12-13]. Abraham's son Isaac continued the trend and also lied to Abimelech king of Gerar in [Genesis 26:7]. Then in [Genesis 27:19-41] Isaac's son Jacob told lies to claim an inheritance that was not supposed to be his. Jacob deceived his father Isaac. Lying was a generational strong man in the family. In [Genesis 27:40] Isaac said to Esau - "by the sword shalt thou live", and in the very next verse [Genesis 27:41] Esau said in his heart - "The days of mourning for my father are at hand; then will I slay my brother Jacob." The prophecy of Isaac over Esau was not yet settled before it became *'life'* in the heart of Esau. This again explains that blurring lies could breed or lead to death. This lying trend advanced a generation further because in [Genesis 37:31-35] Jacob's sons lied to their father by pretending that their brother Joseph had been devoured by a wild beast.

Doubt

The unique thing is that Abraham *'as Abram'* doubted God because God sent him to Canaan but he would then leave for Egypt as seen in - [Genesis

12:1-10 and Genesis 13:1-3] but the good bit was that God was still with him in Egypt. Then again *as Abraham' (father of faith)*, he doubted God because God promised Isaac but he only saw Ishmael and therefore could not believe God's Isaac vision - [Genesis 17:18]. However the single attempt to sacrifice Isaac gave him the star opportunity to land his name in the *' faith hall of fame'* - [Genesis 22:1-18].

For some preachers of the gospel of Christ, growing a Church or ministry established by their parents or grand-parents become their generational war and for some others getting into the ministry is their apparent stumbling block into their destiny and their own generational war. On 13 March 2014 I got a revelation from God that "a preacher that his ministry cannot be numbered for multitude like the stars in the sky or like the sand on the sea shore as God promised the likes of Abraham, Isaac and Jacob; does not count Church members." I thought very long and hard over this and it made some unbelievable sense to me because if you can count members of a particular Church congregation, then that congregation must be small. A congregation or gathering for God is *'estimated'* not counted because whatever God is involved in cannot be numbered or counted. Below are some promises made by God to men of like faith and today we share their testimonies:

Abraham: Genesis 12:3, Genesis 13:14-17, Genesis 15:5, Genesis 16:10, Genesis 17:5-8, Genesis 22: 16-18.

Isaac: Genesis 26:3-4 and verse 24.

Jacob (Israel): Genesis 27:28-29, Genesis 28:3-4 and verse 13-15, Genesis 32:24 and verse 28-29, Genesis 35:10-12 and verse 21.

For many families stepping into their ministry calling is the generational war to the family. I heard my late Dad always say that his Dad (my late grand-Dad) helped bring the Anglican Church to our village. This tells me that there was a genuine passion for God in the family from generations past but for some reason I understand that he equally had some things to do with idol worshipping. That became his strong man. With my late Dad, he equally had a passion for God and even read through the Holy Bible during his life time in the 1980s (he told me), however as the traditional ruler for the local community, he unfortunately had to indulge himself in some traditional and therefore diabolical rituals as required by the culture/tradition that he governed. This again became a barrier for his dedicated pursuit of the living God. This is the aspect of my family blood line that I chose to delete from myself. I made a conscious covenant with the living God that whatever held my parents back from serving him in totality must be broken from my very own lineage. This for me would mean from myself to the generations *upwards*. I made a vow to become the generational warrior in that lineage for myself, my children and the generations following. It has been very challenging but God has equally been very faithful. For instance on 16 December 2014 I went to sleep and woke up on the morning of 17 December 2014 and discovered that I could not breathe properly. I would eventually find myself running to the window to try to gasp some fresh air through my lungs. I had to struggle to breathe through the day and at night it got terribly worse. I started breathing like I was about to give up the ghost but I refused. Very early in the hours of 18 December 2014 around 2am I rang for an ambulance and was rushed to the St Thomas hospital. I'd think this was the most violent attack I've had to endure since I understood what spiritual attacks meant. At the hospital I felt much better and all tests were conducted on me and nothing could be found. My oxygen level remained at one hundred percent (100%) from test results and every blood test that I subsequently had showed that everything was normal. The hospital offered to give me some steroids and to put me on asthma inhalers to keep my airways open but I refused to take the steroids and I got discharged from the hospital later that evening about 5pm. I got home okay again, yet at night the same severe attacks reoccurred. I was now loading my system with inhalers like I was drinking water and it was too frequent to be counted or recorded. I did not know how I could survive this ordeal but I believed God. Setting yourself aside to seek God when you come from a family background that has been in constant contact with the devil and are still in contact to be honest, it can either seem suicidal or self-destructive but at the end victory becomes real. The devil did not want me to see the 2014 Christmas, neither did he want me to enter the year 2015 because he knew that I will be completing major projects for God this year; projects that will glorify

God and put the devil to shame in the name of Jesus and it was a problem for the enemy. Through it all I dared to keep believing and radically kept trusting in the blood of Jesus to deliver me. I totally trusted in the saving grace of Christ. The experience was horrific because I began to ring pastors for prayers that hitherto I had no business contacting them when getting through to my busy pastor was not very easy. Some reluctantly did while others asked for seeds or vows while the rest of them did not. I got a few friends and even my young family to keep praying for me. I thought I had offended God somehow but could not figure out how.

On the Sunday 21 December 2014 I was heading to Church in my condition because I would not miss the Church service being obsessed with presence of God in every meaning of it. I had to struggle breathlessly all the way to Church. I did not even know that I would be able to see the Christmas day just four days later, with constant battles in my mind and I had to gain victory in all. Well that Sunday I had to go out for a *'testimony'* (that I'm still alive) in Church and for one of my pastor (at the time) to pray for me and he did. I thought I felt better but before the service was over the attack started over again and even heavier this time. I tried to get help from Church members to be taken to the hospital but everybody in Church had a *'good* reason' why they could not help me out. I was too sick to get upset with anybody, yet in this frustration I trusted God even more. That was probably the most embarrassing day of my life (21 December 2014) because in faith I'd never have a worse day ever again in Jesus name Amen. While the struggle was going on, I could hear the voice of God saying to me - "*I want you to learn so that when you are in the position to help the sick or weak or anybody, you will not fail. I want you to know how my Church is at the moment so that when you begin to serve me as a minister, you can change and correct it because I will make the ministry I set you over 'a model' in the earth.*" Straight from Church an ambulance eventually came to pick me up after two hours of wait and took me to the Newham General hospital where I was attended to. All tests done again yet all results coming out as normal. They could not help me. This time I pleaded with the medical doctor that saw me to give me some steroid doses and *reluctantly* he did after he determined that there was nothing else he could do to help me. I got discharged again from the second hospital in just four days. A friend of mine came to the hospital after I got discharged and led me and my two sons to the tube station where we caught the tube (underground train) home. I had to take eight tablets of steroids every day for five days which would end on the Christmas day. I wondered '*after the Christmas day, where do I go from here?*' I was so constantly confused with and worried for my life. I only remember repeatedly reminding God – "*Father let your will be done in my life*." That was my prayer all through that ordeal. On Christmas day a friend came to take me to the Anglican Cathedral at Canterbury, but I refused to tell him how sick I was at the time. Prior to this I and my family had intended to spend the Christmas at Canterbury for a few days but we had to cancel that trip because of the severe health attack I was enduring. Yet I had a desire to see Canterbury in 2014 and somehow, just somehow God made it happen for me. We came back from Canterbury on the same day for me to come home and face my reality afresh. I was clueless in my pain, I had taken my last dose of the steroid and I only remembered what David said as written in [Psalm 119:71] – "It is good for me that I have been afflicted; that I might learn thy statutes." I went back to God's word again and again to seek the answers, solace and refuge that I required for my situation. I sure thought I had become hopelessly hopeless.

In the meanwhile I was still ringing and texting all pastors I had their contacts, they were numbers I mainly got from their televised programmes and ministry websites. May I use this opportunity to glorify God again and thank all the pastors that prayed for me with the many others pastors that I even had to send in my incessant prayer requests on-line through their websites to intercede on my behalf and some of them did it every day particularly these three: the Right Reverend Bishop Ngozi Durueke who went into fasting on my behalf and prayed for me every day, Pastor E Isaiah who prayed for me multiple times yet I was not even a member of his ministry, got his Church to pray for me several times and actually gave me a bottle of anointed oil the first day I met him because of that issue, which I cherished so much because the oil came from a man of God who was not even my pastor and then Pastor Paul Oseghale who was based at Glasgow and I had to call every few hours and every day for prayers, sometimes even at midnight hours. I feel sad to say this but these were the pastors who I'm aware were committed to praying for me and prior to this time never knew me except for the Right Reverend Bishop Ngozi Durueke who I've known for twenty (20) years through my parents. I was a complete stranger to Pastor Paul Oseghale and up till this day (of my writing) I haven't met him before yet he prayed for me happily, unreservedly and without bias. My heart cannot express my sincere, heartfelt and profound gratitude to you all and even to those who disappointed their office and God (not me) during this time of my need. God bless you all. The ordeal I went through cannot be properly explained in detail but may the great God reward you all duly and accordingly. During this time I concluded that '**all are men of God but not all are servants of God**' because men of God '*work for God*' while servants of God '*serve God*' and **in the flesh men work but in the spirit men serve**. I also think that if you're a man and a strong believer, you're a man of God because the Holy Spirit resides in you. It is not a pastoral title that makes or qualifies anybody as a man of God, really. Not everybody that preaches the word of God is a servant of God and what must draw the exceptional line in our Church leaderships is *service* because the Lord Jesus was the Son and servant of God. Similarly it is like what the Scripture says in [Matthew 22:14] – "For many are called, but few *are* chosen" and I'm not being critical or judgemental in any way. I really do feel very sad saying this but I promised God I will testify just as it is. Unfortunately the place I regarded as '*my*' very own Church still do not have an inclination of what I went through but it's okay and I can't blame them for this. In 2012 my late Dad gave me about six (6) plots of land in Owerri, Nigeria. During my trying times and attacks, I made a vow to God to sow the entire property as a seed for restoration and restitution to one of the ministries mentioned in this testimony and I've gone on to fulfil this vow in February 2015 by the grace of God. I do not use this as a means to brag about it, rather I use it to emphasize the struggle I endured that caused me to make what I consider as a very 'costly vow' to me. A struggle that triggered me to make and fulfil a vow of that enormity to the living God should explain to people what I went through and I am very happy I did it. If I had died during that ordeal, I wouldn't be thinking about keeping or retaining any land, so it was a privilege that I was alive to sow it as a seed. God allowed me to go through '*death*' for a reason so that I can come out alive to share this testimony that will glorify God and God alone because nobody may ever understand what I experienced through it. Meanwhile I'd spoken to the Right Reverend Bishop Ngozi Durueke briefly about the attack and he'd told me in very precise words – *"It's a spell and it's from your family (in Nigeria). Be encouraged my son because God told me that you will not die in it. Get anointed oil and pour it in warm water before you drink it. Drink it every day and call me every night for prayers until you feel better."*

A few days later I went to meet Pastor E Isaiah for the first time for prayers as already explained above and he gave a very similar picture – *"It's not sickness, it's an attack. You will not die. I can see that sometimes you have to run to the window to get some fresh air. I can see that it's like they tied a rope around your neck and when they think you're feeling better, they go and draw the rope again to try to suffocate you. You will not die, you will get better and God will heal you. Take this bottle of anointed oil. Pour it in warm water and drink it three times a day."* I am sure that these two preachers of the gospel have never met themselves before, maybe not even heard about themselves neither did I discuss what I was going through with them exactly the way they explained it. Hence the need to visit other Churches from time to time because it's not everything about you that God will reveal to your own pastor and what God does not reveal to your pastor, God will surely show to another pastor that you may actually have no business with his ministry, so do keep an open mind about the Church where you worship and don't be too rigid and religious and miss your miracle in the process. Most of our pastors are out to build ministries and gather multitudes in order to make a name, they are not there to make sure that your worries are resolved. The Reverend Bishop Ngozi Durueke is a Nigerian pastor based in Nigeria while Pastor E Isaiah is originally from Ghana but based here in the United Kingdom. So I would believe that they don't know themselves from anywhere yet they saw a glimpse of what I was going through in the spirit. From the very beginning of the Holy Bible we learn of how man became a living being as recorded [Genesis 2:7] – "And the LORD God formed man [of] the dust of the ground, and breathed into his nostrils the breath of life; and man became living soul." After the LORD God had formed the man, the first thing he did was to breath into his nostrils the *breath of life* and that was when man became a living being. Without that breath of life man would have remained dust. Even when babies are born into the world, it is immediately the air (breath) of life breathes or goes into their lungs, this is when babies cry. The reason is not far-fetched, it is because there's a change from what life used to be for them. Prior to this they had what I may call *'supported life'* or *'supported-living'*, helped by their mothers. So *'breathlessness or shortness of breath'* could actually be considered as the toughest affliction that any man could ever suffer from because without that breath there's no life. In very simple words, this was exactly what happened to me.

The New International Version of the Holy Bible confesses in [Psalm 39:11b] – "…each man is but a breath. Selah." If each man is then a breath, then try to picture yourself breathless and then you may understand what I went through during this ordeal of a spiritual attack. A breathless man is already a dead man and this was not even an asthma attack from every indication. The other lesson I learnt from this was how most of the pastors I rang for prayers whose names I've not mentioned here will first ask me – *'what Church do you go to?'* before even praying for me over the telephone and one went on to criticise the Church first and still did not pray for me before she hung up the telephone claiming she was very busy. I told God in these times - *"Lord forgive me for saying I wish to be like certain pastors in the past, Father make me myself and take your glory."* The most stupid and silly wish I ever made was wishing to be like any pastor because most of our pastors urgently need to clean up their acts and being made of flesh makes all men imperfect. I have learnt a lot from my challenges and I wish not to be like any other but like me, the way God has made me. Gradually God brought me through this challenge without my knowledge. Therefore to conquer generational wars as a generational warrior in Christ, we must first understand that *in life we're like birds and every bird flies at their own pace and on their own wings. No bird will lend or offer you a wing to fly on particularly where they can fathom that you're destined to fly higher than them.* So when you can't get help where you expected help from, just remain aware and alert that you did not get help from there because they were not destined to help you. Going into a generational war battle does not often entail that you will go into it with the mind-set or intention that you wish to become the record breaker in your family, however you must pursue every battle with a winning mind-set and in the name of Jesus. There may also not be a record to break especially where the challenge has survived many generations in your family. You cannot break a record where there's no record to break. You simply fight to set new records that will be upheld and emulated, thereby glorifying God.

The place of God's Voice:

The voice of God is not mental assent and having the boldness to declare what God has said or is saying has no basis on pride or arrogance but the word of God must still be declared in boldness. I had this conversation on 18 February 2015 with my older son (Kingdom):

Kingdom: Daddy, God spoke to me!!
Dad: Yeah? What did he say?
Kingdom: He said that I'm a very good boy.
Dad: Laughs.

I laughed not because I did not believe what my son told me as I'm aware that God could speak to anybody, however I laughed because I asked myself within my heart - 'what else could God have said to you if not that?' I found it really amazing indeed that if God had truly not spoken to him, then why would a boy of six start developing such thoughts? If the voice of God was unimportant, how would God speak to people in order to give them direction? God had said in his written Scriptures in [Amos 3:7] that – "Surely the LORD will do nothing, but he revealeth his secret unto his servants the prophets." This word always reminded me that God has directly spoken multiple times about my destiny to me and through his servants the prophets and I had kept a detailed record of these words for a *fulfilment-testimony* and for a memorial, knowing that God cannot lie and waiting for a full manifestation of God's word and will in my life and for his purpose to come through as I move in faith to fulfil this high calling in Christ:

Apostle Ebenezer Ajitena (Christ Light World Outreach Ministries – CLIWOM) on 04 April 2007: "You have a very glorious future. The Lord says you are one of the leaders around and we are going to celebrate you here in this Church. Right here we'd celebrate you. God bless you."

Pastor Chioma Emmanuel (Grace Ministries) on 14 January 2009: "Are you a pastor? There is the calling of God upon your life…a very strong calling. Go and write it down somewhere, because you will remember that I said it. Obey him, the kingdom will call upon you!"

Pastor Alex Omokudu (Victorious Pentecostal Assembly – V.P.A) on 06 December 2010: "I see you with a microphone. I don't know, but I see you with a microphone."

Pastor Ebenezer Ajitena (Christ Light World Outreach Ministries – CLIWOM) at Larnaka International Airport Cyprus on our way to the Holy Land Pilgrimage at Israel on 14 May 2012: "I see something major coming to you very soon. Go and process your British Passport immediately. I don't know what it is but the Lord told me something will happen that will change your life and cause you to be celebrated."

The Lord said to me on leaving the western wall passing through Jews singing just outside the Wailing Wall on 21 May 2012: "Men will sing for you and you will dance like David danced."

Prophet Johnson Akinfewa (Joshua Generation World Outreach Ministries) visited CLIWOM Church on 22 July 2012: "You are like a shining star. A light. The Lord told me that you have what it takes and nobody can stop you."

The Lord said to me (in my dream whilst sleeping on my bed at home) on 21 November 2014: "You are '*Natural Resources*' in the hand of God."

Pastor Alex Omokudu (Victorious Pentecostal Assembly – V.P.A) on 01 January 2015: "There is another Pastor Alex in our midst now. I said there is another Pastor Alex in our midst right now. I heard it very clear." He was speaking to the Church but I knew it was a specific word for my call, not exactly because I want to be like him, but I received that word as a seed to my call for global evangelism and exactly twenty-two days later I was sitting in my living room and the Lord spoke giving me a very clear global vision, which he later confirmed on the same day through a prophet of God (as seen below).

The Lord summoned me (in a vision whilst sitting in my living room at home) on 23 January 2015: "Go and start the ministry now. You are like the '*foolish things*' that I will use as my battle axe in this time to confound the wisdom of the entire world for my glory. All the pastors and other ministers who has ever prayed for you will celebrate you and glorify me for you. Among your friends, family members and the world you will be to them like the stone the builders rejected which has become the chief corner stone and I will watch my word to perform it in your life. Write this date down because you will remember this day forever as the day I spoke to you to start the missions and evangelism global ministry that I have spoken to you about which will be powered by the Holy Ghost for the propagation of the gospel of Christ and for preaching the kingdom of God. Study the book of Acts of the Apostles one chapter a day in every day of February 2015 with a focus on Acts 1:8. I will use this ministry to turn mortuaries into Church buildings because the dead will be raised in record numbers by my power. You are an asset to the Kingdom and have I not called you *Natural Resources*?!" The Lord gave me some other specific details about the ministry and pertinent to this vision which I am not liable to write here.

Pastor Abbeam Danso (God's Solution Centre) on 23 January 2015: "Sir come. Are you a minister of God? Has anybody spoken to you about ministry that God's hands is upon you? Those who were sent to go and talk to you to tell you to do what God wants you to do, they have spoken to you. Let me just give you something, you know the donkey that Jesus wanted to sit on her, you see when the word was given the donkey followed the people. Can you imagine if the donkey sat at the place? The Bible says that nothing sat on the donkey, so if the donkey was still there without following what the people are saying that it should come, do you think Jesus would have sat on that donkey? The Spirit of the Lord said to me, tell him - 'Time! Time!! Time!!! Is now'. But listen, things will turn. All you need to do is follow the instructions. If you are expecting God to come down, even in your dreams you won't get it. He has sent his Prophets to see and to tell you and this is the word. My brother I'm not ready to pray for you. Your money, you are sitting on it. Your life, you are sitting on it. Go and start!!! If you shake, come back. I will tell you what to do; saith the Lord."

Bishop Ngozi Durueke (Powerline Living Water Ministries a.k.a He Reigns Chapel) on 26 January 2015: "I knew about your calling. The Lord told me then that he will use you greatly and I even told your mum about your calling. I wrote it down in my diary. He even told me that I will be a part of it."

Bishop Ngozi Durueke (Powerline Living Water Ministries a.k.a He Reigns Chapel) on 28 January 2015: "God told me two days ago to tell you that whatever you're going through right now, that you should not worry about it because the world will celebrate you. I will encourage you to the last and I will like to be at your ordination whether it's in the United Kingdom or in Nigeria so that I can pour oil on your head and lay my hands on you and bless you."

Bishop Ngozi Durueke (Powerline Living Water Ministries a.k.a He Reigns Chapel) on 09 February 2015: "When you got very sick many years ago, the Lord told me that you will not die. He said that at the fullness of time he will compel you to serve him, he used the word *compel*. He said that you will be very great and that your greatness will attract envy from your siblings, friends and your family members. He said that you will be a succour and a help to them. He told me that you will stand tall over them like an Iroko tree and that I will be like a father and a mentor to you. He said you will go very far and that you will be celebrated all over the world. I could not understand how because I wondered where your parents will be at the time if I will be a father and a mentor to you. In a dream one day I saw you and me in a boat and we were going for evangelism. Then I started to understand what the Lord was saying about you. So I have always known about your calling since then. He told me that you will pass through a cross with hardships and scorching but that at the end [Psalm 1:3] will be manifested and fulfilled in your life. He said that you will be like a tree planted by the rivers of waters. So I can assure you that no matter what you go through you will not die because of that covenant with God."

I've very carefully received, guarded and detailed (in this book and other note-pads) these prophecies for myself and against spiritual-thieves that steal and destroy purposes because effectual doors are opened unto me in ministry (like the Apostle Paul said) and there are many contenders. Destiny destroyers and spiritual-thieves have been real nightmares from ages past. In [Genesis 27:5] the Holy Bible said that – "And Rebekah heard when Isaac spake to Esau his son. And Esau went to the field to hunt *for* venison, *and* to bring *it*." Rebekah rather than Jacob was a destiny-thief and conversations held around destiny-thief prone areas must be curtailed to a minimum. It's a huge error that must be avoided, a costly accident to deal with and some accidents could become enormous mistakes that may eventually take lives or cripple destinies forever. Meanwhile early morning on the 16 January 2015 I over-slept my alarm clock and while still in my sleep I felt someone blow air into my face and nostrils and I woke up immediately. I knew I was experiencing the presence of the Spirit of God. Then again as already mentioned earlier in the 'Dreams and Visions' section of this book, I had a dream on 21 January 2015 where Pastor Benny Hinn laid his hands on my head and prayed for me whilst I knelt down in that dream. I mentioned it to the Right Reverend Bishop Ngozi Durueke and he had told me that it meant *'commissioning'*. Then in a subsequent dream in the early hours of 29 January 2015, someone poured anointed oil on my head. It was being poured on me 'from above' but I could not see the face of the person clearly in that dream. Considering these specific prophetic words and acts over my life the Scripture says in [Psalm 37:23] that - "the steps of a good man are ordered by the LORD: and he delighteth in his way." It says the steps of a good man are ordered (not stagnated) by God. Hence I am confident that the Lord ordered my steps at the times he needed me to hear what he has prepared in my destiny for his glory and majesty. Therefore the Church is the *body of Christ* and the name or title given to the Church is irrelevant as long as it is a Spirit-filled Bible-believing Church. If visiting another Church from time to time will cause the pastor of the main Church where I choose to attend not to pray for me (if I ever need prayers), then so be it because it is the will of God.

After the last attack I had in December 2014, I got to that point where I knew without a shadow of doubt that it is only the will of God that is permitted in my life and family. During that ordeal, the vast majority of pastors that prayed for me were pastors I had never ever set my feet in the Churches that they presided over (as already mentioned). I just watched most of them on TV not knowing that one day God will use them to speak into my life. *That means 'you' refusing to help me tomorrow is actually beyond your control because God must be glorified according to his will*. I told God to forgive me for my past where I've tried to make some pastors to feel like they were God all because I intended to please them.

I concluded that no pastor will ever take God's glory over my life. This is why I chose to be very flexible in my Church attendance whilst maintaining a committed relationship with just one until I eventually started the ministry that the Lord had spoken to me about on 05 April 2015. But whilst I currently function as (what I'd consider) a part-time minister (at the time of this writing), I will keep attending other Churches for special conferences and empowerment as led by God because if I did not visit Pastor Abbeam Danso's Church on 23 January 2015 after God summoned me to his ministry, God will not have confirmed the vision he had given to me on the same day through him and if I did not speak to the Right Reverend Bishop Ngozi Durueke on 09 February 2015 he'd probably not have told me that I have an evangelistic call. Subsequently if I had not visited the V.P.A Church for my first one-to-one counselling with Pastor Alex Omokudu, where on earth would I have received that 'microphone' prophecy from? Although in 1997 I won the '*best rap artist award*' in a singing competition held at the higher institution where I attended during my first (bachelor's) degree. I have always had a gift in music as well which I am yet to develop to its full potential. Yet with all these revelation(s), I mentioned my calling to a pastor I had spent over four years in his ministry (at the time) after he rang me at 07:54 am on the morning of 16 February 2015 and he got so unfriendly and very loud on that conversation that lasted for 2 minutes 13 seconds. The summary of his accusation or rather argument was that '*God cannot call me until I have served in a department in his ministry*'. I tried to explain to him that I heard the Lord speak to me without doubt and that if service in a Church was the criteria or requirement for God calling men to ministry, then God would have called me while I was serving him in the former Church where I worshipped at for over seven (7) years and also served dedicatedly as an intercessor until when I left. The moment I said this, the pastor paused for a while and then hung up the phone because he knew that 'service' is *surely not* a criteria for hearing from God if God was calling you to serve him. How can one's call be based on service if he/she is being called to serve? The argument was not very well articulated. Unfortunately the same pastor had told us in Church several times that when God called him into the ministry nobody believed him, not even his pastors. At that point I started pondering, yet refused to believe that I will be the next victim of such unfounded unbelief system amongst pastors. I refused to tell this pastor (who I will not mention his name because I love and respect him so much regardless) that the day the Lord spoke to me about ministry, that God confirmed his word the same day through his prophet - Pastor Abbeam Danso. If I dared say this during that tense conversation, I can't even imagine what I may have been told. It's not every detail that you should tell those who are not interested in hearing you out or those hell-bent on restricting your call of destiny. They don't have to believe that God has called you because they will see that God has truly called you when God begins to visibly use you and they will have no choice but to glorify God for you. I also contacted another former pastor of mine through email during this time seeking encouragement and he never replied to that email. Prior to this incident, this particular (former) pastor of mine would send me emails inviting me for one Church programme or another and would reply to any emails I sent to him. But the moment I sent him an email telling him about my call, I received an unusual silence from him which I thought was quite absurd. It's goofy to think that he's yet to read my email and I understand better than that. I just knew how wonderful, supportive and Godly our preachers can be yet while I was typing this part of the book I heard the Lord saying to me – "not all pastors will make heaven." I prayed instantly asking the Lord to help me to serve him well and diligently, to avail my call to ministry by his grace and power because I hunger and thirst for righteousness and heaven.

Going further then movement is imperative. It is the same with the rest of the prophecies mentioned above, if I did not move or change my location by listening to the voice of the Lord, who would have spoken to me about them? I made a move and God spoke. If I remained static in one location, there is no way God would have spoken to me the way he spoke through the pastors mentioned above, particularly through those of them who function in a core prophetic office yet humbly address themselves as a pastor. I have decided not to frustrate the Holy Ghost as I am led by him to achieve and fulfil my destiny and ministry in life. No pastor wants to hear that a member of their Church attended another Church gathering or joined the congregation at another ministry without realising that it is not about their ministry but about God. It detests me to think or believe that becoming a preacher of the gospel in full-time ministry leads me into a foul mental motive to try to psychologically '*force*' members of my ministry to remain in my ministry forever because I probably '*think*' that it is the best out there for them. That I think is very selfish because God's word is not domiciled in one place. All 'Churches' belong to Christ and he remains the head and ruler of them all, not the men he's called to lead them. If God speaks through people, through activities, through songs, through visions, through dreams, through the environment, through movies and in so many other ways that means from time to time we must move around for God to speak because God cannot be limited or secluded and it's called positioning or repositioning where necessary. The Church needs to be pragmatic in dealing with Godly affairs because they're not intended to make lives rigid in any way. It is the Holy Ghost (Christ) that heads and controls the Church and the Spirit of God is a free Spirit. This is why very large ministries do not 'force' or intend in any way to '*force*' members to be like sign-posts (stagnant) in their ministry. Actually I've never seen or heard any of the biggest preachers on the planet beg or employ psychological force (directly or indirectly) to retain members in their ministry by often bragging that their anointing is the best *in the market* and hence their ministry, yet their ministries expand every day. No man is endowed with anything called the 'best' anointing. I was ignorant over this in the past because I called some men of God 'best yet' but now I know much better. You could be an acclaimed 'best pastor or preacher' to your members or congregation (in their minds) but you'd never be the best servant of God and God is looking for '*best servants*' of God, not '*best pastors or best men*' of God. People he could easily talk to and get his purpose established in the earth. There's a world of difference between the two authorities. Best pastor or man of God has as its focal point the man, not God. Best servant of God points the focus towards God, not the man. I was not taught this, I discerned this. It's not about what we do as believers, the main point is whether what we do as believers is Biblical and portrays the gospel of Christ? If the Bible is our rule-book, then is what we do in-line with our rule-book? If it is then it is okay, if it's not then there's surely a problem.

The place of Church:

From the foregoing I've always asked myself this simple question – '*Church or cult?*' Personally whenever I start worshipping in a new Church I become totally dedicated, unbelievably committed and I try to be a very loyal member. I also endeavour to be a great student and our pastor(s) being our *physical* teachers most often than not encourage us to remain so. However the Lord opened my spiritual eyes on a particular Sunday morning. I woke up and for the first time in many years I was not very sure where I wanted to worship on this day, then through a revelation it dawned on me that any day our pastor(s) were not in Church, it was because they went to preach or teach in another Church somewhere. I did not think this was hypocrisy, yet I could not understand what it really was. Was I fooling myself with my radical dedication of membership and loyalty to a particular Church building or what? So for so many years I could not attend another Church because pastor(s) had always taught us that it was wrong to visit other Churches and we dared to believe this '*tale*'. Then that Sunday morning I'd woken up and my heart was steering me to go to another Church whose pastor was one of those who was always reachable on the telephone during my health scare cum ordeal and he would pray for me at any time, repeatedly encouraged me hence challenging my spirit to believe God for my total healing. How then would I say 'thank you' to all of them? At this point I heard a word speak to my heart saying – "*if your pastor can go to another Church to teach the word of God every once in a while, why can't you be able to go to another Church as a student to learn the word of God shed from a different light every once in a while? Don't get deceived because you seek God not man or Church building and I never taught my disciples this doctrine. I sent them out to the ends of the earth to preach the gospel to every creature. As a member of the Church you must be flexible even as you adhere to my instructions because I will come to judge the world including your pastor(s) that you seek to please. I made the Church one unit but they have divided my Church into different denominations but I remain the head of all Churches."* I just knew that this was surely not the devil speaking to me. It must have been God's voice. That Sunday I broke that chain of stagnation by attending another Church service in a different location, justified in my spirit that I had done what was right and I felt unbelievably free within me. I felt justified in this revelation because God said to Peter as recorded in [Acts 10:15] – "And the voice spake unto him again the second time, What God hath cleansed, that call not thou common." I believe the word 'common' here means *'condemn'*, therefore - *'what God has cleansed, do not condemn.'* In this perspective it tells me that the Church of God cannot be condemned by the denominations of men. Churches or to be more precise regarding our doctrine I'd say *'Christian Leaders'* sometimes make other Churches and other pastors look small because of a tensely competitive mind-set and (from the way it seems these days) market, forgetting that the Church is not a business or market place. They do not seem to realise that in condemning another Church of God, they (maybe unintentionally) condemn the God that made the Church being Christ. By so doing they also condemn the call on the *'rival'* pastor. I used the word 'rival' consciously because ministry seems to be all about grudge and rivalry today. In the picture of their mind(s) their Churches are always at the top while others are beneath them. I don't write to condemn but this is the reality ravaging the Churches today (wittingly or unwittingly) and there is unavoidably a lot of ignorance still hovering around believers unfortunately as they do not seek to address these issues. The situation has gotten to the stage of normality as we strive to just go with the flow instead of speaking through a change for good. Jesus did not say *'I will build Mr A's Church or Mr Z's Church'*. He did not break up the Church, men did. Jesus said – "…upon this rock I will build **my Church**; and the gates of hell shall not prevail against it" - [Matthew 16:18]. That means the Church of Jesus was one, however after Christ became the head of the Church the denominations crept in, but this was the Lord telling me that they remain his Churches regardless. The Church has seized fighting the devil and have concentrated and therefore made success out of fighting themselves and fellow ministers of the same faith. That is why a believer can be a staunch member of a particular Church and get attacked by the enemy, yet the pastor of the ministry will still boldly claim that - "*nobody gets sick in my Church, they only bring sickness from other Churches here.*" I've heard this so many times and it is totally wrong. Forgive me to think that this is a very naive message and reaction to a hurting and afflicted soul. It does not matter how a sickness started, what matters is that Christ healed it even before it started. I believe this is the reason why God does not speak to many preachers as he used to before, yet they cannot see that God is no longer speaking to and through them as before. Otherwise why would a dedicated member of your ministry get sick and God does not reveal it to you as the spiritual head over that Church, yet God reveals it to other preachers who may not even have met the afflicted individual for the first time. Well I'm responding from experience because it happened to me which I've already narrated in this book.

Ministers of God should seek to remind themselves every day that they must stay conscious that the Church is all about Christ and not whatever name they care to make or whatever preference that they'd assume is right. Christ must be the model while we (as ministers) play the role like Jesus. They say when a child grows in a home where the parents always criticise others, they learn how to criticise people as well. It's just natural and in the same way when a believer gets stock in a Church where the pastor criticises other people, they automatically learn the same. This was one enormous mistake I made in the past as I endeavour to correct myself by seeking wisdom in environments that admonish and encourage real change. When the Spirit of the Lord departed from Saul he did not know. It was his servants that told him - [1 Samuel 16:14-15]. It is important for men of God who should actually be servants to the Church of Christ to understand the times, but it is even more important for men of God to seek a renewal of the mind as they endeavour to become servants of God and the Church instead. The book of [1 Corinthians 3:9] tells us that – "For we are labourers together with God: ye are God's husbandry, [ye are] God's building." If we are '*labourers together*' with God, this implies that we are fellow workers or fellow servants with God because Christ served the Church (albeit as Jesus). If Apostle Paul did not write this unbelievable testament or if it was not recorded in the Holy Bible and I wrote it in this book, somebody may surely have tagged this author with the word *spurious* or worse still *insanity*. All men eventually and inevitably become servants of something. Some men become servants of self, some become servants of wealth, and others could become servants of wife and family. As a man you must be serving something or someone but the servants of God become the servants of the Church automatically. This is when and how they can truly discern 'faults' gradually creeping into their hearts or minds and ministry and then try to curtail it. A spirit that condemns the work of God in a *disguised and/or in an open* manner must be questioned and the day the Lord stops speaking to any of his ministers about the challenges forthcoming to their ministry, they may end up struggling to fulfil their calling. What I have done right now having published this book successfully is a huge part of my ministry or service to God, to help heal and correct the Church. I am not an apostle or a prophet, I am not even a pastor as I type this book, my experiences may be limited in ministry yet the truth is glaring as we endure these challenges rather than enjoying them in our Churches. This possibly limited scope however has clearly not deterred me from serving my God in my own way hence I express myself by writing to the glory of God. As recorded in the New Living Translation of the Holy Bible, Jesus (the Christ) said this to his disciples in [Matthew 20:25-28] – "But Jesus called them together and said, 'You know that in this world kings are tyrants, and officials lord it over the people beneath them. {Verse 26} But among you it should be quite different. Whoever wants to be a leader among you must be your servant, {Verse 27} and whoever wants to be first must become your slave. {Verse 28} For even I, the Son of Man, came here not to be served but to serve others, and to give my life as a ransom for many." I still cannot believe that Jesus really said this because it is very remarkable and largely identify with this sub-chapter. Many pastors in today's Church see service as slander without realising that service is ministry. A lot of pastors get on the altar everyday with the motive to frighten the Church with their recurrent and dreaded old tales of hell fire without checking their own lives to ascertain if they're more at risk than the members of their ministry they preach to regarding this. In so doing they try to shove fear and the tremors of its eventual aftermath down the throats of their loyal members who also willingly swallow the results down without counting the cost. This is *food-for-thought* for them to ponder through in detail. We must advocate the love of Christ over the fear of devil thereby filling our hearts with the resistant power to barricade the streets of our minds from being constantly vulnerable to the atrocities being coined by the enemy. The Church currently seems like a political scene. It now appears to be a joke like most of our friends' exhibit on Facebook and the reality is that the real Facebook is actually referred to by some as the '*fake-book*' because people tend to live a made-up life on Facebook. It's like sharing the secret story of your life in public and the truth is that nobody can share the complete story of their life because you can't remember all anyway. Regardless as much as you even remember, you're only willing to share as much as you deem decent enough to share. The Church is playing this disguised game of '*non-transparency*' today.

The closest description to being a *servant of God* is probably being referred to as the *boy of God* rather than a *man of God* because addressing yourself as the *boy of God* will probably keep your attitude in check, reminding you that you're under Christ in the Church as a servant. The title of *man of God* has caged some and made them become irreverently equal to God. This is why I call myself the *boy of God* and being such, I have no need waiting for a man to decide or determine whether I can or qualify to work for my Father in heaven or not and although men may not think that I am qualified to work for God (I'm just assuming), yet God has qualified me to serve him through my books, ministry and other endeavours which I do diligently. This way I could proudly glorify my God who has qualified me, not men who indirectly want me to glorify them for what they have not done. A lot of men want you to magnify them first and then they can now glorify God for you, but I love glorifying my God directly and not through anybody. In hindsight I consider these experiences malign and inappropriately unacceptable. Having been a very dedicated member of a particular Church for over four years, and then decided not to attend Church service there for over four straight weeks, no leading member in the Church bothered to find out what had happened to me (if anything) and I was a very known face amongst the congregation. It gave me a picture that I am either irrelevant in the Church or possibly unwanted there because there may be more important members who engage more than I do in financial support to the Church. In this same Church I had applied to join a department twice and not once was I contacted regarding it until after I quit attendance, then the calls started coming in to the point that even the pastor rang me eventually after over five weeks and at which point I had already moved on from them in my mind. I've therefore come to the conclusion that today's Church is clogged and surely saturated with more talking, bragging, shouting, threats, bullying and marketing of ministries for arguably financial gain rather than it is for the gospel of Christ. Also being in Church leadership as a minister of God serving in whatever office does not exonerate or excuse anyone from Church membership. As a Church leader, you're still the number one member of the ministry you preside over. You must be a *leading-member*, rather than a *leading-leader*. As a leading-member you make yourself a deep-rooted part of the ministry, which means that you understand the experiences of ordinary members or worshipers who are not actually ordinary because you are one with them in Christ and must align yourselves together to accomplish this task of preaching the gospel.

On the far contrary, as a leading-leader you're at the very top and have no clue what challenges your members go through serving under your very own watch. This position does not truly define you as a servant of God and Church hence other worshippers in *your* ministry are not members of one body together because as things fall apart, the leading centre of the ministry cannot hold. Therefore the Church leader is a member first before acclaiming the office you function in. Your membership role and responsibilities cannot be undermined as much as your leadership role. The reality now is that a lot of ministers no longer seek to satisfy that first and original calling as a member of the household of God, rather achievements in ministry now seems to be based on enhancing the size of the Church congregation. Instead of being passionate about reaching the unreached and telling the untold about Jesus, we tend to deviate into unscrupulous and unethical matters. We neglect calls to reach the people of Iraq, Iran, Pakistan, North Korea, Kuwait, Syria, Afghanistan and the like. We plant our Churches in safe havens – UK, USA, Canada etcetera, proving that we're not ready to die for the Christ who we preach about otherwise why can't we (as the Church) or the pastors organise ourselves and in our songs of faith match together to Syria and the like to declare the gospel of Christ with authority, power and boldness; thereby curtailing the insurgency of these Islamic militants by the word and supremacy of God. If we can't do this, then do we really believe in God as we claim to be? I'd not think so if I were in God's position, but thank God I'm not and that's why he's prompted me to write this letter to the Church. Every member of the Church today is scared of an adventure in Christ, yet we'd venture or rather dare to stand on the altar of God and declare how much we're 'bold as a lion' in our own eyes. We really need to look at ourselves today as a Church and rethink our failing strategies for this gospel. Terrorism is sadly spreading like wildfire, faster than the gospel and the same territories that terrorism has captured today were the same territories once conquered by the apostles of Jesus (the Christ). Today the Church has given them away in fear and in disgusting shame. Believers waste their time and resources preaching to fellow believers instead of reaching out to the Jews, Muslims, Hindus and people of other religions or unbelievers. Apostle Paul wrote in [Romans 15:20] – "Yea, so have I strived to preach the gospel, not where Christ was named, lest I should build upon another man's foundation." He identified that preaching the gospel in the regions where Christ had already reached during his ministry (as Jesus) on earth would be no longer necessary to achieving and fulfilling his requirements as a minister of God. He was less concerned about the unfounded principles in the modern day Church of marketing for Church crowds, but rather his focus was geared towards reaching for lost souls in areas that the gospel had not been preached. Today we call our ministries 'global or international ministries' yet we end up within the walls of the western world. When did global become local? We must understand the distinction the global ministry has over the local one. This urge and need makes me look forward to a time and season when the real servants of God will gather together like Paul and Silas to go into the vilest ends of the earth, planting Churches, healing the sick, raising the dead and performing all manner of miracles, signs and wonders for the gospel and to the glory of Christ. The works and undisputed power of the Holy Spirit should convince the people in these most dangerous and terror-prone regions that Christ is the Lord. This is only when the focus will be reengineered towards taking the kingdoms of the earth and redefining them through seasoned transformation and renewal of the mind into our very sole purpose, thereby winning souls as a community of Christ and for Christ if we truly believe in Christ. The Church is currently experiencing and ridiculed by the challenges of rife misplaced and frivolous priorities and this must be ended. I consider people like the Reverend Cannon Andrew White and I am particularly inspired by such. He is a great example to the Church for the real meaning of servitude, not sitting back in the safe and secure United Kingdom or the United States of America and bragging all day about power if it cannot extend outside these borders. If power is power, then show it in where it's really needed not within safe and secure boundaries.

This is the reason why most men of God will not help their members grow in ministry immediately they have an inclination that there is a calling of God on their life. Instead of encouraging them they get busy thinking (I suppose) that they may leave their ministry and go on to grow a much greater and the real global ministry. They forget that the grace is from God, not from man and therefore nobody can stop nobody. So it's all about them, not all about spreading the word of God and the gospel of Christ. This is why the 'evangelism department' is dysfunctional in many Churches today, yet this is the most important department in any Church. Some pastors even try to enslave their members psychologically, subdue them and/or restrict them for ages. Unknowingly they attempt to kill their call, but the Holy Spirit gives his people the wisdom to know when to make a positive move or leave and where to go. Some men of God are best at telling Church members that there is a strong calling on and in their life yet they are '*intentionally*' not very good at helping these members actualise and fulfil those God's divine callings or purposes for their life. They stop themselves from allowing God to use them to train a kingdom-warrior. The same group (and certainly not all) will still remind the members sitting in the Church pews how other pastors saw and told them that they had a calling for the ministry and never assisted/helped them. They tell members how they were forgotten in the back seats of the Church. However they will intentionally refuse to see that they are now doing the same and these members can't complain because pastors are quick to '*threaten*' the members that God may deal with them *when they speak the truth about their divisive strategies* to restrain them from their call. The '*live and let live*' mantra has been thrown into the garbage for the convenience of such leaders. But I've always known that our Lord is not a beast like they make God look like, neither is he a wicked God or any cookie-monster who waits for occasion to destroy us like some of our pastors '*inevitably*' tell us. That description sounds to me like the devil and I have used the word *inevitably* because the Bible reminds us that "…out of the abundance of the heart the mouth speaketh" - [Matthew 12:34] and [Luke 6:45].

Many pastors expect Church members to be *ordinary* 'members' in their ministry for donkey years and that is called '*service*' to them. They forget they passed through the same routine and they still try to subject members through the same mental chaos, forgetting that the only reason why God allowed them to pass through it was so that they could lead others through it. They threaten them in a disguised language so that the members do not realise that it's a threat. They encourage divorce among quarrelling couples in their ministry and against what the Holy Bible teaches in [Matthew 5:32, Matthew 19:6] and [Mark 10:7-9], rather than teaching reconciliation and love within the Church; however faced with the same marital challenges they divorce not until the devil divorces them. They proudly confess to the Church their joy at separating the husbands from what they call their *unruly* wives. However when their own wives become unruly, they separate not; rather they drag the unruly demonic spirit behind the chaos along. If they then know the right thing to do in their own case, why not in another's? How well we practise what we truly preach indeed in our Churches. I'd humbly advise such leaders of the Church to study the New Living Translation of [Matthew 23] from the beginning till the end of this chapter because it speaks directly to them. In [Matthew 23:3] Jesus said – "So practice and obey whatever they say to you, but don't follow their example. For they don't practice what they preach." If this book will make just one of such pastor(s) to think, reconsider their strategies and change, then it's a great success. These pastors even warn members that if they must leave the ministry, they must leave alone. They tell leaving-members not to take *staying-members* away otherwise God may punish them or they may suffer in their own ministry, but these leaders refuse to remember that those their members were once members '*at*' and '*from*' other Churches. They don't see it that they took another Church's members, prompting me to wonder in awe 'what has the Church turned into'? A business centre or a Church of God?! They blind the eye of their minds to the reality that it is the Spirit of God that convicts people and therefore telling members to stay in a particular ministry/Church becomes an embarrassing sermon to preach on God's altar since we cannot of our self-will convince who the Lord has not convinced to stay. When these leaders need money, they will call for seeds in Church and tell believers all sorts of sweet stories to bring them to come out and give or make a vow, however when such believers cannot afford to fulfil or pay their vows the same pastors get on the altar of God to criticise them saying – "I never forced anybody out, you came out by yourself and now you have refused to pay and you will keep struggling until you pay your vow." Utterly disgusting words that are clearly not from God. A real believer would know that they must fulfil vows they have made to God, not to pastors but these pastors get upset as though Church members owed them money for a business deal that probably became unfruitful. They condemn the members before a God that has not yet condemned them and this is the most annoying part of their *business*. Could our pastors please be conscious of their words on the altar of God in our selfish bids to usurp funds from the members of God's household? I believe a preacher really called by God into the ministry would not deviate from the gospel message by prioritising preaching about money above the main goal of their calling. I'm confident that more than half of the money-preachers seen on our Christian television networks are not anointed men of God, that's actually a fact. They were people who dared to try ministry and once they had some success in it, they started claiming that they were called by God and the proof of their calling seems to be the evidence that their money-advertising ministries are flourishing. That is why they see the call of God on their members as a challenge to them and their ministry. Many Church leaders probably believe that restricting their members or trying to restrict them from manifesting '*over*' them in ministry is their mind's priority, yet it will never stop God from bringing the word he spoke through his servants (including them) to come to pass because they refuse to remember this Scripture in [Romans 11:29] – "For the gifts and calling of God [are] without repentance". This Scripture assures anybody that their gifts and calling are eternal and as such will never change as long as they remain absolutely enthusiastic, faithful and committed to it. I have consciously used the word 'over' above (...manifesting 'over' them in ministry...) because this seems to be their greatest fear. Even Church buildings which are *physical* may change from time to time because of expansion or for so many other reasons, but our positions in Christ which is '*spiritual*' will never change.

Therefore even though the Church should not have been divided into various units, walking into a new Church building does not necessarily entail that we're in a different environment because we're still in the presence of God. Every Church a believer walks into any day is for a particular or specific purpose or phase of their life to be fulfilled. *If Christ is the head of the Church, then it means that the Church is not a place, it is a person and that person has a head which is a symbol of ruler-ship. In the same light a nation is not a place, it is a person (usually a male figure) that multiplied and dominated a place. This is why every nation has a ruler, head, president or prime minister. Every nation started as a real human being that eventually became a people or group of people. That is also why when we think about a place, we think about a certain people with a unique culture. For instance the land of Israel was a person named Jacob but today we call or address Israel as a nation or a place but in reality they are a people. The Church is also 'Jesus multiplied, all with one head which is Christ'.* This is why I have written this journal to explain these things because it holds a catalogue of some of the main challenges of the Church, albeit not completely because the author has avoided issues like *divorce which seems to be the new word for marriage in our Churches* today and I'm sure most of us know members of the Church who have *celebrated* a divorce or more, even some of our pastors unfortunately. I've also avoided certain challenges like *death* which is a kind of spiritual divorce that also manifests itself in the physical because somebody's spirit leaves his body and then his flesh cannot stand without the spirit. So their spirit goes up while their body (flesh) comes down. *Spiritually so, when we accept Christ, our spirit(s) ascend while the flesh descends.* This is why in the school of life, we don't graduate because our graduation day will be the day we die. Let us then be aware that the spirit is as important as the physical because if they were not equally relevant, God will have no need to manifest in the physical as well as in the Spirit. When I was growing up, I would never have imagined or wished to be a preacher. I actually disliked pastors and saw them in this particular light where you behaved in a very weird manner with a somewhat gruesome demeanour until I found myself in a mental state of mind in 1995 which I consider normal today because everybody will surely have a rainy day and when it rains, it really pours down. Then I had no choice but to embrace pastors because the doctors could not help with my condition at the time. It was a revelation and we only make progress in life by revelation. God used a serious challenge I had to show me the need for real servants of God. This is why destinies must be encouraged as well because procrastination kills the time and Scripture reminds us that 'the time is short' [1 Corinthians 7:29]. The Holy Bible says in [Ephesians 5:16] - "Redeeming the time, because the days are evil". Therefore we'd always have to remember the popular saying that 'today was tomorrow yesterday' hence the need to train even more preachers and send them out without bias for the preparation of the coming of our Lord. This is the role of our ministers and pastors, not killing gifts and talents selfishly. When I had that dream where a man standing on the altar in a very large Church shouted out these words from that altar '*You are Natural Resources in the hand of God*', I couldn't recognise anyone in that large congregation but myself and my family. I couldn't immediately understand this dream so I sent an email to one of my pastors regarding that dream and I've refused to delete that email for a testimony because I was expecting some sort of revelation or encouragement from him but never got none until the Lord explained it to me. Considering these challenges we can deduce that the body of Christ (the Church) is not in a perfect state at the moment, however we must also remember that '*the perfecting of the saints*' will only be done by Christ - [Ephesians 5:26-27] and may well happen when Christ comes to judge the world of their righteous deeds and of their sins. Yet we must keep building zealous character in the Churches.

The very significant thing about how I cherish prophesies made over my life is that the passion stirs me to keep holding impromptu deliverance services at my home just for my family before the Lord led me to start the ministry. Prior to this time I also held some imaginary services where I make declarations of victory, healing and freedom over an imaginary audience, casting out demons and healing all manner of sicknesses and diseases in the name of Jesus (the Christ). I preached as though I was actually preaching in a Church yet I was not talking to physical people. It felt quite bizarre sometimes but I had to keep doing it as a born warrior and the words in [Ephesians 6:10-20] give a detailed picture of how to guard yourself as a warrior of Christ and the Church. In [2 Timothy 2:2-4] the Holy Bible says – "And the things that thou hast heard of me among many witnesses, the same commit thou to faithful men, who shall be able to teach others also. {Verse 3} Thou therefore endure hardness, as a good soldier of Jesus Christ. {Verse 4} No man that warreth entangleth himself with the affairs of this life; that he may please him who hath chosen him to be a soldier." From the second verse of this Scripture it can therefore be determined that our race is not a selfish race. It says - 'the same commit thou to *faithful men, who shall be able to teach others also'*. This means as a minister of God if you don't teach others by training them, you are unfaithful. Then it encourages you to be strong as a soldier of Christ. In [2 Timothy 4:5] it gives a similar but more specific picture thus – "But watch thou in all things, endure afflictions, do the work of an evangelist, make full proof of thy ministry." Again you can only make full proof of your ministry through being watchful, enduring afflictions and being an evangelist. I recently considered my family history up to my late Dad's children and was able to see the struggles in the family line. I ascertained that although it is quite a prominent family who have some major contacts and who make efforts to break-through in life, yet little or no major achievements were recorded. Most people on that lineage have sicknesses and diseases in their bodies including their children. I was able to comprehend that the minimum requirement to become a member of the family was *asthma* which (to man) is an incurable disease and then poverty which can seem an impossible challenge (for man) sometimes. Also I was able to see that in spite of very hard work and all efforts, most of the people either died quite young or poor at the time of their death. I sought a change and told the Lord that I and my own seed with the generation after me will not suffer this recurrent curse any longer and spiritually I put a stop to it in the name of Jesus.

So I tried to fast and pray more often, started sowing radical seeds and engaging in numerous spiritual activities. I've sowed thousand pound seeds of faith; made and fulfilled vows, paid tithes, gave offerings and sowed other special seeds. This is not unique or exceptional because every very devoted believer who understands the Scripture does these and the intention is definitely not to brag about these acts of faith, however I don't need a pastor to remind me to sow. I was desperate to come out from the evil altars of the family. I got to a point where I once went on to initiate a change of name using the UK Deed Poll office and then changed my mind about using the new name I had requested. So I had to ring the UK Deed Poll office again when I was advised to simply destroy those papers/documents they had sent to me. Eventually I did not use the names I'd instructed then to change for me which automatically made that change null and void. Sometimes I borrowed or even took out loans just to sow seeds in Churches towards the propagation of the word and the kingdom of God. I was desperate to break every evil spell and demonic connections I had with my late Dad's family line and I still am. I gave away everything I considered valuable to me thinking perhaps that my charity will speak for me before God. In all this God still remained silent, although he guided me through very turbulent times and through the difficult and different raw schools of life that I passed through. Every time I came in contact with an anointed servant of God, my only prayer-anthem became – "Lord I need your anointing and power in my life." I was very desperate and in awe of the power of the Holy Ghost even until this day. I envied genuine servants of God and I mean the good kind of envy because I cherished that power that flowed through them. Hence I determined to start visiting more Churches to experience God's power in a multiplied manner. I was then able to understand that God is movement and movement is God. It is only the living that can move and because life is God, therefore movement signifies life and if God is that life, then movement is God. This ideology and spiritual-spectacle (if you may) has helped me to learn from and grow whilst observing different men and servants of God closely.

The Church is the place where we speak the truth in love as we grow up to become more like Christ and this is recorded in [Ephesians 4:15] – "But speaking the truth in love, may grow up into him in all things, which is the head, [even] Christ." Some of our pastors in our Churches always preach that if you want something different you must do something different, and at the same time they don't believe leaving the building (called 'their Church') for another Church constitutes one of the different things that believers may have to do for a change to occur. This contradicts the gospel they preach and I'm aware that this book may not be popular amongst pastors because they love telling the Church the truth but never like hearing it themselves. When God wants to do a new thing in a believer's life, a lot of times he leads them to a new Church for a new manifestation and for a fresh breath. This may not sound interesting but staying in one Church premises for so long can sometimes make worshipping God *seem* boring, just like staying in the same job for so long. You could easily get fed up hearing a particular kind of message over and over again. This is the reason why people graduate from schools and from courses because you're expected to grow and upgrade exactly the same way that the apostles of Christ had to move from one Church location in a city to another Church location in another city in order to execute the message of the gospel effectively, however the only difference is that it was the same Church for them. Today we have the diverse and unnameable kinds of Churches, thanks to the exploits of religion in our Christianity. But worshipping God is bigger than any Church building or Church rivalry because it constitutes a genuine, heartfelt, undying relationship being exhibited. In [1 John 4:1] we're advised – "Beloved, believe not every spirit, but try the spirits whether they are of God: because many false prophets are gone out into the world." No one believer can achieve this by sitting down in the same Church building. Meanwhile staying in the same Church has its advantages and sometimes disadvantages as much as hopping around Churches do. We must therefore understand that every choice we make in life must have its pros and cons. This message may not be very welcomed by many but every word of truth will have to be criticised by somebody, particularly for it to gain a credible status. As a believer if you were not born in a specific or particular building called Church, why would you consider dying there if Christ has given you a commission to preach to your own world?! This is why the Church is not that building that you worship in, the Church is the presence of God and God can choose to build his presence right in your own home. My advice is that we do not restrict God's move. We've come through an era of divisions and Church politics to eventually and unfortunately become the political Church today and this is why we've managed to encourage gay marriages, envy, strife, malice, bullying, gossiping and hatred, whore-mongering, we build gangs in our Churches and encourage segregations. We're supposed to be apolitical yet today we're more like the political parties which serves as a heavy impediment to any progress in or for the Church. We live and breathe help for Churches instead of using our Churches for help and we jeopardise the message of the gospel of Christ by turning the Church of God into the new business venture. Again I ask how we developed this gang mentality that have crawled into our Churches?! We now celebrate other people's dearth, misfortunes and failures in pretence as though we had sympathy for them. The moment a member leaves a ministry, the Church leader automatically assumes that they're the enemy of their ministry and becomes unfriendly in every way possible. Oh boy! Have we successfully and dramatically but uncharacteristically embraced the phrase David used to mourn the death of Saul and his son Jonathan in [2 Samuel 1:25-27] - "*how are the mighty fallen?!*" What has happened to the founding ethics of the Church? As a result our local communities are now comfortable with evil reports because they're more based around the local pubs much more than around the local Churches. This thought-stimulating catastrophe will be squarely and further addressed as another book.

The place of Experiences and Understanding:

Your experiences have absolutely nothing to do with your age. I'm not talking about the process you go through when bringing your gifts/ talents to life, I'm talking about using your '*common sense prowess*' and the challenges that come with it. Your experiences exercise your common sense by putting them into action. My late mum would very often remind us that '*common sense is not always common*'. It has nothing to do with how old a person is but has all to do with what you've been through in life and how intelligently they've handled it. Sometimes I consider academic education irrelevant and I know quite well that my parents would have disagreed with me if they were still alive. What's the point of being educated if we'd still pass through the school of life or what I may deduce as 'street-education' even though I really dislike that terminology?! It's the school of life that builds your personality and character (not academic education), and these two (personality and character) may be able to determine your common sense level depending on a number of factors which will inevitably include the enormity of the tasks the individual has to deal with at any given moment through life. If you think I'm wrong it's okay, but why do we have a lot of educated people void of common sense? I also discovered that a good number of the greatest men in life did not need to go through the university system. I've also come to the understanding that going through a university does not make one educated, however though, it *certifies* you. Therefore what educates you are your experiences. What you paid for (as education) was actually the certificate. I discovered that going through the university had absolutely no business with my divine calling or my inspiration in life. I started to think and therefore believe that God only allowed me to go through the university so that once I '*become*', no venom of destiny-killers could ever get at me through their criticisms. It is also possible to go through the university and remain a stark-illiterate. By the grace of God I've studied through my Holy Bible a number of times and discerned that even the greatest men in the Holy Bible had no academic education of any sort. Jesus Christ (the greatest) was not learned yet he became a teacher - [John 7:15]. Experience is the greatest education in life and it cannot be bought, whereas academic education is on sale in many places across the globe. Experience is therefore the life-Bible of any man. After the Holy Bible, experience is the next greatest book on earth that anybody could ever read, and it may also be possible or safe to say that 'before the Holy Bible experience leads' because naturally people may gain experiences before they gain knowledge from the Holy Bible.

From the foregoing experience is hence the *growth-Bible* or the Bible for growing up. Through gruesome experiences you learn the principle of 'giving'...that you can give away some of your troubles. That's why I strongly believe that anybody who criticizes 'giving' in any form is unknowledgeable and lacks the kind of common sense that I write about but 'giving' must not be the core of our sermons in the Church. Non-academic related illiteracy is a kind of poverty and poverty is in the mind rather than in one's bank balance. If our wealth and provision must be supernatural then we must think supernatural. Poverty is a thought and as such has nothing to do with what you have because poverty or riches is determined by the wealth of your experiences and understanding. Being Jesus was the experience and riches of Christ and being God was his understanding, that is why Christ qualifies as Lord and saviour today. He had an experience physically and an understanding spiritually. He went through the school of life and death, triumphing over them. It was through the school of experiences and understanding that I got the discernment about the title of this book and some other forces or acts like to 'push', 'envy' and some other challenges that a believer may face daily, good or bad. If 'push' meant *praying until something happens*, that something may be unwanted, catastrophic or critical. Most times when we pray, we find out that we're spiritually attacked the more. That's 'something' but is it the desired result(s)? I'd really not think so. Therefore 'push' could mean *praying until **success** happens*. It's a similar comprehension about 'envy'. Simply put envy has two faces: good envy and bad envy. Good envy is simply admiration. When you believe someone is just classic, posh, crystal, royalty and the like. Here you're very happy for them and what they do. Good envy lifts people before your eyes and it's a spiritual shine because you just love and admire them unreservedly. Good envy encourages and promotes, it appreciates and can be quite peaceful at heart. Good envy is everything because you learn for your own encouragement. It can be a lifestyle. That gives up the picture of bad envy. The very simple understanding is that it kills you, rather than your target. When envy becomes bad, you'd never see great enterprise and call it great. Bad envy is when you hate what someone is doing for themselves for no reason whatsoever, yet you couldn't tell them they made you feel the way you feel because they are not the problem, but you. The truth is that every human being on earth experiences both from time to time but the power of choice within us either encourages or curtails them. I advise my audience (the readers of this book) not to let either of them dominate your spirit(s). The low bill is this: where *good-envy* is dominant (in you), sometimes it could make you feel inferior thereby neglecting or undermining your own innate strengths or abilities and where *bad-envy* is dominant (in you), you die slowly. They're both choices and you would need to strike a great balance. Everything in life has a surface meaning and a deep meaning and most times for understanding to be justified, we must endeavour to ascertain the hidden meanings because more often than not they are the true meaning. Sometimes it may mean that we'd have to over-think, but being trained by the English man will always entail that you read between the lines, in the spirit and then in the physical yet revelations come from God.

Therefore to understand your experiences, it may be imperative to study yourself first because what Christ had to deal with in life (as Jesus) may not necessarily be what we will deal with. It's easy to see the gifts and resilience in somebody else, but very difficult to see the gifts in yourself. The thing is somebody is somewhere watching for your '*making*' to encourage themselves and somebody is equally watching for your '*downfall*' to encourage themselves. Either way your life is a message of encouragement and hope to somebody every day. I've been a son and now I'm a father, I may not be an old man but I think I'm old enough to know what I'm saying. A lot of our biggest problems as human beings (not just for believers) are often our blessings in disguise. Your greatest weakness is usually your greatest strength. I heard one of my pastors once say that '*your worst child is your best child.*' Equally your worst experiences will often turn out to be your best experiences. The things I considered my biggest nightmares are all gradually turning into my best gifts/talents and my writing skills are a great example. People are wondering who you really are but no one can understand you until they come to face your challenges. But how can they even understand you when you don't even understand yourself? Study yourself as you strive to emulate the personality of Christ. But it'd take a lifetime of experiences to understand yourself because you were made for 'only' God to understand you. I discovered that I still don't know me because as human beings we evolve everyday. Sounds irresponsible yet very true. Being a believer does not mean that you are no longer natural or does not mean that you are super-human, it just means that you have the divine nature to be in the flesh and at the same time be in the spirit. I can switch in just one second and I love it because it reminds me that God is in charge of this vessel right here, not me. Radicalism was equally the lifestyle of Jesus (who became the Christ) while he walked the earth. The Bible records in [Matthew 21:12-14] – "And Jesus went into the temple of God, and cast out all them that sold and bought in the temple, and overthrew the tables of the moneychangers, and the seats of them that sold doves, {Verse 13} And said unto them, It is written, My house shall be called the house of prayer; but ye have made it a den of thieves. {Verse 14} And the blind and the lame came to him in the temple; and he healed them." That sounds very radical to me. So one minute he was normal and the very next moment Jesus (the Christ) was acting erratically as he suddenly switched after he saw those traders and moneychangers at the *temple of God* selling doves and he overthrew their tables before he went on to conduct a healing and deliverance service/meeting in the same place. He did not do this to discourage their diligence, his priority was reverencing the house of God. That God is in charge of the believer's life does not mean that we neglect hard work and cling to laziness because I've heard people saying this very often that 'the only place where success comes before work is in the dictionary'. *You're not a summary of whoever gave birth to you or wherever you grew up in.* Different children are raised in a family, yet their secrets remain diverse. This is why the family is a very complex societal structure because in every family there is a major secret, shame, challenge or embarrassment that probably remains undisclosed. Nobody will tell you this secret except they are divinely-insane. Every family on earth has its own major embarrassment, just like the secret embarrassment in the personal life of every human being. You don't have to agree with me, but the reality remains that it's there right now and you've heard it before that one of the greatest apostles of Christ (Apostle Paul) went into ministry with infirmity in his body. That was his own shame. Our victory over life will always come from sharing those embarrassments to the world for a tangible testimony to God's glory. This is why I write. The moment you summon the courage to share about a shame you have or once had to endure, you stand tall over that shame. This (again) is why I will keep writing and then I will keep speaking too. I believe that writing is a kind of freedom of speech because it involves making expressions about oneself and life.

The identity that became Christ was a superior person but whether you prosper or you don't prosper, there is a time in your life when you will feel inferior. It is a feeling, it is not reality because the Christ that you were made in his image is superior and again what influences these feelings are mainly the people around you. This is why we must choose right because God's blessing is not your wealth, God's blessing is a person who is the *right* person sent to help you or bless your life. God uses a person to bless you and the devil uses a person to curse and afflict you with recurrent demonic/spiritual or even physical attack(s). There are agents of light as much as there are agents of darkness and we must discern how to deal with each group. When Jesus said - "…pray for them which despitefully use you, and persecute you" in [Matthew 5:44], he left the prayer line open to choice and that choice was between either praying for their peace or praying for vengeance on them. Jesus was particularly specific all through the instructions that preceded this one. I therefore believe he intended the 'prayer of vengeance' here even though he did not spell this out, because we must always be on the offensive against the enemies that come against us. Knowing this now, I believe that the preparation for tomorrow stands on the platform of yesterday. The things that looked or sounded like gibberish to people regarding our past, may become relevant and very meaningful to God as finished products. I look at my past today and see an empty vessel but still I know that by tomorrow I'd look at today (as yesterday) and probably see the same. Circumstances and events always do improve and change for the better. I had an experience growing up, my Dad would flog us with the cane when we were quite young for attending Church services with our mum. He was a core heathen at the time and the drama went on for years until (I believe) he had a personal encounter with God. Prior to this (assumed encounter with God), my Dad would always say (even on live television broadcast) that - "Jesus Christ is a mere concept". However out of the blues the tide suddenly changed for good as he became the one scolding us for not attending Church services when we were required to. During these years he began to have an understanding of the truth and I believe that was when he read through the Holy Bible for the first time. It may have taken quite some experiences for him to be able to understanding or comprehend that *in me is Christ and in Christ I'm Jesus*. Scripture tells us in [Colossians 3:11b] – "…but Christ *is* all, and in all." *Christ is all* talks about Jesus and *Christ in all* talks about Holy Spirit and his indwelling presence in us. The Holy Bible writes in [Galatians 3:27] that – "For as many of you as have been baptized into Christ have put on Christ." If it then be true that we are wearing Christ through baptism, then it is a verified truth that we are in Christ. Therefore Christ becomes a covering as seen in [Romans 13:14] – "But put ye on the Lord Jesus Christ, and make not provision for the flesh, to [fulfil] the lusts [thereof]."

The Apostle Paul began his preaching ministry with a sickness in his body as mentioned earlier and I could not understand why a great apostle would have sickness in his body yet be able to heal the sick. Apostle Paul actually became proud of his sickness boasting thus as recorded in the New King James Version of [2 Corinthians 11:30] – "If I must boast, I will boast in the things which concern my infirmity." Instead of shame, he bragged through his challenges and in the same version of the Holy Bible (NKJV), Apostle Paul continued from [2 Corinthians 12:5] – "Of such a one I will boast; yet of myself I will not boast, except in my infirmities." The only reason behind his boasting is that he sought to glorify God knowing that what he experienced were mere symptoms and as such they were not permanent. Most times men of God prophesied to me about my calling I was either having one affliction or going through another. In an affliction God gave me the vision (not a dream) of ministry in my living room while I was wide awake and the very same day I visited a Church for the first time and the prophet of God there confirmed the same word from God and prior to this day he'd never met me anywhere before. I believed, yet, I was too scared to start even after the Lord had spoken to me directly. *I strongly believe that you cannot give what you don't have but the symptoms of the affliction I was facing was not a confirmation that I was not yet healed, however it was a confirmation that I may not have believed that I was healed even though I knew I was.* This was my psychological drama until I read through Apostle Paul's words in the book of Galatians and it started making sense to me why God would say *"start now"* and I quote from [Galatians 4:12-14] – "Brethren, I beseech you, be as I *am*; for I am as ye *are*: ye have not injured me at all. {Verse 13} Ye know how through infirmity of the flesh I preached the gospel unto you at the first. {Verse 14} And my temptation which was in my flesh ye despised not, nor rejected; but received me as an angel of God, *even* as Christ Jesus." In the (New International Version) the same reads – "{Verse 12} I plead with you, brothers, become like me, for I became like you. You have done me no wrong. {Verse 13} As you know, it was because of an illness that I first preached the gospel to you. {Verse 14} Even though my illness was a trial to you, you did not treat me with contempt or scorn. Instead, you welcomed me as if I were an angel of God, as if I were Christ Jesus himself." From {Verse 13} we'd conclude that a sickness '*forced*' Apostle Paul to take up his Holy Bible and walk the word of God. If my understanding is right, he did this unwillingly. Whether he was referring to the encounter he had with the Lord or some other afflictions he may have had in his body remains a mystery, however what we do know is that he took up the Holy Bible in pain and preached home his healing.

Therefore Apostle Paul being flesh yet '*lived in the spirit and therefore walked in the spirit*' - [Galatians 5:25], into the very successful ministry that he had and became the victorious leader that he was. This meant that by experience and the understanding that his infirmity was a symbol of his calling, he was not deterred by the discomfort in his body but was rather encouraged by the saving grace that comes from serving Christ. This was why he was able to declare with such authority in [Galatians 6:17] that – "From henceforth let no man trouble me: for I bear in my body the marks of the Lord Jesus." Why would he lay emphasis on his body? I want to believe that through preaching the gospel of Christ, he had received faith to be healed in his body and actually got healed; then and only then was he able to declare his freedom from trouble because he bore the marks of the Lord Jesus in his body. This truth became possible because Apostle Paul through preaching the gospel of Christ through the word of God had been soaked in the word of God, hence the words of the Scripture in [Romans 10:17] thus – "So then faith cometh by hearing, and hearing by the word of God." I believe Apostle Paul was sharing about his health challenges, otherwise how would the '*brethren*' have known about his personal challenges for them to be encouraged? If this were not the case, then I would dare to believe that Apostle Paul must have been plagued with an obvious or *evidently* terminal affliction because this is the only reason why he would speak to the '*brethren*' about an affliction he had that they already knew of. Apostle Paul had saturated his mind with the thoughts and testimonies of an overcomer and regarding this new mind-set he wrote in [2 Corinthians 12:8-10] of the New King James Version – "Concerning this thing I pleaded with the Lord three times that it might depart from me. {Verse 9} And He said to me, 'My grace is sufficient for you, for My strength is made perfect in weakness.' Therefore most gladly I will rather boast in my infirmities, that the power of Christ may rest upon me. {Verse 10} Therefore I take pleasure in infirmities, in reproaches, in needs, in persecutions, in distresses, for Christ's sake. For when I am weak, then I am strong." With this sort of boldness, no infirmity, needs or reproaches could have conquered Paul. This is the lesson that as believers we must understand our experiences and their relevance or the need for them helping to shoot us into our destinies because in Christ (as Jesus) we no longer have *secrets, shame or embarrassments to hide* because our experiences have now become *stories to tell* for Christ to be glorified. Above all, this sub-chapter is some general knowledge for all.

The place of Eternity:

The Church was instituted for service and Apostle Paul in [2 Corinthians 8:23] said – "Whether [any do enquire] of Titus, [he is] my partner and fellowhelper concerning you: or our brethren [be enquired of, they are] the messengers of the churches, [and] the glory of Christ." The Church must therefore be willing and humble enough to produce messengers or servants in service for the glory of Christ to be manifested in full measure towards eternal glory. Therefore no matter how much longer we as a Church wallow in our self-righteousness, we may often be chastised by this truth that 'God is the one who draws men to Jesus', not will-power. But does this undermine evangelism if it means that the unbelievers were destined for destruction from time immemorial? I wouldn't assume such conclusions just yet until we get a clear picture of what God really had in mind when he said this; but from a natural perspective the only way you can get a picture of what people have conceived about you off their minds is time; in the same light we need time for God to unravel his plans in the individual lives he has created. Many times when believers think about eternity, they get into a judgemental mind-set towards unbelievers without thinking back on the words recorded in [John 6:44] – "No man can come to me, except the Father which hath sent me draw him: and I will raise him up at the last day." Jesus was speaking a revelation of God's authority which was being manifested in the lives of men. His words were clear and precise that no one becomes saved except the Father draws him and this then explains to me that even before the foundation of the world, eternity may have already been declared by the Father who arguably could have chosen who and who will make eternity and who will not. That may mean that the unbelievers may just be manifesting a destiny that was already pre-ordained, pre-written, pre-planned and/or panned-out for them from the beginning. But God cannot be wicked to draw some and not draw some. Again as human beings made in the image of God we have been given the mind of God to make our choices according to what we believe is the right way for us and these choices may be summarised between eternal glorification and eternal damnation. This argument may contradict the words in [Acts 13:48] – "And when the Gentiles heard this, they were glad, and glorified the word of the Lord: and as many as **were ordained** to eternal life believed." This again seems to conclude that not all men are appointed to or for eternal life, thereby giving the express impression or possibly confirming the (I believe 'unfounded') notion that God already chose his people for eternity even before the ages began. Someone may also conclude that this is right because Christ has the power to change all men but how come he does not change all? But I want to believe that the many that were '*ordained*' to eternal life are those who have made the right choice(s) for eternal life over eternal damnation. The issue of eternity has made a lot of people more conscious of **leaving life** rather than **living life**. They ponder exiting life rather than existing and enjoying the life. This makes then constantly scared of life-absence and aware of death-presence. If then that Christ is life and the road to eternity, how could we then be scared of life instead of being cared for by the same life that gave us life?! The need to think right may be similar to mandates in men's lives, some have a global, multi-national or what we may call the inter-continental vision from heaven which could be attributed to *life-unlimited* while some others have a local or maybe national mandate therefore they'd probably exhibit a humdrum or prosaic assertion about the person with the global vision which could be attributed to a *life-limited* perspective and *you don't mingle with small thinkers when you're a big talker, neither do you mingle with small talkers when you're a big thinker.* This is hugely because light will always over-shadow darkness. Jesus who became the Christ gave the men God had created a global and heavenly mandate and that global-heavenly mandate is all about life-unlimited.

Eternity is a glorious treasure and therefore an adventure from what I call the realm of Jesus-hood to that of Christ-hood and [2 Corinthians 3:18] tells us – "But we all, with open face beholding as in a glass the glory of the Lord, are changed into the same image from glory to glory, even as by the Spirit of the Lord." The process of eternity is a change process that is able to transform flesh to spirit and that ability is already in man because [2 Corinthians 4:7] says – "But we have this treasure in earthen vessels, that the excellency of the power may be of God, and not of us." Eternity is therefore of God, created and resident in our spirit. For instance you can visit or live in a lot of places during your lifetime but you can only call one home which is probably where you were born. As believers we were born from eternity into eternity. The life that Christ gave us as Jesus on the Cross of Calvary was eternal life and we rely on and live by this life made of God and came from God. The book of [1 John 5:20] explains this – "And we know that the Son of God is come, and hath given us an understanding that we may know him that is true, and we are in him that is true, [even] in his Son Jesus Christ. This is the true God, and eternal life." So it came from God and continues in the earth until we meet the Lord in the air [1 Thessalonians 4:16-17]. Therefore eternity for a believer is home and a realm of experiencing heaven right from the earth even before we get to heaven. This is the distinguishing phenomenon and excelling factor that differentiates the believer as light from the unbeliever as darkness. I remember preaching to my cousin *'Babaa'* and some other people in my dream in the early hours of 13 February 2015, my message was from [Acts 1:8] and I said to him "the Bible says 'And I shall receive power after that the Holy Ghost is come upon me and I shall be witnesses unto the Lord in Jerusalem and in Judea and in Samaria and unto the uttermost ends of the Earth.'" Babaa (my cousin) asked me in that dream – "But who has received this power?" I responded – "Me! I received power after the Holy

Ghost came upon me and now I am the witness of the Lord Jesus Christ all over the world." All the people I was preaching to in that dream just kept staring at me because they could not comprehend the global vision I was attempting to unveil to them that I had acquired through the grace and the power of God. They could simply not visualise or capture the picture I was trying to show them. I don't want to sound derogatory in any way but the mundane or dreary look on their faces just sold them off and I realised that I was preaching to the wrong people and that was when I woke up from that sleep. I was showcasing to them what could be attributed to as an eternal vision from God, but because they held a more local and curtailed view, it became as though I was reading the forecast or the prophecy of a heavy snow storm right in the middle of summer. I just wasn't communicating!! An eternal mind-set has a strong correlation with righteousness which automatically breeds prosperity and [Proverbs 15:6] says – "In the house of the righteous *is* much treasure: but in the revenues of the wicked is trouble." The thought of eternity often frightens people instead of stirring them up in faith because eternal life is the knowledge and fear of God that pushes us towards righteous living with the assurance and hope of a peaceful end in Christ and [John 17:3] identifies that – "And this is life eternal, that they might know thee the only true God, and Jesus Christ, whom thou hast sent." This is an evidence that eternity has to do with the knowledge, the knowing, the mind-set and the understanding of who God really is and the infinitely global vision of the gospel of Christ. We have this summarised in [Psalm 112:1-3] – "Praise ye the LORD. Blessed *is* the man *that* feareth the LORD, *that* delighteth greatly in his commandments. {Verse 2} His seed shall **be mighty upon the earth**: the generation of the upright shall be blessed. {Verse 3} Wealth and riches *shall be* in his house: and his righteousness endureth for ever." A life of eternity begins from the earth. This can also be proven further from Scripture in [Proverbs 11:31] – "Behold, the righteous shall be recompensed in the earth: much more the wicked and the sinner." It encapsulates a holistic understanding and therefore the mind-set of a good life that transcends time and the natural life for the supernatural and everlasting life. When you are manifesting within the will and the framework of God, you are without doubt experiencing eternal life in its fullness and entirety because as much as we believers believe in heaven, the Holy Bible says that we will reign in the earth, as found in [Revelation 5:10] – "And hast made us unto our God kings and priests: and we shall reign on the earth." *In summary, our eternity begins from our reality.*

The place of Seeds and Sacrifices:

This is quite different from charity or love as these (seeds and sacrifices) may be acceptable as direct or indirect forms of worship to God although as much as charities to some extent. **However the distinction is that in charity *'we give'*, in love *'we show and we share'*, then, in seeds *'we sow'* while in sacrifices *'we make'*; in the same way in offerings *'we give'*, in pledges *'we make'*, in vows *'we fulfil'*, in tithes *'we pay'* and in first fruits *'we covenant'*, yet we use all these interchangeably.** Christ has a history that bears the symbol of an incorruptible seed and the image of a sacrifice, hence [Galatians 3:13] defined the testimony thus – "Christ hath redeemed us from the curse of the law, being made a curse for us: for it is written, Cursed [is] every one that hangeth on a tree…" Although Christ never died, yet Christ died as Jesus and this remains about the most incomprehensible yet distinctive truthful conundrums of this generation, many would argue. All through the Scriptures we have read about seeds and sacrifices which subsequently builds a mental picture of their relevance in our faith as believers. Abraham the patriarch obeyed the instruction of God when he attempted to sacrifice his *only* son Isaac and it was accounted to him for righteousness in [Genesis 22:1-18], with Isaac (although) being considered the only son of Abraham (even though he was not) because he was the child of the promise. Similarly a lengthy encyclopaedia for sacrificial giving could be endorsed for David who was a regular in the giving hall of fame. Could it be that David's sacrificial seeds recorded thus in – [1 Chronicles 22:14] "Now, behold, in my trouble I have prepared for the house of the LORD an hundred thousand talents of gold, and a thousand thousand talents of silver; and of brass and iron without weight; for it is in abundance: timber also and stone have I prepared; and thou mayest add thereto", became the light of him being identified to have the resemblance as an angel of God as recorded in [1 Samuel 29:9] – "And Achish answered and said to David, I know that thou [art] good in my sight, as an angel of God: notwithstanding the princes of the Philistines have said, He shall not go up with us to the battle"? Sacrifices provoked God on numerous occasions recorded in the Holy Bible. David made an enormous amount of radical sacrifices and the Holy Bible time and time again accorded him the regard and recognition of being wise like an angel of God in [2 Samuel 14:20] – "To fetch about this form of speech hath thy servant Joab done this thing: and my lord [is] wise, according to the wisdom of an angel of God, to know all [things] that [are] in the earth." He further triggered the mercy of God to the point that God attributed him to being after the heart of God [1 Samuel 13:14] and [Acts 13:22]. These were men who sacrificed regularly to God and had tangible evidences of their sacrifices during their time(s). Could the attitude in the Church today be the bane of unproductive sacrifices or unfulfilled vows/pledges amongst worshippers?

David identified that there is a more excellent sacrifice far beyond burnt offerings and seed offerings in [Psalm 51:15-17] – "O Lord, open thou my lips; and my mouth shall shew forth thy praise, {Verse 16} For thou desirest not sacrifice; else would I give [it]: thou delightest not in burnt offering. {Verse 17} *The sacrifices of God [are] a broken spirit: a broken and a contrite heart, O God, thou wilt not despise.*" This is single-handedly one of the best (if not the best) schooling there is in the Holy Bible and the New International Version of the Holy Bible gives a similar rendering of this in [Psalm 50:14, 15, 23] – "Sacrifice thank offerings to God, fulfill your vows to the Most High, {Verse 15} and call upon me in the day of trouble; I will deliver you, and you will honour me. {Verse 23} He who sacrifices thank offerings honours me, and he prepares the way so that I may show him the salvation of God." The express understanding through a devout relationship (with God) that seeds and sacrifices move God is essential in the believer's walk of faith, yet not as much as a broken spirit in thanksgiving would. Many scholars of the Holy Bible avoid or maybe neglect drawing attention to this. David by divine knowledge through revelation knew the mind of God more than any man that ever walked the earth (but Jesus) because of a justifiable, unquestionable and undeniable spirited-cohesion with the supernatural deity and he exhibited this relationship particularly by that line in [Psalm 51:17]. On a number of occasions David insisted that he will not offer anything to God that cost him nothing and this we find in [2 Samuel 24:24] – "And the king said unto Araunah, Nay; but I will surely buy [it] of thee at a price: neither will I offer burnt offerings unto the LORD my God of that which doth cost me nothing. So David bought the threshingfloor and the oxen for fifty shekels of silver." He iterated this consciousness in [1 Chronicles 21:24] – "And the king David said to Ornan, Nay; but I will verily buy it for the full price: for I will not take [that] which [is] thine for the LORD, nor offer burnt offerings without cost." David insisted and was completely adamant that he will never offer to God what does not cost him anything. This tells any believer that the value we place on our gifts to God really do matter to God.

Solomon also had a free hand to giving which he probably either inherited or learnt from his father David although we're not given the facts. In [1 Kings 3:4-5] the Scripture wrote about one of King Solomon's largest acts of sacrifice "And the king went to Gibeon to sacrifice there; for that [was] the great high place: a thousand burnt offerings did Solomon offer upon that altar. {Verse 5} In Gibeon the LORD appeared to Solomon in a dream by night: and God said, Ask what I shall give thee." We have a very detailed account of the outcome of David's several radical sacrifices and acts of faith because he was exalted to the throne of the kingdom of Israel as king and above all David was chosen over his brethren, but the Holy Bible records that God had to '*intervene*' in order to determine what Solomon intended by that seed. Then Solomon spoke in this manner answering God with a *wise* and very calculated suggestion-question [1 Kings 3:9] – "Give therefore thy servant an understanding heart to judge thy people, that I may discern between good and bad: for who is able to judge this thy so great a people?" Solomon's response showed that he was already endowed with wisdom even before he asked for it. God therefore confirmed to Solomon that *wisdom* had already been released in his spirit [1 Kings 3:12-13] – "Behold, I have done according to thy words: lo, I have given thee a wise and an understanding heart; so that there was none like thee before thee, neither after thee shall any arise like unto thee. {Verse 13} And I have also given thee that which thou hast not asked, both riches, and honour: so that there shall not be any among the kings like unto thee all thy days." Solomon's wisdom became more pronounced after God spoke about it and from God's response it sounds as though Solomon was even exalted above his father David and many of our teachers in the Churches and Bible schools avoid making this comparison because of how *too much wisdom* became *unwise* and probably ruined Solomon bringing him to arguably an inevitable and eventual destruction. However I believe this wisdom was domiciled in his spirit even before God spoke, for surely it was the wisdom within him that steered him to make a sacrifice of a thousand burnt offerings and indeed ask for wisdom. Not satisfied with what Solomon had asked for which he already had (I believe), God went on to enhance the offer with a conditional add-on in [1 Kings 3:14] – "And if thou wilt walk in my ways, to keep my statutes and my commandments, as thy father David did walk, then I will lengthen thy days." Long life was not an original part of Solomon's package of honour, although Solomon would go on to write about wisdom in [Proverbs 3:16] thus – "Length of days is in her right hand; *and* in her left hand riches and honour." From this detail one could easily discern that wisdom has a lot to do with long life and therefore God may have seen that Solomon would not walk in the ways of the Lord like David his father walked, so he gave it as a condition for long-life in order to keep Solomon from sinning against him but this promise still did not prevent Solomon from sinning against the God of his father David.

The book of [Ecclesiastes 7:12] writes this – "For wisdom *is* a defence, and money *is* a defence: but the excellency of knowledge *is, that* wisdom giveth life to them that have it." The whole point is that wisdom is a seed that is *supposed* or rather *intended* to give *more* life to the **recipient** of the gift of wisdom (the wise). Wisdom makes stars and exalts to stardom. Therefore seeds and sacrifices should then not be viewed as a 'money-doubler' or a 'health-enhancer' like some believe, rather as a covenant fulfilment by man with a zealous expectation thereby trusting in the Lord for the desired results. There is a joke that *the safest way to double your money is to fold it in half.* I personally had a strong view for so many years that sowing seeds was a strategy for doubling my income as being taught by many of our pastors today. It's not an automatic grab and go. This idea strongly undermines investments in the kingdom of God and would only remain acceptable to worshippers for so long because of our seemingly cantankerous sermons driven by pride and sometimes selfish lusts. Investing money in God's kingdom is very vital because money represents blood since we sweat from doing our work in the process of money making or conducting business activities and other ventures. Even preachers of the Scriptures sweat during sermons and this is only because there is a living blood in humans that excretes sweat when we're active. Therefore our money can build an altar to God on our behalf if we can use them as sacrifices to God, yet over-echoing sermons dedicated strictly to money undermines the value of the Church and the preacher. Hence we cannot appease God if we come to the throne with the mind-set of money-doubling encouraged by pastors instead of a sacrificial mind-set as led by the Spirit of the Lord. My take is that if sowing is preceded by the hopes or messages that the money must be doubled, then we seem to lie against God when these don't seem to happen within the time-frames that pastors and believers set and such realities frustrate the ministry as much as it does the worshippers. When we sow a seed in faith, we may have sown such seeds believing God for some divine healing. However God knows where we need our seeds most importantly, so he directs our seeds by himself. This is not an antidote for worrying since we are assured that Christ has his best will at heart towards us and also because worrying will not take away tomorrow's troubles, what it does however is to take away today's peace.

Having said this, it is imperative that we sow into good grounds if we must reap a bountiful harvest from our seeds. I also realised that the inheritance and gifts men give to their children and family members are gifts, but the ones men give to others that are not blood relatives to them become seeds. The Lord Jesus (who later became the Christ) taught us parables about the sower in the book of [Matthew 13], however it was recorded that the seeds that became fruitful only reproduced when they were sown on good ground while others failed to yield depending on the soil where they had been planted in. This parable of sowing into good grounds can be seen in [Matthew 13:8] – "But other fell into good ground, and brought forth fruit, some an hundredfold, some sixtyfold, some thirtyfold." Also the Lord Jesus who became a seed himself and yielded or sprung up as the Christ, would later testify in a later parable of another man who sowed good seed in his field and in the darkness of the night the enemy came and sowed tares among them. What this parable does not insinuate is whether those good seeds were sown in good ground or not. A good argument could be that it must have been good ground for it to be able to nurture both the good seeds sown by the man and the tares sown by the enemy, but let's consider this Scripture in [Matthew 13:24-25] – "Another parable put he forth unto them, saying, The kingdom of heaven is likened unto a man which sowed good seed in his field: {Verse 25} But while men slept, his enemy came and sowed tares among the wheat, and went his way." Therefore from these two slightly distinct parables we could assume that a good seed may not yield if planted in a bad ground, however a bad seed will possibly yield (depending on how bad it is) in good ground but it will only yield a bad harvest according to its quality because the quality of the seed as much as that of the soil it is planted in matters. The reality then lies in the obvious that we must nurture and prepare good seeds as we also endeavour to sow those good seeds in good grounds cheerfully and [2 Corinthians 9] speaks in much detail about our attitude towards seeds. These two parables could be likened to the lives of human beings (believers and unbelievers alike) as seeds that are either consciously plant in the Church or outside of the Church, hence each yields according to its quality (the seed and the soil) but the quality that justifies a man (believer or not) as good seed is character and by this I mean the character of Christ examined from the beginning of this chapter because a lot of the unbelievers nowadays prosper exceedingly while the tongue-talking believers struggle through to live. Sacrifices therefore must be placed on good grounds (altars) but the sacrifices must also be of good quality in order not to hinder a great harvest and I'd refer back to the instance given about David and Solomon (above).

Summary

Bearing the name of Jesus does not come cheaply for the believer because it is a passage that every representative of Jesus must pass through. Jesus has paid the price, but bearing his name '*in the name of Jesus*' attracts a price as well if we must fulfil our destiny and finish well like Jesus finished because he was then glorified. However this complex requirement and divine responsibility is not always fully comprehended by the believer.

The name of Jesus being the name of man and God further complicates the comprehension of this narrative and the author has engaged *ideas from God* to ensure a thorough understanding of the roles and personalities of 'Jesus – man of God' and 'Jesus – God of man' which is Christ.

From this work we also get the understanding of two pertinent habits of God exhibited from the beginning of the Old Testament (*To Speak*) through to the New Testament (*To Give*) Scriptures and the two chapters of this book each ends with a detailed summary (sub-chapters) of the later (*To Give*) which is 'the place of Charity and Love' and 'the place of Seeds and Sacrifices' respectively. In the book of Genesis God taught us how to speak (not just talk) because speaking brings breath and therefore life, it also commands value unlike talking which has no value. God spoke light [Genesis 1:3] into being. In the book of Matthew God taught us how to give. He gave his best seed and only begotten Son Jesus who died to save us from our sins and then rose again from the dead for our justification [Matthew 1:21] and [Matthew 27 – Matthew 28]. We'd also remember that that 'light' which God spoke into being was the '*light of the world*' which was Jesus [John 8:12]. This therefore unwinds the truth that the same light-bearing word-seed of God was sown twice, first as a 'Word' and then as a 'Seed'. Therefore words became seeds that gave birth to the breath of life. Hence the life in us which is Jesus Christ.

Shalom.

Prayer Points

1. Abba Father may I, my wife and our children's health worship you and let our wealth glorify you in Jesus name Amen.
2. Supernatural King just as you did to Sarah, give me a testimony that has no point of reference in history in the name of Jesus Amen.
3. Ancient of Days by the power and authority of the Spirit of God I declare that the same people that said that I will never make it in life are the same people that will help me and lift me into my next level in supernatural destiny (knowingly or unknowingly) in the name of Jesus Amen.
4. Holy Spirit of the living God let your name be named upon my life and family indefinitely and from eternity to eternity in the awesome and beautiful name of Jesus Amen.
5. Unchangeable God give me a good conscience, a clear conscience that reflects you Lord I need in the name of Jesus Amen.
6. Alpha and Omega in your majesty turn my 'no' into a 'YES' according to your will in the name of Jesus Amen.
7. I AM cause these hands that I lift up to you in worship, that I will never use them for sins or evil against you; restrain me Lord in your love, mercy and integrity from committing sins or evil with these hands in the name of Jesus Amen.
8. Omnipotent God it is written in your word that I and the children who the Lord has given me are for signs and for wonders in life and that we shall not die but live to testify; therefore I decree and declare that I will not bury any of my children and that they will bury me in my ripe old age in the name of Jesus Amen.

9. Holy One of Israel may you reap every investment you've made in my life; Daddy every talent you put in I and my family will lift up your majesty and honour in the name of Jesus Amen.

10. The Beginning and the End be merciful to me a sinner, Magnificent God put your fear in me in Jesus name Amen.

11. Supernatural God put your zeal in my heart, confuse the world with my life and magnify your word and compassion in my home in Jesus name Amen.

12. Create in me a clean heart O God and renew a right spirit within me; Cast me not away from thy presence and take not thy Holy Spirit from me; Restore unto me the joy of thy salvation and uphold me with thy free spirit (culled from Psalm 51:10-12).

Saviour find me, call me, choose me, anoint me, appoint me, send me, defend me and make me for your honour, glory and majesty in Jesus name Amen.

Where Is Knowledge?! (A Poem)

Calls came ringing while birds kept singing
asking if the funeral still holds?
I just reply we'd wait and see.
Polygamous battles ensued…
From every indication the journey so far has seemed futile and barren!
From adults taking very unintelligent steps to
men not knowing who to ask what.
A sojourner in a 'foreign land turned home' being asked
about souvenirs for a funeral that may not hold.
How disturbing it was to hear from a second
caller that no cheques had been signed?!!
The result, an enormous void of the power called wisdom on
every possible nook and cranny of the process. How grand!!
The hopes told tales, the rage raved on…
yet our replies all void of wisdom.
Who will rescue this lost Sheep from the land of the
dead but the great and terrible hand of God!
Moves erupted more chaos as we stretched to save the dying grace.
How terrible art thy works O God; through the greatness of
thy power shall thine enemies submit themselves unto thee.
Voices are made of words, words are sounds
but meanings determine results.
Oh how I've learned that the end justifies the means,
though means sometimes do justify the end.
So we wait and watch this sparrow flee!
Again, probably into the Eagle's nest.
And we brew more drama yet to unfold.

How majestic art thy secrets Holy Ghost.
We stand and watch while none pursues!
Yet as the days dawn our flights escape to where just only God will tell.
Mysteries revealed, visions repelled.
But the Glory still withstands in God.

- Chimezie Okonkwo - completed at 00:00 hours on 12.06.2014 (Dedicated to and in the loving memory of my late Dad HRM Eze Professor Chuka Okonkwo. R.I.P Dad).

Other Titles From The Author

Kingdom, Freedom and Wisdom
(Three Mysterious Forces and Treasures of the Trinity)

An exceptional piece of art work...thrilling, engaging and intellectually stimulating. This book is a must-read for the God-fearing and adventurous mind.

Printed in the United States
By Bookmasters